T0146993

WALTER BENJAMIN

Radical Thinkers ▼

WALTER BENJAMIN

or Towards a Revolutionary Criticism

Terry Eagleton

VERSO

London • New York

First published by Verso 1981
© Terry Eagleton 1981
Reprinted 2009
All rights reserved

3 5 7 9 10 8 6 4 2

Verso
UK: 6 Meard Street, London W1F 0EG
US: 20 Jay Street, Suite 1010, Brooklyn, NY 11201
www.versobooks.com

Verso is the imprint of New Left Books

ISBN-13: 978-1-84467-350-6

British Library Cataloguing in Publication Data
A catalogue record for this book is available from the British Library

Library of Congress Cataloging-in-Publication Data
A catalog record for this book is available from the Library of Congress

Printed in the United States

Contents

Deny to working-class children any common share in the immaterial, and presently they will grow into the men who demand with menaces a communism of the material.

Sir Henry Newbolt, Government report on *The Teaching of English in England*, 1921

[Cultural history] may well increase the burden of the treasures that are piled up on humanity's back. But it does not give mankind the strength to shake them off, so as to get its hands on them.

Walter Benjamin, *Eduard Fuchs, Collector and Historian*

for TORIL

Note

Parts of this book have been previously published in different form in *New Left Review*, *Social Text*, *Contemporary Literature* and *Literature, Society and the Sociology of Literature* (University of Essex, 1976), and I wish to thank the editors of those publications for their permission to reprint.

Works by Walter Benjamin cited in the text have been abbreviated as follows:

O *The Origin of German Tragic Drama*, translated by John Osborne, NLB 1977.

OWS *One-Way Street and Other Writings*, translated by Edmund Jephcott and Kingsley Shorter, with an Introduction by Susan Sontag, NLB 1979.

UB *Understanding Brecht*, translated by Anna Bostock with an Introduction by Stanley Mitchell, NLB 1973.

CB *Charles Baudelaire: A Lyric Poet in the Era of High Capitalism*, translated by Harry Zohn, NLB 1973.

I *Illuminations*, translated by Harry Zohn, edited and with an Introduction by Hannah Arendt, London 1973.

GS *Gesammelte Schriften*, edited by Rolf Tiedemann and Hermann Schweppenhäuser, 4 vols., Frankfurt am Main 1972.

B *Briefe*, edited by Gershom Scholem and T.W. Adorno, 2 vols., Frankfurt am Main 1966.

Preface

One afternoon, Walter Benjamin was sitting inside the Café des Deux Magots in Saint Germain des Prés when he was struck with compelling force by the idea of drawing a diagram of his life, and knew at the same moment exactly how it was to be done. He drew the diagram, and with utterly typical ill-luck lost it again a year or two later. The diagram, not surprisingly, was a labyrinth.

This book is not that diagram restored. It is neither an introduction to Benjamin's writing nor scholarly exegesis; nor is it quite a 'critical account', since even where I seem to be 'explicating' Benjamin's thought I am hardly ever actually summarizing or transcribing his texts. I am trying rather to manhandle them for my own purposes, blast them out of the continuum of history, in ways I think he would have approved. The relation between Benjamin's discourse and my own is not one of reflection or reproduction; it is more a matter of imbricating the two languages to produce a third that belongs wholly to neither of us. It would be difficult in any case to know what an adequate 'critical account' of Benjamin would look like, given his own hostility to the academic mode of production, and the complex strategies whereby his texts resist such reductiveness. Benjamin's sardonic distaste for conventional book-production is closely linked to his politics, and I should say that the formative impulse of this book too is political rather than academic. I wrote it because I thought I could see ways in which Benjamin's work might be used to illuminate some key problems now confronting a 'revolutionary criticism'. In the manner of Benjamin himself, the book is deliberately not an 'organic unity': the logic of its second part in particular is as much to be constructed by the reader as given by the text.

In these ways, then, the book marks a development from my *Criticism and Ideology* (NLB, 1976), which was less overtly political in timbre and more conventionally academic in style and form. That development, however, is not merely my own. What seemed important when I wrote my earlier book, at a time when 'Marxist criticism' had little anchorage in Britain, was to examine its pre-history and to systematize the categories essential for a 'science of the text'. I would still defend the principle of that project, but it is perhaps no longer the focal concern of Marxist cultural studies. Partly under the pressure of global capitalist crisis, partly under the influence of new themes and forces within socialism, the centre of such studies is shifting from narrowly textual or conceptual analysis to problems of cultural production and the political uses of artefacts. Interwoven with that general mutation is my own individual evolution since writing *Criticism and Ideology*. What intervened between that book and this was a play, *Brecht and Company* (1979), which both in its writing and in the final product raised questions of the relations between socialist cultural theory and cultural practice, the relevance of both to revolution-ary politics, the techniques of intellectual production and the political uses of theatre and comedy. This shift of direction was in turn obscurely related to certain deep-seated changes in my own personal and political life since the writing of *Criticism and Ideology*.

There are other reasons why a book on Benjamin seems appropriate. Bred as a bourgeois intellectual, Benjamin buckled himself to the tasks of revolutionary transformation; so that whatever the individual class-provenance of Marxist intellectuals within the academy today, his life and work speak challengingly to us all. This is true above all at a time of historical upheaval, when every materialist intellectual labour must deliberately examine its own political credentials. Moreover, Benjamin's work seems to me strikingly to prefigure many of the current motifs of post-structuralism, and to do so, unusually, in a committedly Marxist context. The book is therefore intended among other things as an intervention into those particular disputes. But I have written what I believe is the first book-length English-language study of Benjamin in order also to get at him before the opposition does. All the signs are that Benjamin is in imminent danger of being appropriated by a critical establishment that regards his Marxism as a contingent peccadillo or tolerable eccentricity. Were it not for his premature death, suggests Frank Kermode, Benjamin 'might now, at eighty-six, be a distingu-ished American professor emeritus'.[1] One can envisage the glee with which Benjamin would have greeted this prospect. 'Had he lived', asserts George Steiner, 'Walter Benjamin would doubtless have been sceptical of any "New Left". Like every man committed to abstruse thought and scholarship, he knew that not only the humanities, but humane and critical intelligence itself, resides in the always-threatened keeping of the very few'.[2] These words, which are the exact reverse of the truth, seem to me an insult to Benjamin's memory. My final and most simple reason for writing the book, then, is to pay homage to Walter Benjamin, who in a dark time taught us that it is the lowly and inconspicuous who will blast history apart.

I am grateful to Francis Mulhern, Bernard Sharratt and Paul Tickell, who commented valuably on the manuscript of this book. I must also thank Faculty and students at the Universities of Oregon, British Columbia, and Deakin University, Australia, with whom I have discussed these matters, and the Society for the Humanities, Cornell University, for appointing me to a visiting senior research fellowship during which the last stages of work were carried out. Toril Moi argued some of these ideas with me to the point where it is impossible to say whether they are 'hers' or 'mine'; but I cannot hold her responsible for typing the manuscript, tolerating prolonged periods of unsociability with patience and good humour, or keeping me sane.

T.E.

Wadham College
Oxford

1. 'Every Kind of Intelligence', *New York Times Book Review*, July 30, 1978.
2. 'Introduction', Walter Benjamin, *The Origin of German Tragic Drama*, NLB 1977, p. 24.

ONE

Walter Benjamin

Walter Benjamin found it demeaning
To leave more than fragments for gleaning;
His *Ursprung* explains
That God gave us brains
To deem meaning itself overweaning.
ALAN WALL

The progressive discovery of Walter Benjamin that has marked the past two decades is not really very surprising. For who could be more appealing to Western Marxists than a writer who manages marvellously to combine all the vigorous iconoclasm of a materialist 'production aesthetics' with the entrancing esotericism of the Kabbala? Who indeed could speak to us more persuasively, torn as we are between media technology and idealist meditation? In the doomed, poignant figure of a Benjamin we find reflected back to us something of our own contradictory desire for some undreamt-of emancipation and persistent delight in the contingent. *The Origin of German Tragic Drama* stands at the confluence of these impulses—for nothing could be at once more boldly dialectical and more intriguingly arcane than the seventeenth-century *Trauerspiel*.

For an English critic in particular, Benjamin's return to the seventeenth century inevitably recalls the apparently similar gestures of T.S. Eliot and F.R. Leavis. Restless with an eighteenth century that it has already rewritten as 'Augustan', thwarted by its own ideological creations, twentieth-century English criticism peers back beyond that artificially pacified epoch to glimpse in its turbulent predecessor an image it can call its own. Far from merely paralleling that project, however, Benjamin's recourse to the *Trauerspiel* neatly exposes its ideological basis. Writing of John Donne in *Revaluation*, F.R. Leavis suggests that his 'utterance, movement and intonation are those of the talking voice . . . [exhibiting] a natural speaking stress and intonation and an economy that is the privilege of speech . . .'.[1] Pope's verse is similarly expressive: 'above every line of Pope we can imagine a tensely flexible and complex curve, representing

[1] London 1949, pp. 11 and 13.

4

the modulation, emphasis and changing tone and tempo of the voice in reading . . .'.[2] It is this trace within script of the living voice that the linguistic disaster of Milton has fatally erased. Milton's language 'has no particular expressive work to do, but functions by rote, of its own momentum, in the manner of a ritual'; his diction at its worst is a 'laboured, pedantic artifice', in which the obtrusive sign draws imperiously onto itself that attention to 'perceptions, sensations or things' that it is its business to foster.[3] Milton's arid, factitious discourse suggests a medium 'cut off from speech—speech that belongs to the emotional and sensory texture of actual living and is in resonance with the nervous system'.[4] What is 'natural' about Donne, by contrast, is precisely his subtle rootedness in 'idiomatic speech'. Eliot, who is similarly in pursuit of a poetry that infiltrates 'the cerebral cortex, the nervous system, and the digestive tracts',[5] also finds such a bodily semiotic in Donne rather than in Milton, whose 'remoteness . . . from ordinary speech'[6] is for the early Eliot grievously disabling.

For both critics, the contrast between Donne and Milton is cast in terms of the 'visual' versus the 'auditory' imagination. What both in fact find corrupting in Milton is an irreducible surplus of signification that deflects the sign from its truly representational role—and reveals, in Leavis's phrase, 'a feeling *for* words rather than a capacity for feeling *through* words'.[7] That surplus of signification we can designate as *écriture*; and for Benjamin it lies at the heart of the *Trauerspiel*. Seventeenth-century allegory, obsessed as it is by emblem and hieroglyph, is a profoundly visual form; but what swims into visibility is nothing less than the materiality of the letter itself. It is not that the letter flexes and effaces itself to become the bearer of 'perceptions, sensations or things', as Leavis would have us believe of Donne; it is rather that 'at one stroke the profound vision of allegory transforms things and works into stirring writing'.[8] The allegorical signifier is 'not merely a sign of what is to be known but it is in itself an object worthy of knowledge':[9] its denotative force is inseparable

2 *Revaluation*, p. 31.
3 Ibid., p. 49.
4 Ibid., p. 51.
5 'The Metaphysical Poets', *Selected Essays*, London 1963, p. 290.
6 *Selected Prose of T.S. Eliot*, Frank Kermode, ed., London 1975, p. 268.
7 *Revaluation*, p. 50.
8 O, p. 176.
9 O, p. 184.

from its complex carnality. The writing of *Trauerspiel*, Benjamin remarks, 'does not achieve transcendence by being voiced; rather does the world of written language remain self-sufficient and intent on the display of its own substance'.[10]

This is not to say that such writing is not 'voiced' at all—that sound is merely quelled by its material thickness. On the contrary, the baroque signifier displays a dialectical structure in which sound and script 'confront each other in tense polarity',[11] forcing a division within discourse that impels the gaze into its very depths. That division, for Benjamin, is ontological: spoken language signifies the 'free, spontaneous utterance of the creature',[12] an expressive ecstasy at odds with that fateful enslavement to meaning which the language of allegory entails. What escapes such enslavement is shape and sound, which figure for the baroque allegorist as a self-delighting, purely sensuous residue over and above the meaning with which all written language is inexorably contaminated (and here, of course, 'written language' can mean nothing less than 'language as such'). Seeking in the fullness of sound to assert its creaturely rights, language is nonetheless grimly subdued to significance; the 'semiotic', in the Kristevan sense of that babble or prattle of loosely articulated impulses below the threshold of meaning, enters the constraints of the 'symbolic' but just manages to remain heterogeneous in relation to it.[13] No finer image of such constraint can be found than in the baroque echo-game, in which the echo, itself quite literally a free play of sound, is harnessed to dramatic meaning as answer, warning, prophecy or the like, violently subordinated to a domain of significance that its empty resonance nonetheless threatens to dissolve.

What Benjamin discovers in the *Trauerspiel*, then, is a profound gulf between materiality and meaning—a gulf across which the contention between the two nevertheless persists. It is precisely this which Eliot detects in Milton: 'to extract everything possible from *Paradise Lost*', he comments, 'it would seem necessary to read it in two different ways, first solely for the sound, and second for the sense'.[14] The semiotic contradiction that Benjamin singles out is resolved into separate readings.

---

10 O, p. 201.
11 O, p. 201.
12 O, p. 202.
13 See *La Révolution du langage poétique*, Paris 1974.
14 *Selected Prose of T.S. Eliot*, p. 263.

For Leavis, the 'Miltonic music' is little more than an external embellishment, clumsily at odds with the springs of sense. That this should be scandalous for both critics is hardly surprising, given their commitment to the very aesthetic ideology that Benjamin so ruthlessly demystifies: that of the *symbol*. Ineluctably idealizing, the symbol subdues the material object to a surge of spirit that illuminates and redeems it from within. In a transfigurative flash, meaning and materiality are reconciled into one; for a fragile, irrationalist instant, being and signification become harmoniously totalized. It is impossible that allegory should not appear prolix, mechanical and uncouth in the light of such glamorous notions, and indeed Benjamin is only too aware of the fact; what else is his entire book but an effort to salvage allegory from the 'enormous condescension' of history, as allegory's whole striving is itself for the painful salvaging of truth? Symbolism has denigrated allegory as thoroughly as the ideology of the speaking voice has humiliated script; and though Benjamin himself does not fully develop the connection, it is surely a relevant one. For the allegorical object has undergone a kind of haemorrhage of spirit: drained of all immanent meaning, it lies as a pure facticity under the manipulative hand of the allegorist, awaiting such meaning as he or she may imbue it with. Nothing could more aptly exemplify such a condition than the practice of writing itself, which draws its atomized material fragments into endless, unmotivated constellations of meaning. In the baroque allegory, a jagged line of demarcation is scored between theatrical object and meaning, signifier and signified—a line that for Benjamin traces between the two the dark shadow of that ultimate disjoining of consciousness and physical nature which is death. But if death is in this sense the final devastation of the sign, the utter disruption of its imaginary coherence, so too is writing itself, which happens at the sliding hinge between signifier and signified, and with which, as we shall see later, death itself is intimately associated.

Since Benjamin, like Bertolt Brecht, believes in starting not from the good old things but from the bad new ones,[15] he does not mourn the bereft condition of the baroque world, sundered as it is from all transcendence. It is true, as we shall see, that he considers such barrenness to contain the seeds of its own redemption; but even so he welcomes the *Trauerspiel* as figuring the real, demystified form of 'man's subjection to nature'.[16] For

15 See UB, p. 121.
16 O, p. 166.

Eliot and Leavis, on the other hand, this drastic dissociation of sensibility—for that, after all, is another jargon for what we are discussing—is an ideological menace. The world of the *Trauerspiel* is not one in which characters feel their thought as immediately as the odour of a rose; and even if the typewriter had been invented they would hardly have combined hearing the noise of it with the experience of reading Spinoza. The *Trauerspiel*, with its habitual disarticulation of elements, knows nothing of that fetishism of the 'organic' which haunts an Eliot or Leavis, and which informs the German Romantic criticism Benjamin so courageously challenged. In the baroque, 'the false appearance of totality is extinguished',[17] even if it then yields grounds to a fetishism of the fragment. Eliot and Leavis, gripped by the good old things, return wistfully to the time when the intellect was at the tip of the senses and the social relations of exploited farm-labourers constituted a 'right and inevitable' human environment.[18] Indeed what is the Metaphysical conceit but the organic society in miniature, a *Gemeinschaft* of senses and intellect, a transfiguring flash in which the material object is rescued from its facticity and offered up to the ephemeral embrace of spirit? It is no wonder that the criticism of Eliot and Leavis betrays such a deep 'phonocentric' prejudice—in favour of what Jacques Derrida has described as an 'absolute proximity of voice and being, of voice and the meaning of being, of voice and the ideality of meaning'.[19] For if poetry is to slide into the cerebral cortex, nervous system and digestive tracts to perform its ideological labour there, it must free itself from the thwarting materiality of the signifier to become the subtilized medium of the living body itself, of which nothing is more symbolically expressive than the 'spontaneous' speaking voice. Unless the 'thing' is ripely, unmediatedly present within the word, it will fail to be borne subliminally to that realm which for both Eliot and Leavis is the very heartland of 'human experience', and which historical materialism knows to be the very terrain of the ideological.

Benjamin, by contrast, does not fall prey to the illusion that the voice is any more spontaneous or immaterial than script. 'That inward connection of word and script', he quotes Johann Wilhelm Ritter as reflecting, 'so powerful that we write when we speak . . . has long interested me. . . .

17 O, p. 176.
18 F.R. Leavis and Denys Thompson, *Culture and Environment*, London 1933, p. 87.
19 *Of Grammatology*, trans. Gayatri Chakravorty Spivak, Baltimore and London 1976, p. 12.

Their original, and absolute, simultaneity was rooted in the fact that the organ of speech itself writes in order to speak. The letter alone speaks, or rather: word and script are, at source, one, and neither is possible without the other. . . . Every sound pattern is an electric pattern, and every electric pattern is a sound pattern'.[20] In the *Trauerspiel*, Benjamin continues, 'there is nothing subordinate about written script; it is not cast away in reading, like dross. It is absorbed along with what is read, as its "pattern"'.[21]

That Leavis should manifest such hostility to Milton is itself a profound historical irony. For his animus against Milton is among other things the irritation of a petty-bourgeois radical with a thoroughly 'Establishment' figure—a poet solemnly venerated for his rhetorical grandeur by generations of patrician academics. But with the exception of William Blake, English literature has produced no finer petty-bourgeois radical than John Milton.[22] Leavis's own signal virtues—his unswerving seriousness and nonconformist courage, his coupling of trenchant individualism and social conscience—would not have been historically possible, in the precise configurations they display, without the revolutionary lineage of which Milton was such an heroic architect. Leavis cannot perceive this grotesque irony, partly because the Milton he assails remains the construct of the ideological enemy, partly because his formalism necessarily blinds him to the 'content' of Milton's work. In this, Leavis and Eliot are at one: the former is largely indifferent to the theological and political substance of Milton's texts, while the latter, in so far as such substance concerns him at all, finds it 'repellent'. Such resistance to 'ideas' stems logically from the empiricism and irrationalism that both critics variously championed throughout their careers; few critics have betrayed such programmatic anti-intellectualism as the formidably erudite Eliot. But it also has a more particular root in their

20 O, pp. 213–14. Cf. Marx and Engels: 'from the start the "spirit" is affected with the curse of being "burdened" with matter, which here makes its appearance in the form of agitated layers of air, sounds, in short, of language' (*The German Ideology*, London 1965, p. 41). In a conversation recorded by Gershom Scholem, Benjamin sharply rejected a distinction between writing and the voice, 'with such animosity as if someone had touched a wound' (Preface to B, 1, p. 16). Scholem comments elsewhere that Benjamin spoke as though he were writing.

21 O, p. 215.

22 A fact in some sense obvious to the soldiers of the first Russian revolution of 1905, who carried copies of the poem with them and read it enthusiastically as a libertarian text.

ideological construction of seventeenth-century England. For their shared linguistic idealism impels them to locate the mourned *Gemeinschaft* primarily in language itself. Not entirely, to be sure: 'health' of language must signify cultural sanity, and Leavis, rather more than Eliot, is concerned to give such sanity a social habitation. But both are forced to 'bracket' the ideological content of the texts they admire to an astonishing degree: the desirable wedlock of being and meaning manifest in the verbal form of a Donne poem or Webster tragedy must be celebrated in systematic inattention to the flagrant dislocations of their content. If the Donne of *Songs and Sonnets* centres himself as a dramatic voice, a colloquially expressive subject, it is not least because he is concerned to construct a defiant 'imaginary' coherence across a decentred, Copernican world of 'symbolic' differences. His mechanism of sensibility may indeed be capable of devouring any experience, but usually only to spew it back again as an inferior metaphor of the imaginary subject-position he can achieve with his mistress. Both Eliot and Leavis, it is true, discern in such seventeenth-century *Weltanschauungen* relevant paradigms for contemporary experience; but this is not the most typical focus of their interest. Eliot may draw upon such paradigms in *The Waste Land*, but his criticism is remarkable for its almost comic lack of interest in what a poet actually has to 'say'. Such formalism is the concomitant of a necessary depoliticizing, as Raymond Williams has shrewdly noted: 'let me take a case which was very important in clarifying my attitude to Leavis. I said to people here at Cambridge: in the thirties you were passing severely limiting judgments on Milton and relatively favourable judgments on the metaphysical poets, which in effect redrew the map of seventeenth-century literature in England. Now you were, of course, making literary judgments—your supporting quotations and analysis prove it, but you were also asking about ways of living through a political and cultural crisis of national dimensions. On the one side, you have a man who totally committed himself to a particular side and cause, who temporarily suspended what you call literature, but in fact not writing, in that conflict. On the other, you have a kind of writing which is highly intelligent and elaborate, that is a way of holding divergent attitudes towards struggle or towards experience together in the mind at the same time. These are two possibilities for any highly conscious person in a period of crisis—a kind of commitment which involves certain difficulties, certain naïvetés, certain styles; and another kind of consciousness, whose complexities are a way of living with the crisis without being openly part of it. I said that when you were making your judgments about these poets, you were not only arguing about their literary practice, you were arguing about your own at that time.'[23]

The triumph of Benjamin's text, by contrast, lies in its subtle imbrication of form and motif. In the jaded, secularized world of the *Trauerspiel*, rife as it is with sluggish melancholy and pure intrigue, the leakage of meaning from objects, the unhinging of signifiers from signifieds, is at once a matter of *énoncé* and *énonciation*, as the features of an already petrified, primordial landscape undergo a kind of secondary reification at the hands of the 'fixing' hieroglyph. Those features, indeed, include 'psychology' itself, which, elaborately encoded as it is, attains to a kind of dense objectivity in which 'the passions themselves take on the nature of stage-properties'.[24] Signifieds metonymically displace themselves onto their signifiers, so that jealousy becomes as sharp and functional as the dagger with which it is associated. If this domain of thickly reified signs is predominantly spatial, it is nevertheless propelled slowly forward by an ineluctable temporality; for allegory, as Fredric Jameson has remarked of the *Trauerspiel*, is 'the privileged mode of our own life in time, a clumsy deciphering of meaning from moment to moment, the painful attempt to restore a continuity to heterogeneous, disconnected instants'.[25] Benjamin distinguishes three kinds of temporality: the 'empirical' time of empty repetition, which belongs to the *Trauerspiel* and, as we shall see later, to the commodity; 'heroic' time, centred upon the individual tragic protagonist; and 'historical' time, which is neither 'spatial' as in the *Trauerspiel* nor individual as in tragedy, but which prefigures his later concerns with the '*nunc stans*' or *Jetztzeit*, in which time receives its collective fullness. The freezing of time achieved by the *Trauerspiel* signifies the need of the absolutist state to bring history to an end; the absolutist monarch himself becomes the primary source of signification in a world drained of historical dynamic. This theme, too, will find a later echo in Benjamin, in that ultimate abolition of history which is fascism. Such significant temporality as there is, however, belongs more to hermeneutic practice itself than to its objects; the time of the *Trauerspiel* is as empty as its *realia*, the negation of that teleological vision which

23 *Politics and Letters*, NLB 1979, pp. 335–6.
24 O, p. 133.
25 *Marxism and Form*, Princeton 1971, p. 72.

Benjamin will later denounce as 'historicism', listlessly open to the *Jetztzeit*—the totalizing, transfiguring moment—that never comes. As the petrified stage-properties are ritually shuffled, time is almost folded back into space, dwindled to a recurrence so agonizingly empty that some salvific epiphany might indeed just be conceived to tremble on its brink. If there is a moment in the *Trauerspiel* that resembles the *Jetztzeit*—the apocalyptic point at which time stands still to receive the plenitude of hitherto dismembered meaning—it resembles it only as caricature: 'the narrow frame of midnight, an opening in the passage of time, in which the same ghostly image constantly reappears'.[26]

Benjamin's treatment of the *Trauerspiel* might suggest, in contrast to Leavis and Eliot, an approach to *Paradise Lost* that has moved beyond formalism. For Milton's text too, remote as it is from those that Benjamin examines, is the drama of a jagged line scored by some primordial catastrophe between *physis* and meaning, the plot of a history reduced by God's apparent withdrawal to certain signs and fragments urgently in need of decipherment. The withdrawal *is*, of course, merely apparent: an eschatology unknown to the baroque is still active, and will finally usher into history the transcendental signifier that already lies concealed in its midst. But for all that, the transcendental signifier *is* concealed, and to justify its dealings with humankind demands an awkwardly discursive hermeneutic that is the precise reverse of the conceit. The conceit 'naturalizes' its incongruous couplings, amazing us with a 'spontaneity' that we appreciate all the more because its artifice is kept cunningly in view; wit is intellect without labour. Milton's God is equally unlaborious, pure symbolicity whose 'material' acts have the immediacy of spirit; but he is so only from the standpoint of eternity. Viewed from the fallen realm of a revolutionary history gone awry, those acts must be painfully decoded, elaborated and reassembled, in a narrative that can expose their logic only at the cost of laying bare its own devices.

The slippages and lacunae entailed by such a practice are precisely what Milton's critics have denounced. The poem is not really very realistic: at one moment Satan is chained to the burning lake, and before you can look again he is making his way towards the shore. George Eliot would have handled the whole thing incomparably better. Leavis, significantly, is much preoccupied with such Waldockian points,[27] upbraiding the poem for its lapses of consistency. It is not fortuitous that a phonocentric criticism, concerned to chart the very anatomy of feeling in the sinuous flexings of speech, should pull a naive representationalism in its wake: for both ideologies, the signifier lives only in the moment of its demise. What is fascinating about *Paradise Lost* is precisely its necessary lack of self-identity—the persistent mutual interferences of what is stated and what is shown, the contradictory entanglements of 'epic' immediacy and hermeneutic discourse, the fixing of significations at one level that produces a sliding of them at another. All of this, for Leavis, is simply offensive: he cannot see that it possesses that quality of *provocative* offensiveness which Benjamin discerns in the baroque, any more than he can read the harsh laboriousness of some of the poem's language as anything but a violation of sensuous immediacy. In fact, the language of *Paradise Lost* is a labour that works athwart the 'natural' texture of the senses, failing or refusing (it is immaterial which) to repress its own artifice. Nothing could be further from the swift fusion of the conceit than the calculated self-conscious unfurling of the epic simile, with all its whirring machinery of production unashamedly on show. And nothing could be closer to one aspect of Benjamin's *Trauerspiel*, in which 'the writer must not conceal the fact that his activity is one of arranging'.[28] What is perhaps most surprising about Leavis's attitude to *Paradise Lost* is his failure to be surprised by it. For few English literary works could surely be more bizarre, more boldly exotic, more massively and self-consciously 'literary'. The poem is so defiantly resistant to a merely realist reading, so scarred and contorted by the labour of its own production, that this very form becomes its most crucial signified.

Leavis's response to this weird phenomenon is to complain that the sound distracts him from seeing what is going on. Fredric Jameson has suggested another way of viewing this form of artifice: 'unlike prose narrative, artificial epic takes as its object of representation not events and actions themselves but rather the describing of them: the process whereby such narrative raw materials are fixed and immobilized in the heightened

---

27 See A.J.A. Waldock, *Paradise Lost and Its Critics*, Cambridge 1947, for a characteristically 'realist' reading of the poem. Waldock's book, however, shows in unconsciously Machereyan style how the official ideology of Milton's poem is ruptured and embarrassed by the formal figurations (narrative, character and so on) it is constrained to assume.
28 O, p. 179.

and embellished speech of verse. There is thus already present in epic discourse a basic and constitutive rift between form and content, between the words and their objects. . . . It can therefore be asserted that the poet of artificial epic does not compose immediately with words, but rather works, as with his most fundamental raw materials and building blocks, with just such perceptual or gestural signifiers, juxtaposing and reunifying them into the sensuous continuity of the verse paragraph.'[29] What is true of 'artificial epic' is true also of the *Trauerspiel*. There too the relative fixity of the component parts—which as Benjamin points out 'lack all "symbolic" freedom of expression',[30] belonging as they do to some great storehouse of subjectless script—compels attention, in a way equivalent to the phenomenological bracketing, to the act of interpretation itself. Milton's resounding litanies of proper names have the effect of Jameson's pre-fashioned blocks; and Benjamin himself comments how the baroque uses the capital letter so as to break up language and charge its fragments with intensified meaning. 'With the baroque the place of the capital letter was established in German orthography'.[31] Milton's sonorous names, aimed at the impressionable ear, might still of course be claimed as part of a phonocentric strategy. Yet what we have in effect is an ear without a voice: what speaks is the names themselves, discrete and monumental, uninflected by the tones of a punctual subject and grandly excessive of any strict regime of sense.

This is not a common occurrence in the literature of the time. We have become accustomed since Derrida to associating a Western prejudice for 'living speech' as against script with a metaphysic of the human subject, centred in the plenitude of its linguistic presence, the fount and origin of all sense. It is in this refusal of the materiality of the sign, this ineradicable nostalgia for a transcendental source of meaning anterior to and constitutive of all sign-systems, that Derrida finds the Western tradition most deeply marked by idealism. The speaking voice, obliterating its own materiality in the 'naturalness' of its self-production, opens a passage to the equivalent 'naturalness' of its *signata*—a passage blocked by the materiality of script, which (for this lineage) is thus destined to remain external to the spontaneous springs of meaning.

---

29 *Fables of Aggression: Wyndham Lewis, the Modernist as Fascist*, Berkeley, Los Angeles and London, 1979, pp. 76, 78.
30 O, p. 166.
31 O, p. 208.

It could then hardly be otherwise than that the dense corpus of *writing* we know as the eighteenth-century English novel should find itself plunged into a severe dilemma, given the influence upon it of that ideological discourse we loosely term 'puritanism'. For installed at the very centre of puritanism is the living word—the word preached, proclaimed, consumed, obeyed and violated, the word valorized by its roots in the authentic experience of a subject, and radiant with the full presence of the divine Subject of subjects. The living Word of God, the pure expressivity of the Father, creates that sacred space in which speaking and listening persons are constituted as pure subjects for themselves and others, in a ceaseless redoubling of that transcendental intersubjectivity which is the Trinity. Of course, for the puritan tradition, *script* has a privileged status. But that is no more than to say that the enigmatic materiality of the biblical text must be dispersed by the power of grace, so that the living speech of its Author may be freed from its earthly encasement. *Texts* become *voices*, for the anguished John Bunyan of *Grace Abounding*: writing itself becomes a Subject, to be 'heard' rather than 'read', a living flesh to be cherished as the presence among men and women of the Word of words. The Word is fully present within all his words, as the principle of their unity; yet for individuals struggling in the opaqueness of history, the primordial Word is refracted amongst his various texts, which thus demand scrupulous decodement for the life-giving discourse of their Author to sound through. The meaning of that vast, cryptic sign-system which is history must be constantly displaced to be discovered—ceaselessly referred to a supportive system of trans-cendental *signata*, in an act whose literary name is allegory. In a double hermeneutic, historical significations must first be referred to the privileged signs of scripture, which must then be themselves dis-encumbered of their polyvalence to reveal a unitary Truth.

It is not surprising, then, that what strikes us most about the 'puritan' fiction of Defoe is precisely the weightlessness of its signifiers, which efface themselves in a potentially infinite metonymic chain to yield up all the material immediacy of their signifieds. Yet this instantly involves us in a contradiction at the very heart of the puritan ideology. For if the 'innocence' of Defoe's dematerialized writing marks the presence of a privileged autobiographical subject, a lonely Cartesian ego radically anterior to its material embodiments, the same device so foregrounds the material world itself as to threaten constantly to reduce the subject to no more than a reflex or support of it. The subject's epistemological security of position is in contradiction with its 'real' precariousness and contingency; safely lodged in its *retrospective* account of its turbulent experiences, it nonetheless dwindles more than once within its own narration to a cypher as empty as its signs, a mere formal motivation of plot, a perfunctory 'suturing' of heterogeneous material events. An idealism of the literary sign fatally inverts itself into a mechanical materialism of the subject: Defoe's 'degree zero' writing clears a space for that subject's expressivity, only to find that space then crammed with material *signata* which threaten to engulf and confiscate subjectivity itself.

It is this contradiction within puritan ideology, between the privilege and precariousness simultaneously assigned to the subject, that finds a different form in the novels of Samuel Richardson. For what could serve as a more dramatic image of that duality than the sight of the puritan serving-maid Pamela, cowering in her bedchamber before the rapacious advances of Mr B, yet at that very moment *writing it out*, scribbling a desperate letter, centring herself in the expressive plenitude of 'written speech' at the very instant her subordinate petty-bourgeois status is about to be sexually exploited? Fascinated by print, yet deeply embroiled in the ideological modes of the 'living', evangelizing word, Richardson discovers in the epistolary novel a breathtakingly ingenious 'solution' to his dilemma—a literary form in which 'writing' and 'experience' are absolutely synchronous, given spontaneously together, in which the act of script can become exactly contemporaneous with the very point and genesis of experience itself. For Richardson, there is nothing that cannot be *written*; but this is the precise opposite of that deconstruction of the subject into the play of *écriture* with which Derrida's work concerns itself. On the contrary, it is nothing less than the wholesale dissolution of script into the originating subject—a triumphant victory over the 'alienations' of writing, which are ceaselessly recuperated in that unity of subject and object which is the identity between Pamela as writing subject and the 'I' of whom she writes.

Except, of course, that such an identity, constituted as it is by that 'mirror relation' of Pamela to herself which is writing, is merely imaginary, as Henry Fielding in *Shamela* was the first to see. There *is* no such unity between the Pamela who writes and the Pamela whom she reveals; and it is part of the interest of Richardson's psychologism, which stakes all signification in the living subject, that when produced in fictional form it cannot help but betray those material determinants of the subject's construction that the subject speaks only to deny. For nothing could be more flagrant than what Fielding, in his own way, saw—that if we submit the epistolary texts of a Pamela or a Clarissa to a symptomatic reading, alert to their palpable absences and resonating silences, then we can begin to construct alongside the cohesive 'phenomenal' text the 'latent', mutilated text that forms the very matrix of its production. Indeed nothing could be easier to hear than the ideological and psychoanalytic discourses that truly 'write' Pamela and Clarissa, discourses that resound scandalously through the cohering letter of the subject. The phenomenal text exists to 'write out' (cancel) those discourses—to displace the guilty, inarticulable contradiction between the petty bourgeoisie's simultaneous desire for and aversion to the fertilizing embrace of the aristocracy. It is the subject constituted by the repression of that contradiction (and of others) which figures for Henry Fielding as the very mark of ideological degeneracy—Fielding, whose own fictions install the reader in the gap between their 'latent' and 'phenomenal' levels, baring the mechanisms by which a resolution of contradictions may be *arbitrarily* achieved by the forms of fictive discourse.

It is an index of the reversibility between the subject Pamela and her 'expressive' account that the very text of *Pamela* assumes the status of a subject within the novel itself—a 'character' of mystery, scandal and intrigue that at one point is actually lost. But this confrontation of the text with itself does not assume the form of an inquiry into the conditions of its own possibility, as it does, most notably, with Sterne's *Tristram Shandy*. That the famous 'rise of the novel' in England should produce almost instantaneously the greatest 'anti-novel' of all time should not seem fortuitous, in the light of what has been said: for Sterne's fiction is nothing less than a flamboyant exposé of the impossible contradictions inherent in a representational writing that can fulfil its function only by abolishing itself. *Tristram Shandy* centres itself in a benevolistic (rather than puritan) ideology of the subject, fighting the anonymity of script to invest all in expressivity, in the search for which even typography itself must be wrenched into submission. Bemused as it is by the problematic relations between matter and spirit, the novel finds the major trope of that dilemma in itself: by what Cartesian miracle can black marks on white sheets become the bearers of meaning? How can there conceivably be a passage from 'book' to 'text'? How can the materiality of language and the 'artifice' of aesthetic device hope to leave unimpaired the full presence of the author to his readers? Inexorably 'alienated' by the 'externality' of *écriture*, the reader must be ceaselessly re-centred, so that Tristram's project of self-recuperation through some form of infinite autobiography is at the same time the reader's continuously re-totalized possession of the materials. Yet this, of course, is the sign of an enormous irony, for this potentially boundless plethora of signification in fact produces an endless deconstruction of the fiction, jamming the narrative and radically decentring the reader. To pursue the logic of 'representation', to insure against the problematic bond between 'ideal' signifier and 'material' signified by anxiously explicating every iota of possible meaning and forestalling every conceivable misreading, is to load representational discourse with a weight under which it buckles and all but collapses. And this movement of construction/deconstruction is nothing less than the process by which Tristram produces himself as a 'writing subject' by a constant decomposition of himself into the material determinants that went into his making, thus undermining his security of position as subject with every step he takes to consolidate it. Every taking up of position involves both Tristram and the reader in an instant displacement, just as every attempt at representation dissolves into a spawning infinity of significations. It is this uncontrollable discourse—the endless, sprawling mesh of possible other words that each of Tristram's enunciations drags fatally in its wake—that constitutes the 'unconsciousness' that deconstructs his efforts to centre himself in speech. The 'imaginary' relation between the Tristram who writes, and the Tristram he writes of, is ruptured and confounded with every proposition; there is no way in which his writing can round on itself, *à la* Pamela, in a moment of total self-recuperation, no way in which the discourse of the writing subject can inscribe within itself the lost, secret mechanisms of that subject's process of construction. The desperate hunt for the moment of genesis of all meaning—Tristram's attempts to isolate the inner structure of his psychic wounding, Uncle Toby's physical reconstructions of the very instant of his impotency—is a mere hurtling from one signifier to another, a ceaseless spiralling within language that can never emerge into some transcendental sense. The privileged mechanisms of production evade exposure, dissolved as they are in the endless play of signs mobilized in their pursuit. They must of necessity be absent, for *writing itself* is the very sign of their repression—the displaced potency and *ersatz* manhood produced by some primordial sexual crippling that resists reconstruction. The moment of Tristram's entry into the symbolic order—into language—cannot be reproduced *within* that order, any more than the eye can reproduce itself within the field of vision; it can be alluded to only in the *form* of the symbolic, in its infinite play of difference and absence. The castrated narrative of *Tristram Shandy* is the sign of its castrated author, but—since it *is* his impotency—can tell him nothing of the 'real' causes of that lack. The novel's discourse thus installs itself in the space of a primordial absence—a bodily mutilation—which is nothing less than the *nature of literary discourse itself*, and which can consequently never quite round on its repressed origins.

For Sterne, then, the problematical structure of the sign itself—how can it be both meaning and materiality?—opens out into another question, that of the structure of the subject. It is a question posed on the terrain of that immense irony which is autobiography: how can the subject's discourse signify his material determinants when it is itself the product of their repression? Or—to re-pose the question as the problem of literary representation—how can the signified be captured other than in an infinite chain of signifiers within which it will itself assume the status of one more signifier? To turn back from Sterne to Swift is to see how, in *A Tale of a Tub*, all of these problems are already adumbrated—how, indeed, they thrust themselves forward as inescapable corollaries of that new, obsessionally subject-centred literary *genre* which, much to Swift's ideological disgust, was in process of arising. *Gulliver's Travels* is Swift's major riposte to that *genre*—a work which, tempting the reader into its space with the bait of the 'coherent subject' Gulliver, does so only to reveal Gulliver as an area traversed and devastated by intolerable contradiction. Like Sterne, Swift locates the material/ideal contradiction of his theological problematic in the sign itself, which seems to recognize no middle ground between elaborating its referent out of sight, and evaporating into it (those Laputans who hold up material objects to one another rather than exchange words). It is these material/ideal contradictions that the fourth book of *Gulliver's Travels* detonates within the reader, ruthlessly dispersing him or her amidst mutually incompatible discourses. Gulliver despises men as Yahoos and identifies with the Houyhnhnms; the Houyhnhnms despise the Yahoos and regard Gulliver as one of them; we are amused by the Houyhnhnms and by Gulliver's delusions, but are close enough to the Yahoos for the amusement to be uneasy; and to cap it all there are some respects in which the Yahoos *are* superior to humans. There is no way for the reader to 'totalize' these contradictions, which the text so adroitly springs upon him or her; he or she is merely caught in their dialectical interplay, rendered as eccentric to himself as the lunatic Gulliver, unable to turn to the refuge of an assuring authorial voice. To deconstruct the reader, reducing him or her from positioned subject to a function of polyphonic discourses: this is the *ideological* intervention accomplished by all of Swift's writing. And it is here that a discourse concerned with Derrida circles to the name of Brecht.

There is no doubt that when Benjamin writes of the doleful tainting of language by meaning, its leashing to logicality, he betrays a nostalgia for the pure, prelapsarian word.[32] But this is not quite Eliot's 'dissociation of sensibility' or Leavis's organicist delusions. For Eliot and Leavis, a 'prelapsarian' language is one transparent to the body: it is thus 'material' only by derivation. In the postlapsarian Miltonic era, language disentwines itself from the digestive tracts and falls into its own clogging material mode. For Benjamin, the Edenic word is likewise bodily, expressive and mimetic; but it never ceases to manifest a materiality of its own. 'Language communicates the linguistic being of things. The clearest manifestation of this being, however, is language itself. The answer to the question "*What* does language communicate?" is therefore "All language communicates itself"'.[33] Ironically, this materialism of the word is nowhere more evident than in the 'postlapsarian' language of baroque. The more things and meanings disengage, the more obvious become the material operations of the allegories that fumble to reunite them. Such unity, to be sure, can be won only at the cost of a grievous reification: emblem and hieroglyph paralyse history to print, and the body achieves its deepest signification as corpse. But if experience is in this way converted to a stilted, repetitive text, it is only the more dramatically to reveal that it is, in some sense, 'text' in the first place. The lumbering action of the *Trauerspiel* writes large or plays through in slow motion something of the nature of language 'as such'. The matter-laden letters of such drama press an Edenic materiality of the word to a point of grisly caricature; and this differs sharply from a Leavisian view of the relations between Donne and Milton.

32 See 'On Language as Such and on the Language of Man', OWS, pp. 107–23.
33 OWS, p. 109.

It is certainly true that we cannot imagine the shattered world of the *Trauerspiel* without itching to construct some pre-given unity from which it has lapsed away; in this sense Benjamin's text confronts us with the familiar problem of trying to think difference without positing the unity it denies. But if allegory 'enslaves objects in the eccentric embrace of meaning',[34] that meaning is irreducibly multiple. The very arbitrariness of the relations between signifier and signified in allegorical thought encourages 'the exploitation of ever remoter characteristics of the representative objects as symbols, so as to surpass even the Egyptians with new subtleties. In addition to this there was the dogmatic power of the meanings handed down from the ancients, so that one and the same object can just as easily signify a virtue as a vice, and therefore more or less anything'.[35] In an astounding circulation of signifiers, 'any person, any object, any relationship can mean absolutely anything else'.[36] The immanent meaning that ebbs from the object under the transfixing gaze of melancholy leaves it a pure signifier, a rune or fragment retrieved from the clutches of an univocal sense and surrendered unconditionally into the allegorist's power. If it has become in one sense embalmed, it has also been liberated into polyvalence: it is in this that for Benjamin the profoundly dialectical nature of allegory lies. Allegorical discourse has the doubleness of the death's head: 'total expressionlessness—the black of the eye-sockets—coupled to the most unbridled expression—the grinning rows of teeth'.[37] The mortified landscape of history is redeemed, not by being recuperated into spirit, but by being raised, so to speak, to the second power—converted into a formal repertoire, fashioned into certain enigmatic emblems which then hold the promise of knowledge and possession.

History, then, as always for Benjamin, progresses by its bad side. If there is a route beyond reification, it is through and not around it; if even apparently dead objects, in the sepulchral splendour of the *Trauerspiel*, secure tyrannical power over the human, it remains true that the tenacious self-absorption of melancholy, brooding upon such husks, embraces them in order to redeem them. For Benjamin, such redemption is finally Messianic; but even his Messianism has a kind of dialectical structure.

34 O, p. 202.
35 O, p. 174.
36 O, p. 175.
37 OWS, p. 70.

The baroque renounces eschatology: it shows no immanent mechanism whereby earthly things are even now being gathered in and exalted. Instead, the rich profusion of mundane objects is seen as a kind of plundering of the hereafter: the more history is thoroughly secularized, the less possible it is to characterize heaven in its terms. Heaven, accordingly, is reduced to a pure signifier, an empty space, but this vacuum will one day engulf the world with catastrophic violence.[38] If this apocalypticism is for us one of the least palatable elements of Benjamin's thought, it nonetheless marks a kind of 'negative dialectics' that, for all its idealism, comes close to the productively pessimistic side of historical materialism. Indeed to 'begin from the bad side' is a methodological premise for Benjamin, as is clear enough from his study of Baudelaire: 'sundering truth from falsehood is the goal of the materialist method, not its point of departure. In other words, its point of departure is the object riddled with error, with *doxa*'.[39] It is by submitting itself to the mixed substance of the empirical object, not by transfiguring that object at a stroke into its appearance 'in truth', that the progressively discriminative movement of inquiry proceeds. It is not always easy, admittedly, to distinguish this clearly from the positivist tendency for which Adorno chides Benjamin, the 'wide-eyed presentation of mere facts'[40] that in the very density of its description seems to pass right through the object and emerge on the other side as a sort of ghosted theorizing of it. 'There is a delicate empiricism', Benjamin quotes Goethe as writing, 'which so intimately involves itself with the object that it becomes true theory'.[41] Whatever the limits of this emphasis, it belongs with the Benjamin who acknowledged the mixed substance of his own political situation, stranded between Communists and bourgeoisie—who recognized that 'right' in such a condition could only mean 'necessarily, symptomatically, productively false'.[42] To begin from the bad side is to reckon loss, ambiguity and *mauvaise foi* into the calculation; and Benjamin began his own writing career with a book that turned such things to productive use.

What Benjamin asserts of the allegorical object—that at its nadir of blank inertia, purged of all mystified immanence, it can be liberated into

38 See 'Theologico-Political Fragment', OWS, pp. 155–6.
39 CB, p. 103.
40 *Aesthetics and Politics*, NLB 1977, p. 129.
41 'A Small History of Photography', OWS, p. 252.
42 B, 2, p. 530.

multiple uses—has more than an echo of Georg Lukács's *History and Class Consciousness*, which in similar idealist fashion sees the reduction of the proletariat to the paradigmatic commodity as the prelude to its emancipation. The *Trauerspiel* ransacks heaven and ruins all transcendence, marooning its characters in a world of paranoid, patriarchal power; but by the same token it disowns all facile teleologies, ruptures the imaginary relations of myth and scatters free those symbolic fragments from which the emblem may forge fresh correspondences. Released from the ideological tyrannies of Nature, the subject can find no consolation in a compensatory myth of history, for that too has shrunk to sheer ritual repetition. If discourse has been similarly debased to a mere permutation of properties, an arbitrary *bricolage* of elements, this itself subverts the logocentrism of the symbol and unmasks the speaking voice as yet another inscription. The more the signifier becomes fetishized in the ceaseless pedantries of emblematic correspondence, the more suggestively arbitrary it comes to seem: the very laborious effort expended on asserting its iconic or 'motivated' relations with the signified comes curiously to demystify itself, revealing how usably unmotivated it actually is. The enigmas of history force the techniques of their decipherment into peculiar self-consciousness, so that concealment on one level produces exposure on another: a fetishized reality gives birth to a fetishized hermeneutic, but one so palpably so that it lays bare its own devices. And trembling on the brink of this historical collapse, waiting in the wings for its redemptive entry, is, precisely—nothing: the pure signifier of a paradise that never comes, an utterly destructive apocalypse that is at once everything and nothing, a spasm of empty space that consummates all those deaths and absences that are language itself.

The truly materialist version of Benjamin's redemptive hope will come not through his mentor Lukács but through his friend Bertolt Brecht. For nothing is quite so striking as the way in which the *Origin* recapitulates, even before they had properly initiated, all the major themes of Benjamin's later championship of Brechtian drama. Baroque allegory lays bare the device, posing motto and caption in blunt, obtrusive relation to the visual figure, defeating the mystifications of symbolism. In the dense hieroglyphics of this genre, *writing* comes to receive all its material weight—but this in a dialectical way, since as we have seen any figure or object can come to mean absolutely anything else. Objects in such spectacles are always strictly coded, in a discourse as far as Jacques Derrida himself would wish from the speaking voice; and images, far from being hierarchically ranked, are piled in a seemingly haphazard way one on the other, with no 'totalizing' aim in mind. Yet for all that the drama is ostentatiously a construction, though of a notably decentred kind: its diverse, elaborate features submit inexorably to a structure that yet forever refuses to unite them, allowing them their jarring particularity and glittering ornamentation. 'Shock' is thus an essential quality of such texts: the baroque, for Benjamin, is nothing if not provocative and offensive. The allegorist is spontaneously anti-Hegelian: the 'essence', rather than lurking behind the object as its repressed secret, is dragged into the open, hounded into the brazen status of a caption. The relation between object and essence is metonymic rather than metaphorical: 'in the context of allegory the image is only a signature, only the monogram of essence, not the essence itself in a mask'.[43]

If it is true that the action of such melancholic dramas moves with a certain heavy-handed slowness, it is also true that situations can change in a flash. Objects in such texts are fanatically collected, but then slackly and indifferently dispersed in their arrangements; and the very form of the *Trauerspiel* reproduces this irregular impulse, since it builds act upon act in the 'manner of terraces', repulsing any suave linearity of presentation for a syncopated rhythm that oscillates endlessly between swift switches of direction and consolidations into rigidity. The imagery of the *Trauerspiel* rudely dismembers the human body in order to allegorize its discrete parts, sundering its organic unity (in a manner analogous, perhaps, to Freud's) so that some meaning may be rescued from its parcelled fragments. Like Benjamin's own later philosophy of history, the *Trauerspiel*, obsessed with the transience of the present and the need to redeem it for eternity, blasts coherences apart in order to salvage them in their primordial givenness.

It is surely clear that what we have here are all the seeds of Benjamin's later defence of Brecht. The drama as fragmented, device-baring, non-hierarchical, shock-producing; theatre as dispersed, gear-switching and dialectical, ostentatious and arbitrary yet densely encoded: what Benjamin discovered in Brecht was precisely how you might do all this and be non-

43 O, p. 214.

melancholic into the bargain.[44] And the secret of the *Origin* is not merely that it speaks of these qualities; it is that it is itself constituted by them. For there is hardly an epithet used by Benjamin to describe his object of study that does not glance sideways at his own critical method. That this is so, yet that he succeeds in displacing rather than reproducing the texts in question, is surely one of the book's most remarkable triumphs. Since the text believes that the task of philosophy is to divest phenomena of their empirical trappings so that they may be lifted into a realm of essences whose mutual interrelations constitute truth, this is a triumph it doubtless needs; though even this epistemology, as we shall see later, has a materialist seed.

44 What Angus Fletcher has to say of allegory in his unsurpassed study is particularly appropriate to Brechtian theatre: 'the price of a lack of mimetic naturalness is what the allegorist, like the Metaphysical poet, must pay in order to force his reader into an analytic frame of mind. . . . The silences in allegory mean as much as the filled-in spaces, because by bridging the silent gaps between oddly unrelated images we reach the sunken understructure of thought . . .' (*Allegory: The Theory of a Symbolic Mode*, Ithaca 1964, p. 107). The whole cluster of concerns that Fletcher delineates—allegory, multiple meaning, didacticism, montage, surrealistic surface textures—is of the closest relevance to Benjamin's cultural interests.

2

The death of the symbol in the dismembered body of script will become, for the later Benjamin, the decline of the 'aura' in the age of commodity production. Indeed the term 'commodity' is the eloquent silence of the *Origin*, the secret link between baroque allegory and the later anatomizing of Baudelaire. The allegorical stance towards objects is on the one hand abstract and arbitrary: since any one of them may be exchanged for another, all are indifferently levelled to relative insignificance. Yet if reality is thus devalued at a stroke, it is elevated in the same instant. For those objects in fact selected as signifiers are invested by baroque with fetishistic force: whatever it picks up, the *Trauerspiel's* Midas-like touch reifies into numinous meaning. The baroque figure thus displays the dual structure of the commodity, which atomizes Nature to abstract equivalents only to recharge each fragment with a kind of grisly caricature of the magical 'aura' it has driven from social production in general. Viewed from another angle, the commodity can be seen to blend the qualities that Benjamin assigns respectively to emblem and to symbol: if it has something of the stark, solitary flatness of the one, it also glows with the alluring radiance of the other. In this, it finds an echo in what Benjamin sees as the provocative blend of Baudelaire's poetry, with its brusque coincidence of allegory and lyricism.

The *flâneur*—that drifting relic of a decaying petty bourgeoisie who for Benjamin bulks so large behind Baudelaire's texts—has something of the allegorist's way with things. Strolling self-composedly through the city, loitering without intent, languid yet secretly vigilant, he displays in living motion something of the commodity's self-contradictory form. His solitary dispossession reflects the commodity's existence as fragment (Benjamin speaks of the commodity as 'abandoned' in the crowd), and his meanderings are as magically free of physical traces as the commodity is absolved from the traces of its production. Yet at the same time his painstaking production of himself as 'personality', his genteel-amateur distaste for the industrial labour through which he glides, signifies the protest of a fading aura in the face of commodity production—just as the commodity itself, that glamorous, eternally self-possessed 'subject', offers itself as compensation for the very drab division of labour of which it is the product. Both *flâneur* and commodity tart themselves up in dandyish dress.[45] The *flâneur* at once spiritually pre-dates commodity production—he strays through the bazaars but prices nothing—and is himself the prototypical commodity, not least because his relationship to the masses is one of simultaneous complicity and contempt. In this, indeed, the *flâneur* resembles the allegorist, for both dip randomly into the ruck of objects to single out for consecration certain ones that they know to be in themselves arbitrary and ephemeral. The *flâneur* 'becomes deeply involved with [the crowd], only to relegate them to oblivion with a single glance of contempt';[46] and this ambivalence, for the baroque writer, is 'the most dramatic manifestation of the power of knowledge'.[47] A woman on the street, glimpsed momentarily in a Baudelaire poem, is a sign of this ambiguity in the commodity structure. On the one hand she is abstractly anonymous, a serialized apparition in the crowd, dissolved back into it at the very moment of 'exchange' with the poet's eyes; yet that moment is then sealed with the uniqueness of the aura, imbued with the flash of the mutely revelatory symbol. 'Love at last sight' is the typical urban experience. 'Separation', Benjamin comments in *One-Way Street*, 'penetrates the disappearing person like a pigment and steeps him in gentle radiance'.[48] In the symbol of the *Origin*, 'destruction is idealized and the transfigured face of nature is fleetingly revealed in the light of redemp-

---

45 In a letter of 1913 to an English friend Herbert Belmore, Benjamin protests against what he sees as Belmore's fetishistic cult of the prostitute as a form of 'insipid aestheticism', a Romantic idealization of what is in reality a form of commodity-exchange. Prostitute, aura and commodity are already subtly linked in his thought. His own declared views on sexuality differ from what he takes to be Belmore's spiritualizing of the whore: 'Europe is made up of individuals (each comprising the masculine and the feminine), not of men and women' (B, 1, p. 65). It could hardly be said, on the other hand, that Benjamin always practised what he preached.

46 CB, p. 128.

47 O, p. 184.

48 OWS, p. 53.

tion'.[49] Translated to the city, however, this eternal moment of the symbol, the hallowed space scooped out of time, is also the vacuum through which other such moments may metonymically rush, each casually effacing itself for the next.

The commodity's relation to its potential buyers contains something of this contradiction. If the *flâneur* knows the delights of possessing unpossessed and seeing unseen, of tasting transiently so as to remain self-composed, the commodity disports itself with all comers without its halo slipping, promises permanent possession to everyone in the market without abandoning its secretive isolation. Serializing its consumers, it nevertheless makes intimate *ad hominem* address to each. Its 'soul', Benjamin remarks, would, if it existed, be the most empathetic ever, 'for it would have to see in everyone the buyer in whose hand and house it wants to nestle'.[1] It is obvious, then, that the *flâneur* cannot compete with the commodity, for though both are ironically aware of the abstractly quantified nature of the masses from whom they beckon out certain privileged subjects, such quantification is for the commodity the very condition of its existence. The *flâneur*, by contrast, fights a losing battle against the crowd's impersonality, struggling to maintain his *sang froid* in the rush, imbuing the masses with the last tattered vestiges of an aura he will then be able narcissistically to recoup from it. Just as his life-style represents a desperate last-ditch domestication of the urban, turning shop-signs into wall ornaments and news-stands into private libraries, so his faltering gaze strives to aestheticize the city, in a prelude to that later, more radical rebuff of social experience which, with *l'art pour l'art*, will resist the commodity only to reproduce something of its own arcane rites in doing so. It is also, more remotely, a prelude to that ultimate aestheticizing of the political which is, as Benjamin saw, fascism.

Capitalist society, whose social relations are stripped of an aura everywhere reinstated by the commodities they generate, is in some ways an even more degraded version of the corrupt world of the *Trauerspiel*. In an implausible analogy, Benjamin sees the drudgery of the gambler as a counterpart to the drudgery of labour: both involve discrete, repetitive, manipulative operations that entail the death of 'experience', in the auratic or Proustian sense of a richly recollected inwardness. But if the work of both gambler and labourer is devoid of substance, so is that of the baroque intriguer, whose manipulative practices are wholly without historical logic. Indeed it is not difficult to read the faithless opportunism of the intriguer, whose life burns itself out in a pure repetitive present, as a kind of lack of Proustian remembrance; and a similar deficiency infests the texts in which he appears, which like their characters seem to know no 'experience' beyond the extrinsic shuffling of fixed elements. But whereas the dialectic required to overturn the world of the *Trauerspiel* is, as we have seen, of an unutterably transcendental kind, this is clearly not the case with capitalism. For the technology that conspires in reproducing the aura can also be used to demystify it. The baroque, rigorously encoded as it is, reduces the scope of imaginative play to an ingenious quibbling on unwieldly hieroglyphs; it is concerned with the expression of conventions rather than with the conventions of expression. The techniques of mechanical reproduction similarly reduce the scope of 'free expression'— hence Baudelaire's unnerved response to the daguerreotype. But such reproduction differs from the repetitions of a history drained of substance. The mechanical reproduction of an object, which for Benjamin undermines its unique aura, promises to undo a fetishism that finds its highest form in, precisely, repetition. Jacques Lacan has reminded us that in Freud's texts repetition (*Wiederholen*) is never reproduction (*Reproduzieren*);[50] and in Benjamin's writing they might be said to be antithetical. The epitome of repetition is the cult of *nouveauté* or ritual of fashion—that final triumph of commodity fetishism in which, as Benjamin puts it, the living body is prostituted to the inorganic world and succumbs to its sex appeal. Novelty is independent of the use-value of the commodity, and so causes it to appear at its most fetishistic; it marks the frozen dialectic of history, projecting its illusion of infinite renewal in the mirror of infinite sameness.

The secret of this arrested dialectic may be found in the fact that the commodity, which flaunts itself as a unique, heteroclite slice of matter, is in truth part of the very mechanism by which history becomes homogenized. As the signifier of mere abstract equivalence, the empty space through which one portion of labour-power exchanges with another, the commodity nonetheless disguises its virulent anti-materialism in a carnival of consumption. In the circulation of commodities, each presents to the other a mirror which reflects no more than its own mirroring; all that is new in this process is the very flash and dexterity with which mirrors are interchanged, the *Trauerspiel's* ostentatious 'activity of arrangement'. As with Proust, we are dealing with what Benjamin calls an 'impassioned cult of similarity'.[51] The exchange of commodities is at once smoothly continuous and an infinity of interruption: since each gesture of exchange is an exact repetition of the previous one, there can be no connection between them. It is for this reason that the time of the commodity is at once empty and homogeneous: its homogeneity is, precisely, the infinite self-identity of a pure recurrence which, since it has no power to modify, has no more body than a mirror-image. What binds history into plenitude is the exact symmetry of its repeated absences. It is because its non-happenings always happen in exactly the same way that it forms such an organic whole. Since the significance of the commodity is always elsewhere, in the social relations of production whose traces it has obliterated, it is freed, like the baroque emblem, into polyvalence, smoothed to a surface that can receive the trace of any other commodity whatsoever. But since these other commodities exist only as traces of yet others, this polyvalence is perhaps better described as a structure of ambiguity—an ambiguity that for Benjamin is 'the figurative appearance of the dialectic, the law of the dialectic at a standstill'.[52] The duplicity of the commodity lies in the fact that it is at once bafflingly esoteric and absolutely eccentric to itself. Hollowed to the empty receptacle of traces of other traces, without a particle of autonomous matter in its economic make-up, the commodity is an orphaned nonentity with nothing to call its own; but like the *flâneur* in his last shabby-genteel peregrinations, sucking from the city a substance as frugal as Baudelaire's rag-picker, it brazenly cloaks this paucity with the panache of an impenetrable self-sufficiency. The process of commodity-exchange is infinitely metonymic: each commodity is defined only by its displacement of another, constituted only by the endless circulation of the 'trace' that is the mechanism of its movement. Yet as with the secretly 'spatial' time of the *Trauerspiel*, this metonymy is constantly folded back into an enormous immobile meta-phor, since each commodity merely seeks out in its partner that essence in which it can find itself securely mirrored. And this steady inversion of metonym into metaphor at the level of *exchange*, this veering of the substitutions of displacement into the substitutions of substitutions, has

51 'The Image of Proust', I, p. 206.
52 CB, p. 171.

its root in the process of commodity *production*, where the causal, metonymic relation between that process and its products is concealed, in the body of the commodity, as one of mere substitution.

In this sense, perhaps, the commodity can be understood as the baroque emblem pressed to an extreme. The meaning of the emblem is also always elsewhere, in the continual metamorphosis of signifiers, but this polyvalence is harnessed to hermeneutic ends: the more polyvalent the signifier, the greater its forensic force in deciphering the real. And the more intricate in structure it grows, the more its materiality is foregrounded without it in the least ceasing to denote. Indeed it is precisely by becoming material talisman that it has the power to unlock Nature's secrets. In the commodity, by contrast, the materiality of the signifier has on the one hand degenerated to esoteric self-reference, and on the other hand has been evacuated by exchange-value to mere abstraction. The commodity is the 'bad side' of the emblem, grossly swelling its material density at the same time as it robs it of referential value. This, indeed, is the commodity's inherent contradiction—that the more the vacuum of exchange-value at its centre inflates its material skin to garish proportions, the more this very excess of materiality comes to signify nothing but itself, collapsing the object back upon itself as a monstrous tautology. In this way, the secret of the object's truly tautological status within the process of commodity exchange is betrayed.

If the commodity is the bad side of the emblem, so is it of the modern semiotic signifier. For it is surely not difficult to see how contemporary semiotics, once it has cut itself loose from (or failed to encounter) historical materialism, is liable at its most euphoric to reproduce at the level of the sign that blend of formalistic idealism and vulgar materialism that Marxism locates in the very structure of the commodity. On the one hand, such semiotics may valuably re-materialize the signifier—but only at the risk of collapsing history into it and conflating all materialisms into one. The sign becomes the commodity of the petty-bourgeois intellectual, who succumbs to its sex appeal not least because it tantalizingly combines the fleshiness of the stripper with her elusiveness. To those who protest that strip-shows are a substitution for genuine sexuality, the petty-bourgeois semiotician will reply that nothing could be more material. On the other hand, semiotics may usefully defetishize the signifier—but only at the risk of reducing it to the instantly effaced moment of a discourse that, like commodity exchange, speaks of nothing but itself. Nor is this a mere analogy: for it is surely the case that the productive impasse to which semiotics has brought us, in trying to think signification coherently at all, was in a sense there all along, shaped as it is by a history of commodity production confronting us daily with the problem of deciphering signs that appear to repress their materiality on one level only to parade it on another.

The ambiguities we are discussing are perhaps nowhere more sharply focused than in Benjamin's concept of the 'trace', a term which turns on its axis within his work to present several faces. The traces of himself preserved by the bourgeois in his odds and ends of domestic articles are a kind of shabby compensation for the diminution of private life, an *ersatz* aura whose luminousness has now dwindled to a heap of fossilized fragments containing the barest imprint of life. It is, in its own way, a transition from metaphor to metonymy: unable any longer to totalize his experience in some heroic figure, the bourgeois is forced to let it trickle away into objects related to him by sheer contiguity. In the aura or symbol, connotations are always fused, instantaneous; in allegory they are laid out alongside one another, pedantically explicated. It is such traces that Benjamin sees as expunged by the 'destructive character'—the figure who, as in his romanticized image of Brecht, has purged himself of 'experience' in order to become the faceless, cheerful, non-visionary agent of a revolutionary violence that will blast out of history the apocalyptic empty space within which the new may germinate.[53] Such a character must efface both the fossilized traces of others and his own, including those of his own destructiveness: he is the revolutionary antithesis of the *flâneur*, whose trackless ambulations among the crowd likewise clear a provisional space, but that of the magic circle in which his solitary subjectivity may disport itself. The destructive character, by contrast, is the *Unmensch*, the radical dismantling of the bourgeois humanist subject, who has renounced all truck with bourgeois 'Man' for a sober, efficient, inconspicuous intercourse with the 'people'.[54]

The trace, then, belongs in one sense with the aura, either as its petrified physical residue or, as we shall see in the case of Benjamin's Freudian theory of remembrance, the unconscious track, fraying or *Bahnung* which psychoanalytically speaking is the aura's very mechanism. But more

53 See 'The Destructive Character', OWS, pp. 157–9; and Irving Wohlfarth's excellent essay on this piece in *Diacritics*, June 1978, pp. 47–65.
54 See 'Leute', GS, 2/1, pp. 216–17.

generally the concept stands directly opposed to the aura, to indicate those elements of the productive process which, in still clinging to an object, help to defetishize it—elements which in the case of mechanical reproduction lend it a kind of fruitful anonymity or pliability of feature, equivalent in the realm of things to the *Unmensch* in the realm of individuals. But the trace is also what marks an object's historicity, the scars it has accumulated at the hands of its users, the visible imprint of its variable functions. The traces inscribed on an object's body are the web that undoes its self-identity, the mesh of consumptional modes in which it has been variously caught. The erasure, preservation or revival of traces, then, is a political practice that depends on the nature of the traces and contexts in question: the object may need to be treated as a palimpsest, its existent traces expunged by an overwriting, or it may secrete blurred traces that can be productively retrieved. In any case, it seems clear that the metaphor of trace is in the end too external for Benjamin's purposes— that what is at issue is not just a rubbing or inscribing of surfaces but a recognition that all objects are *written* in their deepest being, internally constituted by the changing script of their social relations, which never adds up to a fully coherent text. Objects, like the human subject, are 'written' before they 'speak', a fact that in both cases accounts for their crisis-ridden history.[55] The human subject, who is already scored over by a network of unconscious signifiers before it comes to assume its signifying place within what Lacan has termed the 'symbolic order', finds itself fissured in precisely that painful transition, divided between its allotted place and its subversive desire. But the Law or 'Name of the Father', which joints the subject to that place under threat of castration, at the same stroke opening up the unconscious, is in a sense operative also in the history of objects and artefacts. Its names in that history are 'aura', 'authority', 'authenticity'—names which designate the object's per- sistence in its originary mode of being, its carving out of an organic identity for itself over time. 'The authenticity of a thing', writes Benjamin, 'is the essence of all that is transmissible from its beginning, ranging from its substantive duration to its testimony to the history which it has experienced. Since the historical testimony rests on the authenticity, the former, too, is jeopardized by reproduction when substantive duration ceases to matter. And what is really jeopardized when the historical testimony is affected is the authority of the aura'.[56]

Yet we know that such persistence of the origin is ideological delusion. The statue of Venus venerated by the ancient Romans is only for the chemist the 'same' statue denounced as idolatry by medieval clerics. Mechanical reproduction—which may figure here as a metonym for cultural revolution—destroys the authority of origins, but in doing so writes large a plurality that was there all along. It signifies the invasion of multiplicity into the object, shattering that illusory self-identity which one might risk calling the object's 'ego'. For just as the psychoanalytic subject is able to designate itself as a homogeneous entity over time only by repressing the traces of its unconscious desires, so the auratic object, whether it be cultural artefact or state apparatus, continually rewrites its own history to expel the traces of its ruptured, heterogeneous past. The political task of 'liberating' an object, then, takes the form of opening up its unconscious—detecting within it those chips of heterogeneity that it has been unable quite to dissolve. 'Even though chronology places regularity above permanence, it cannot prevent heterogeneous, conspicuous fragments from remaining within it'.[57] When Benjamin looks at a photographic portrait, what fascinates him is precisely not the composed aura of stillness and distance in which its subjects bathe, but those stray, tell-tale, irreducible symptoms of 'reality' that flicker on its edges—symptoms which, in linking the photograph's present to a putative 'real' future for its subjects, constrain us, viewing that photographed past from the future, into constellating our own present time with its. 'No matter how artful the photographer, no matter how carefully posed his subject, the beholder feels an irresistible urge to search such a picture for the tiny spark of contingency, of the Here and Now, with which reality has so to speak seared the subject, to find the inconspicuous spot where in the immediacy of that long-forgotten moment the future subsists so eloquently that we, looking back, may rediscover it'.[58]

There is another sense in which the superficiality of the 'trace' image is potentially misleading. For it may suggest something as easily wiped clean as a snail's slime, rather than—as in Benjamin's own implicit image—a

56 'The Work of Art in the Age of Mechanical Reproduction', I, p. 223.
57 CB, p. 144.
58 'A Small History of Photography', OWS, p. 243.

snail's fossilized imprint in rock. It can conspire, in other words, with that now fashionable epistemological 'constructivism' for which the object—since we have all agreed to abolish the *Ding-an-sich*—can seem pure possibility in the hands of the subject, offering not the slightest resistance to the subject's designs upon it. Properly understood, 'trace' reminds us among other things of exactly that resistance to reconstruction which is a sign of the object's materiality, and of the fact that it is not just anybody's ideological dupe. It reminds us that the business of erasing, preserving or rewriting traces is always one of political *struggle*, a struggle in which the object itself is no mere paper tiger.

When Benjamin writes of commodity fetishism as a succumbing to the sex appeal of the inorganic, it is difficult not to feel that he is quoting indirectly from a text that plays a major role in the study of Baudelaire: Freud's *Beyond the Pleasure Principle*. In that work, Freud speaks of the pleasure principle as a tendency 'operating in the service of a function whose business is to free the mental apparatus entirely from excitation or to keep the amount of excitation in it constant or to keep it as low as possible'.[59] The concern of this function is 'with the most universal endeavour of all living substance—namely to return to the quiescence of the inorganic world'. Death, so to speak, is the ultimate aura, in which the organism can at last discover secure refuge from the shocks that batter it; and it is possible to speculate that the erotic enthralment to the commodity provides a foretaste of this condition. Eros, in Freud's metapsychology, is in the service of Thanatos, or the death drive, in that it continually seeks a discharge of stimuli that anticipates the quiescence of death; and to this extent commodity fetishism might be said to have a contradictory psychoanalytic meaning. In so far as it is fetishism, it constitutes a flight from death—an attempt to plug that minatory gap, first unveiled in the castration complex, with an imaginary object. In so far as it is an erotic sport with inorganic matter, it allows us a glimpse of Eros's lethal purposes. Repetition partakes of those purposes, as a mechanism that helps to secure the 'binding', or mastery, of stimuli preparatory to their successful discharge; and it is therefore not surprising that Benjamin should associate both repetition and Thanatos with the commodity. The commodity is a death's head that, unlike the skull of the *Trauerspiel*, has

59 *The Standard Edition of the Complete Psychological Works of Sigmund Freud*, James Strachey, ed., vol. 18, London 1955, p. 62.

ceased to know itself as such. In the presence of fashion, that supreme cult of the commodity, we are in the presence of death—of a hectic repetition that gets precisely nowhere, a flashing of mirror upon mirror that believes that by thus arresting history it can avoid death, but in this orgy of matter succeeds only in being drawn more inexorably into its grasp. What is reflected in the mirror of the commodity is the absence of death in a double sense: its erasure, but also its sinister blankness. And this contradiction is for Benjamin at the very heart of the dialectical or utopian image, which in searching out the new always finds itself rapidly regressing, prefiguring the future in the idiom of the archaic.

However, Benjamin's chief use of Freud in *Charles Baudelaire* relates to his counterposing of 'aura' and 'shock'. In the process of perception, only those stimuli that consciousness does not vigilantly register will sink into the unconscious to lay memory traces there; and these traces, once revived, are at the root of the auratic experience. 'Living' an event with full awareness, parrying the shocks of stimuli rather than allowing them to penetrate, is therefore inimical to the aura, as the *Unmensch* is inimical to the *flâneur* and mechanical reproduction to 'authenticity'. Freud's theory of memory traces allows Benjamin to press the scandal of the *Trauerspiel*, in which 'experience' is subordinated to the *écriture* of emblem, to even greater lengths—for now writing has rudely invaded the inmost sanctum of experience itself, whose productive mechanism lies exposed as nothing more than a set of inscriptions. In both cases, at any rate, it is clear that writing and experience can never coincide, and this whether 'experience' is taken to denote the directly lived (*Erlebnis*, 'shock') or privileged inwardness (*Erfahrung*, 'aura'). In the first case, writing and experience inhabit two quite separate systems: what is lived cannot be traced and what is traced cannot be lived. In the second case, experience is divided by the trace between consciousness and the unconscious: the moment when the stimulus implants itself in the latter is disjunct from the moment when it comes to fruition in the former. Auratic experience can only be recollection. What we have here, then, is an adumbration of the contemporary theme of the non-coincidence of signification and being, whether in the form of Michel Foucault's flamboyant assertion that Man and language can never be coterminous, or in Jacques Lacan's reflections on the 'fading' of the subject in language, its Hobson's choice between meaning and being. Writing scoops out the organic interiority of the bourgeois-humanist subject: the very act whereby the subject designates itself in the signifying chain is no more than a perpetual standing-in for its own absence. 'When you name yourself', as Brecht writes in *A Man's a Man*, 'you always name another'.

Benjamin does more than adumbrate this theme, however; he lends it political meaning, in advance of the depoliticization it is now suffering at the hands of intellectuals who will cheerfully subvert every transcendental signifier but the state. Perhaps this can be best seen by contrasting Benjamin, somewhat improbably, with another critic much concerned with stimuli: I.A. Richards. Like Matthew Arnold before him, Richards is a conscious ideologue: in an era of bewildering social change, traditional habits are crumbling, religion has lost its hegemony and impulses are becoming disequilibrated. What is needed, Richards proclaims, is a 'League of Nations for the moral ordering of the impulses';[60] and poetry is called upon to fulfil this role. The moral impulses, cramped by conventional ethics and bemused by the increasing complexity of social life, have been getting out of hand, transforming themselves into a lawless horde of uncouth libertarians; and poetry, with its attendant science of criticism, must inject a little law and order into this mob of appetencies. 'No life can be excellent in which the elementary responses are disorganized and confused',[61] and under the pressures of what Richards terms 'commercialism' the confusion of stimuli assailing our senses has lately grown serious. What is needed is a central administrative body that will discipline the laxer stimuli, force some of the least valuable of them into involuntary redundancy, and organize the rest into an efficient work-force. This central body is poetry. It is, however, a meritocratic rather than authoritarian form of government, concerned to promote the conditions in which 'success' can be obtained for the greatest number of stimuli; and such success clearly cannot be left to the operations of the psychic free market. Something of social-democratic intervention or eugenic planning is obviously needed, by which criticism can evaluate which stimuli are most likely to succeed in life and which should be repressed as socially harmful. The function of poetry is essentially conciliatory, holding the ring between competing interests, eliminating as far as possible any subversive struggle between antagonistic impulses: the artist's experiences 'represent conciliations of impulses which in most

60 *Science and Poetry*, London 1926, p. 35.
61 *Principles of Literary Criticism*, London 1963, p. 62.

minds are still confused, intertrammelled and conflicting'.[62] Without such centralized arbitration, standards of value are likely to collapse beneath the 'more sinister potentialities of the cinema and the loud-speaker'.[63] Modern science is quite correct to be positivist, but emotionally it leaves something to be desired; it does not pose the deeper questions of 'what' and 'why'. Richards does not believe in these questions himself, but he generously concedes that many people do—indeed that if the masses are not supplied with pseudo-answers to them they are likely to grow restless. The task of poetry, in brief, is to provide such pseudo-answers to such pseudo-questions, bringing the emotive equipment of men and women into line with their new cognitive apparatus. The closest modern equivalent to this aesthetic position is probably to be found in Stalinism, where feelings are likewise to be harnessed by art to new functions. For Richards, then, the role of art is to defuse the shock-effects of stimuli by selective organization; for Benjamin, it is to exploit such shocks to their full political potential, disrupting imaginary unities in the process.

The effect of the commodity is to suppress difference beneath repetition; and this is as much as to say that it is, in Lacan's sense, an essentially 'imaginary' object, one which bolsters the subject in an illusory self-identity by ceaselessly reflecting back to it an image that is at once itself and another. For Benjamin, this imaginary interchange is grasped primarily in terms of vision. 'What was inevitably felt to be inhuman, one might even say deadly, in daguerreotypy was the (prolonged) looking into the camera, since the camera records our likeness without returning our gaze. But looking at someone carries the implicit expectation that our look will be returned by the object of our gaze. Where this expectation is met (which, in the case of thought processes, can apply equally to the look of the eye of the mind and to a glance pure and simple), there is an experience of the aura to the fullest extent'.[64] Auratic objects, like the roses of T.S.

62 Ibid., p. 61.
63 Ibid., p. 32.
64 CB, p. 147. 'Benjamin is here . . . he says: when you feel a gaze directed to you, even behind your back, you return it (!). the expectation that what you look at looks back at you, provides the aura, the latter is supposed to be in decay in recent times, together with the cultic. . . . it is mysticism mysticism, in a posture opposed to mysticism. it is in such a form that the materialistic concept of history is adopted! it is rather ghastly.' (Bertolt Brecht, *Arbeitsjournal*, vol. 1, Frankfurt-am-Main 1973, p. 16).

Eliot's *Burnt Norton*, have the look of things that are looked at; but when the aura disintegrates, Benjamin comments in a curiously Eliotian image, one begins to encounter 'eyes of which one is inclined to say that they have lost their ability to look'.[65] 'The things I see, see me just as much as I see them', writes Valéry of dream-perceptions;[66] and this indeed is the courtesy of the commodity, which tenderly returns the gaze of every potential customer while frostily withholding it from the destitute.

In his eleventh seminar, Jacques Lacan recounts an anecdote strikingly parallel to Benjamin's meditations. Out fishing with a friend, he sighted a glittering can floating on the waves. 'You see that can?' asked his friend. 'Do you see it? Well, it doesn't see you!'[67] This feeble narrative turns out to have a point. For Lacan, the imaginary enclosure of lovers' looks is always fractured by a lack: the fact that I can never look at her from the place from which she sees me. The 'symbolic'—the possibility of alternative subject-positions, contradictory articulations—enters the imaginary to disrupt it from within. Once the field of vision is thus robbed of its imaginary unity by the gaze of the other, it becomes libidinally cathected: it is now configured around a lack which deprives the insatiable look of full satisfaction. The gaze is always an interplay of light and opacity, as the translucent imaginary is stained by the intrusion of the symbolic; it has the ambiguity of Baudelaire's city crowd, 'in which no one is either quite transparent or quite opaque to all others'.[68] Indeed this is the perverse pleasure of the *flâneur*—to strive to salvage the imaginary on the very brink of its being swallowed up by the symbolic, wresting a last gleam of aura from faces about to dissolve into difference and anonymity. One may place the ambiguity of the Baudelairean crowd beside Benjamin's comment on the surrealists, who acknowledge 'the everyday as impenetrable, the impenetrable as everyday'.[69]

What Lacan calls the 'pacifying, Apollonian effect of painting'[70] is the object's attempt to tame the greedily libidinal gaze, coyly offering itself to it as a satisfactory partner. 'You want to see? Well, take a look at this!' is how Lacan imagines the object's address to the psychoanalytic subject,

65 CB, p. 149.
66 CB, p. 149
67 *The Four Fundamental Concepts*, p. 95.
68 CB, p. 49.
69 'Surrealism', OWS, p. 237.
70 *The Four Fundamental Concepts*, p. 101.

beguiling it into 'laying down its gaze' by dissimulating its own lack. 'We recognize a work of art', writes Valéry, 'by the fact that no idea it inspires in us, no mode of behaviour that it suggests we adopt could exhaust it or dispose of it'. 'According to this view,' Benjamin comments, 'the painting we look at reflects back to us that of which our eyes will never have their fill. What it contains that fulfils the original desire would be the very same stuff on which the desire continuously feeds'.[71] He recognizes, in other words, that the condition idealized by Valéry as infinite plenitude is better described as the infinite lack of desire, which as in the empty hankerings of the *Trauerspiel* will never rediscover its imaginary homeland. As in Baudelaire's poetry, 'the expectation roused by the look of the human eye is not fulfilled';[72] the object which seeks to seduce us back to the narcissism of the imaginary cannot but remind us in that very act that our gaze is 'castrated', a function of that unassuageable desire set in motion by the 'shock' of our first encounter with absence, difference and death in entering the symbolic order.

Benjamin associates the aura with distance, a connection which may seem at first sight at odds with the claustrophobic exchanges of the imaginary. But the aura opens up distance only the more effectively to insinuate intimacy: 'the deeper the remoteness which a glance has to overcome, the stronger will be the spell that is apt to emanate from the gaze'.[73] In the aura as in the imaginary, there occurs a mystifying interplay of otherness and intimacy; and this is nowhere more marked than in the commodity, which combines the allure of the mythically untouchable madonna with the instant availability of the mythical whore. The intimacy of the mechanically reproduced object, however, is of a different kind. Whereas the traditional painting maintains a cool distance from reality, the film camera penetrates deeply into its web, deranging the 'natural' viewpoint by its ability to probe and isolate, freezing, magnifying or disarticulating the fragments of an action in order to reassemble them in multiple forms. And this demystifying familiarity, one that may be in the strict sense cognitive—who knew the precise structure of reaching for a spoon until we could film it in slow motion?—has its correlative, unauratic distancing. If the camera penetrates, it does so with the clinical motion of the surgeon's scalpel, whose involvement with its object cannot be thought

71 CB, pp. 146–7.
72 CB, p. 149.
73 CB, p. 150.

through in terms of auratic empathy. Surrealist photography 'gives free play to the politically educated eye, under whose gaze all intimacies are sacrificed to the illumination of detail'.[74] In such images, indeed, Benjamin offers us ways of conceiving the morality of revolutionary political practice itself, which similarly can be thought neither under the bourgeois-humanist sign of empathy nor (the imaginary obverse of that) as a dehumanized indifference.

If the commodity breeds the infinite sameness of narcissism, it might seem strange that Benjamin should attribute precisely this quality to mechanical reproduction: 'the stripping bare of the object, the destruction of the aura, is the mark of a perception whose sense of the sameness of things has grown to the point where even the singular, the unique, is divested of its uniqueness—by means of its reproduction'.[75] But reproduction, once more, is not repetition. By surrendering the object into the close possession of the subject, as with the postcard reproduction of an Old Master, reproduction can defetishize the aura of the original, which condemns its history to a mere compulsive repetition of itself. Origin and repetition are themselves locked in imaginary collusion: the 'original' moment is bound to reduce what follows to mere repetition; repetition itself is the empty pulsation of a process striving to return to an origin it continually displaces. At the same time, Benjamin's use of the phrase 'the sameness of things', with its inescapable hint of the commodity, is a sign of his belief in history's progression by its bad side. For the technology that produces the commodity under one set of social relations can disintegrate the aura under another; like the effective (as opposed to the Romantic) nihilist in Benjamin's thought, it is a question of entering 'into [the] opponent's strength in order to destroy him from within'.[76] The vital distinction is that between the eternal recurrence of myth or ideology, which for Benjamin includes those modern historicist mythologies of the perpetually same, and the ceaseless 'differencing' which results from smashing the aura and deploying the object in specific conjunctures. It is not, however, a question of fetishizing difference either: for dialectical thought, once released from the frozen correspondences of myth and historicism, must begin to weave its own 'magical' network of similarities

74 OWS, p. 251.
75 'A Small History of Photography', OWS, p. 250.
76 GS, 2/2, p. 481.

across the face of history, seeking the dialectical image or shocking confrontation in which a present moment may re-read itself in the past and allow the past to interpret itself anew in the present. As Jürgen Habermas has pointed out, the problem of Benjamin's project is to restore the possibility of symbolic correspondences while liquidating that world of natural mythology of which such correspondences are a part.[77] The perception of similarities in Benjamin has a regressive root in his mimetic theory of language, in which word and thing were once magically, instantaneously one; now that this primacy of the living word has lapsed into linear discourse, however, it is left to allegory, or dialectical thought, to forge usable correspondences from its shattered pieces. Neither the 'natural' totalizing of the symbol, nor the mere consecration of linear repetition (historicism), are possible; if the sign has been rendered arbitrary, torn from its mimetic intimacy with the thing, it has nevertheless been released into a new freedom with which fresh 'iconic' correspondences may be constructed. Mechanical reproduction rejects both the unique difference of the aura and the endless identities of myth: in levelling artefacts to a sameness subversive of the former, it frees them for distinctive functions repugnant to the latter.

Writing of Henri Bergson's auratic philosophy of *durée*, Benjamin protests that such a metaphysic must inevitably suppress death. It is the quintessence of the homogeneous time of historicism, from which all rupture has been eradicated. 'The *durée* from which death has been eliminated has the miserable endlessness of a scroll. Tradition is excluded from it. It is the quintessence of a passing moment (*Erlebnis*) that struts about in the borrowed garb of experience'.[78] The imaginary in general cannot accommodate death: its plenitude must resist that traumatic moment in which, confronted with lack and difference, I recognize that I can die because the world is not dependent on me for its existence. This is the equivalent of Baudelairean spleen, which 'exposes the passing moment in all its nakedness',[79] as it is of the death-obsessions of the *Trauerspiel*. The aura, which binds subject and object in claustral exchange, belongs to this extent with myth, which encodes a passive dependency upon Nature, and this in turn is for Benjamin the secret of all ideology. Three strategies are

77 See his 'Bewusstmachende oder rettende Kritik—die Aktualität Walter Benjamins', in *Zur Aktualität Walter Benjamins*, Siegfried Unseld, ed., Frankfurt-am-Main 1972, p. 205.
78 CB, p. 145.
79 CB, p. 145.

then possible for the libidinal drive that has sought out and unmasked its own castration behind the seductive fullness of the object. The first is to regress to an imaginary past: 'insofar as art aims at the beautiful, and, on however modest a scale, "reproduces" it, it conjures it up (as Faust does Helen) out of the womb of time'.[80] The second is to remain disconsolately marooned in the symbolic order, like all those melancholiasts from the *Trauerspiel* to the *Fleurs du Mal*, therapeutically demystified but to the same degree impotent. This, for Benjamin, is a notable advance on the first: few writers have expended so much energy on the patient, destructive, non-visionary task of clearing away the imaginary so that something might germinate in the space left behind. But there is also a third strategy, Benjamin's own, for which this second is a *sine qua non* yet with which it forms no obvious continuum. This is to re-channel desire from both past and present to the future: to detect in the decline of the aura the form of new social and libidinal relations, realizable by revolutionary practice.

80 CB, p. 147. The criticism of Northrop Frye exemplifies this regression. Frye values the genre of romance because it furnishes, in Lacan's sense, an imaginary sphere of 'natural' rhythms in which desire may be vicariously fulfilled. Frye goes one step further, however, and eliminates from the imaginary its constituent structure of *paranoia*: the fact that the 'other' in the mirror is indissociably *alter ego* and rival. The stature of romance characters, for Frye, is such as to ensure that they will incarnate our desires without entering into the least rivalry with us. See *Anatomy of Criticism*, Princeton 1957, pp. 186–203.

3

'A popular tradition warns against recounting dreams on an empty stomach. In this state, though awake, one remains under the sway of the dream. For washing brings only the surface of the body and the visible motor functions into the light, while in the deeper strata, even during the morning ablution, the grey penumbra of dream persists and indeed, in the solitude of the first waking hour, consolidates itself . . . The narration of dream brings calamity, because a person still half in league with the dream world betrays it in his words and must incur its revenge. Expressed in more modern terms: he betrays himself. He has outgrown the protection of dreaming naïveté, and in laying clumsy hands on his dream visions he surrenders himself. For only from the far bank, from broad daylight, may dream be recalled with impunity. This further side of dream is only attainable through a cleansing analogous to washing yet totally different. By way of the stomach. The fasting man tells his dream as if he were talking in his sleep.'[81]

To narrate the dream on an empty stomach is to remain under the sway of the past rather than to release it productively into the present. Dream may fructify in history, but only if it is first subjected to a certain violence—ruptured, distanced, purged, and only thus refracted into the vigilance of conscious life. Those who avoid a 'rupture between the nocturnal and the daytime worlds'[82] (Benjamin may well have the dangers of surrealism in mind) bring calamity, since in folding history back into the unconscious, in reducing the present to a mere stuttering repetition of the past, they rob both past and unconscious of their emancipatory force,

81 OWS, pp. 45–6.
82 CB, p. 46.

which is to be always elsewhere. It is only through the radical discontinuity of past and present, through the space hollowed by their mutual eccentricity, that the former may be brought to bear explosively upon the latter. Any attempt to recuperate the past directly, non-violently, will result only in paralysing complicity with it.

This, perhaps, is also one of the morals of a cryptic parable which Benjamin appends as a postscript to a letter to Gershom Scholem:

'I would like to tell in a different way the story of the Sleeping Beauty:

'She is asleep in her thorn bush. And then, after so many years, she awakes.

'But not to the kiss of a prince charming.

'It was the cook who awakened her, when he smacked the kitchen boy; the smack resounded with all the pent-up force of those long years and re-echoed throughout the castle.

'A fair child sleeps behind the thorny hedge of the pages which follow.

'The last thing to come near her should be a prince charming, in the shimmering garments of science. He would be bitten as he kissed his betrothed.

'It is left to the author, in his role as master-chef, to wake her up. For too long now we have been waiting for the smack which must resound ear-splittingly through the halls of science.

'Then too will awaken that poor truth which pricked itself on an outmoded distaff when, despite the prohibition, she wanted to weave for herself, among the tattered rags, a professor's robe.' [83]

Stung by her complicity with bourgeois academicism, truth has sunk into a deathly sleep from which only a further violation will awaken her—but this time the enlightening smack of Zen rather than the seductive embrace of science. The sound that will stir her to life is the rough noise of class violence, issuing from the lowliest quarter of the castle; and the author, culinary transformer of raw materials into nourishing texts, must cuff truth into his service with all the casual high-handedness with which Benjamin himself here manhandles a revered tale. Benjamin's thorny parable protects the truth dormant at its centre from any too-facile release, as tenderly chivalric as the prince charming it spurns; and if it is sexist enough in this assumption, so is it in another. For truth—the woman—is at once smooth and bristling, passive and minatory; and the sound of the smack to which she awakes is also the smack of a rape performed upon her. The woman, like truth itself, is both the fair untouchable child and, metaphorically, the assaulted kitchen scullion, just as the author as chef is both lowly—a class alternative to the ineffectual prince charming—and, in his dominative violence to even lower orders, the prince's alter ego. As the scholar who tried to weave himself a professorial gown only to have his *Habilitationsschrift* rejected, the author is also poor truth herself, pricked by an archaic mode of academic production.[84]

The waking dreamer of whom Benjamin writes resembles those who fall under the sway of an organicist theory of history; and in one of the theses on the philosophy of history, he is implicitly contrasted with the image of the rapist: 'the historical materialist leaves it to others to be drained by the whore called "Once upon a time" in historicism's bordello. He remains in control of his powers, man enough to blast open the continuum of history.'[85] The narrational device of 'Once upon a time' is auratic: it opens up distance only the more effectively to insinuate intimacy. In a single gesture, the past is at once relegated to a safe distance and, robbed of its turbulence, surrendered to the hegemony of the present. The very structure of the phrase, implying as it does the double assurance of a finished yet historically indeterminate moment, enacts something of the structure of myth. It is interesting that this imaginary conception of history is cast in sexual terms, even if it is also unpleasant: the passage has a virile swagger about it, evoking as it does the image of the icy male haughtily withholding his seed from the vampiric female. Indeed it is not difficult to feel that there is, as Harold Bloom might say, an anxiety about this image. Homogeneous history—history that has expelled the trace of rupture and revolution—is whorelike both in its instant availability and in its barren emptiness; the ease with which it can be penetrated is the very sign of its sterility. It is also whorelike in its endless repeatability, since for sexist mythology all whores are essentially one: the delusion of difference, of erotic adventure, is reduced by the static enclosure of the bordello to the oldest story in the world. The duplicity of the mythological whore, however, is that she is always penetrated but never ravished, ceaselessly filled but continually empty; the openness of homogeneous history is both

---

84 See Werner Fuld, *Walter Benjamin: Zwischen den Stühlen*, Munich 1979, pp. 162–3, for a discussion of the relevance of this fable to Benjamin's own academic situation.
85 'Theses on the Philosophy of History', I, p. 264.

seductive invitation and frustrating refusal, since in entering its gaping void you are entering precisely nothing. The immediate echo is T.S. Eliot's *Gerontion*:

> After such knowledge, what forgiveness? Think now
> History has many cunning passages, contrived corridors
> And issues, deceives with whispering ambitions,
> Guides us by vanities. Think now
> She gives when our attention is distracted
> And what she gives, gives with such supple confusions
> That the giving famishes the craving. Gives too late
> What's not believed in, or if still believed
> In memory only, reconsidered passion. Gives too soon
> Into weak hands what's thought can be dispensed with
> Till the refusal propagates a fear.

The refusal certainly seems to propagate a fear in Benjamin. What it generates is the sexual violence of 'blast[ing] open the continuum of history', which is officially an alternative to erotic entanglements but unconsciously a way of possessing the whore and thereby being revenged on her. The 'continuum' signifies her endless, meaningless amenability, but also the hymen—the smooth membrane that prohibits penetration, and which must be ruptured in an act of rape. The whore of history is a virgin, her indifferent reception of all comers the mere obverse of the virgin's inviolability; she thus displays the insidious ambiguity of the commodity, and indeed doubles that ambiguity, for like the worker under capitalism she is both seller and commodity in one. Alternatively, the image suggests a kind of coitus interruptus, breaking open history but then letting the seed spurt free in empty space—a space that is not the sterile womb of historicism, but that womb transfigured by violence into the *Jetztzeit* or arrested moment of time forced to its revolutionary crisis, which is empty only in so far as it teems with unformed possibilities. This, indeed, is how Benjamin sees Brecht's epic theatre: 'the damming of the stream of real life, the moment when its flow comes to a standstill, makes itself felt as reflux: this reflux is astonishment. The dialectic at a standstill is its real object . . . Epic theatre makes life spurt up high from the bed of time and, for an instant, hover iridescent in empty space. Then it puts it back to bed'.[86]

86 UB, p. 13.

There is a connection between the industrial working class and the act of killing one's children. The act is called prolicide, from *proles*, or offspring. *Proletariat* means those too poor to serve the state by property, who serve it instead by producing children as labour-power. It is the proletariat, not ruling-class history, who is a woman. It is women, not men, who are the most exact image of the oppressed; it is in child-birth and child-rearing that the desolate condition of the workers is most graphically figured, a condition in which one is stripped of everything but one's own flesh. Woman, notwithstanding Benjamin's fantasy, is not the whore of history but the ultimate image of violation. She embodies the final loss, that of the fruits of the body itself.[87]

There are several ways in which Bloom's aesthetic of anxiety would seem to illuminate Benjamin's reflections upon history.[88] When Benjamin writes that 'In every era the attempt must be made anew to wrest tradition away from a conformism that is about to overpower it',[89] it is not difficult to rewrite this insight in Bloom's terms, as the process of troping or psychical defence whereby the present seeks to displace a patriarchal past by creatively misreading it, undoing the powers of a castrating precursor by entering his strength from within in a moment of victorious self-substitution. Bloom's trope of *apophrades* or the 'return of the dead' recalls Benjamin's insistence that 'no matter what [the present] is like, one must firmly take it by the horns to be able to consult the past. It is the bull whose blood must fill the pit if the shades of the departed are to appear at its edge'.[90] Nor is Bloom's notion of 'misprision' far from Benjamin's belief in 'quoting out of context', to which I shall refer later. For all that, however, Bloom's aesthetics represent an impoverishment of Benjamin's politics. Indeed if Bloom is related to Benjamin at all, then it is as a 'latecomer' who has emptied out the revolutionary vision of his precursor and put the feeble *tessara* of literary history defensively in its place. Bloom's history is a literary battle of lonely sons and fathers; for Benjamin, by contrast, each 'latecoming' present has two rival precursors, begotten as it is by a complex coupling of 'history' and 'tradition'. History is the

---

87 A point that Benjamin—to do him justice—fully acknowledges in his review of Brecht's *The Mother*: see 'A Family Drama in the Epic Theatre', UB, pp. 33–6.
88 See in particular *The Anxiety of Influence*, New York 1973.
89 I, p. 257.
90 'Wider ein Meisterwerk', *Schriften*, Theodor W. and Gretel Adorno, ed., vol. 2, Frankfurt-am-Main 1955, p. 314.

homogeneous time of the ruling class; tradition belongs to the oppressed and exploited, who know, as ruling classes do not, that states of emergency are not the exception but the rule. If there are precursor fathers, then there are also for historical materialism precursor brothers and sisters; and the 'father' whose influence threatens to overwhelm us, from whose death-dealing grasp tradition must be ceaselessly wrested away, is himself anxious, marked with the sign of castration, not only by virtue of his rivalry with his own forebears but by the historical insurrections of his sons and daughters. The strength of the political revolutionary is not just the resource won by entering the father from within, but the accumulated force of all the past conquests and attritions of the ruling class by those who, as our brothers and sisters, signify our true parentage. The Oedipal image is a potentially treacherous one to use of the class struggle, for fathers are rarely destroyed by their offspring other than in fantasy; ruling-class cultures, however, have often been and may still be. Nor does the revolutionary proletariat aim at assuming the father's role: its intention, as Lenin writes in *The State and Revolution*, is not to take over the state but to destroy it.

'Tradition' is not secreted within 'history' as the essence within the phenomenon. It is not an alternative history which runs beneath the history of the exploiters, silently ghosting it. If it were, it would be no more than another homogeneity which merely denied or inverted the first, as some corporatist historiography of the working class would suggest. Tradition is nothing other than a series of spasms or crises within class history itself, a particular set of articulations of that history, not the scattered letters of an invisible word. History and tradition form a dialectical unity: 'there is no cultural document that is not at the same time a record of barbarism'.[91] Yet if the crises that constitute tradition cannot be subsumed into simple unity, they can nevertheless be drawn into a complex constellation; and the task of historical materialism is to 'brush history against the grain',[92] reconstructing it in the image of that constellation: 'historicism contents itself with establishing a causal connection between various moments in history. But no fact that is a cause is for that very reason historical. It became historical posthumously, as it were, through events that may be separated from it by thousands of years.

91 'Eduard Fuchs, Collector and Historian', OWS, p. 359.
92 I, p. 259.

A historian who takes this as his point of departure stops telling the sequence of events like the beads of a rosary. Instead, he grasps the constellation which his own era has formed with a definite earlier one. Thus he establishes a conception of the present as the "time of the now" which is shot through with chips of Messianic time.'[93]

Such a constellation, which rejects both linearity and discreteness, can be constructed in the field of 'cultural history' from those dramas that present us with the 'untragic hero': the medieval mystery plays, the *Trauerspiel*, Lenz and Grabbe, Strindberg, Brecht.[94] This is not, as its bizarre heterogeneity suggests, a 'tradition' in the sense of a conscious, unbroken set of influences; it is not a grid of relations given by historical reality to the inspecting gaze. To map this territory means blasting through the mountains and clearing the jungles of ideological criticism, shifting and flattening its familiar landscapes. And what is then discovered is not a secret river that flows beneath the obscuring foliage of German bourgeois aesthetics, but a range of far-flung peaks of various shapes and sizes which from a particular vantage-point may nonetheless be configurated into complex unity. An image in *One-Way Street* contrasts the aerial view of a terrain, in which 'the passenger sees only how the road pushes through the landscape', with the same prospect seen on foot: the view from on foot brushes the smooth continuity of the aerial view against the grain, so to speak, opening up irregular perspectives and sudden clearings concealed from the deceptively homogeneous vantage-point of the flier.[95] The tradition of the non-tragic is produced, not reflected, by a theoretical concept; and what produces that concept in turn is the (theoretically determined) necessities of the historical present. If the *Origin* seeks to blast open the continuum of history, it can do so only because its own epoch, in the exaggerated violence of its Expressionist styles, is ripe for arresting into constellation with that particular past, and must be so if its true character is to be determined. The book is itself a *nunc*

---

93 I, p. 265. It is notable that Benjamin's anti-historicism and his use of the term 'constellation' go back at least as far as his early fascination with Kant. 'For Kant,' he wrote in a letter to Scholem in 1917, 'it is a question less of history than of certain historical constellations that have an aesthetic interest' (B, 1, p. 161).

94 See UB, pp. 17–18. See also Benjamin's essay 'Literaturgeschichte und Literatur-wissenschaft': 'it is not a question of representing works of literature in the context of their time, but of bringing them to representation in the time in which they emerged, which knows them—that is our time. (GS, 3, p. 290).

95 OWS, p. 50.

stans, a violent suspension of the bland continuum of bourgeois criticism, which allows the forces of the present to rip through it so as to confront themselves in the image of a past they configurate into sense. It is the joining of what can be seen in the light of Benjamin's later work of the 'class struggle at the level of theory' (Althusser); for this early assault on a German academy that can see little in the baroque drama but a distasteful declension from classical norms is an indispensable preliminary to Benjamin's later apologia for the anti-tragic revolutionism of a Brecht. Indeed what Benjamin finds in the Brechtian *Gestus*, the verbal and bodily gesture that crystallizes the social gist of a dramatic event, is a theatrical version of the dialectical thought that forces history to its crisis. The *Gestus* of epi(sodi)c theatre is an irregular interruption of the action, a shocking suspension of its onward flow that transforms it into a conjuncture or, as Benjamin calls it, a 'monad'. 'Where thinking suddenly stops in a constellation pregnant with tensions, it gives that constellation a shock, by which it crystallizes into a monad. A historical materialist approaches a historical subject only where he encounters it as a monad. In this structure he recognizes the sign of a Messianic cessation of happening, or, put differently, a revolutionary chance in the fight for the oppressed past'.[96] If the dead are a cessation of happening, repressed by violence into the past, then there is a chance that a converse violence, the Zen-like smack or abrupt *Gestus* of dialectical thought, may make them happen again. The 'fight *for* the oppressed past' is fruitfully ambiguous: a fight *on behalf* of it—not even the dead, Benjamin warns, will be safe from the enemy if he wins—which can be waged only by ceaselessly salvaging that past, causing the shades of the dead to congregate around the empty pit of a slaughtered present.

That slaughter, for Benjamin, is the work of a particular form of class society—fascism—that seeks to rescue monopoly capitalism by abolishing history itself. Fascism is the 'new ice age', the 'epoch without history' of which Benjamin speaks in his conversations with Brecht. It is the dialectic at its most deathly standstill; and Benjamin's own most arduous dialectical feat will be to differentiate this form of annihilation from the 'cheerful' destructiveness of the revolutionary. For the blood that fills the pit of the present is not only that spilt by fascism; it is also the blood of a present consciously sacrificed by dialectical thought to the revolutionary invo-

96 I, pp. 264–5 (translation amended).

cation of tradition, a tradition whose liberation demands the liquidation of 'history'. The present can become traditional only if it violates history by laying violent hands upon itself; through this metaleptic movement, the past can be reconstructed as striving to turn towards the sun of revolution that is rising in the future. This is not a teleological image, even though it is deliberately made to sound like one: Benjamin's anti-teleology is affirmative enough to occupy that figurative terrain too, wrest those tropological spoils from its opponent. It is the practice of the present that turns the past upon its axis, not some immanent *telos* of the sort Benjamin's Messianism specifically denies. Dialectical thought, then, might almost be tempted to say that the empty space into which it will move is the past that dissolves beneath the Führer's boot. This—the line of the 'Third Period'—is of course unacceptable, not least because in pulverizing history fascism destroys tradition along with it; but it is as though it were necessary to *think* this possibility, to acknowledge the apparent relations between the fascistic and revolutionary erasures of history, so that the full contradictions of this 'monad' may be unleashed. Fascism cannot be defeated by teleology because it is in one sense the grotesque enthronement of the *telos* itself, the coming of the Antichrist that brings history to its grisly consummation; yet because this particular *telos* must extirpate its past, it is also an anti-teleology, consummating nothing. This is why it can only be vanquished by an anti-teleological excavation of the past.

If fascism eradicates history by rewriting it in its own image, historical materialism rewrites the past in order to redeem it in its revolutionary validity. Colin McCabe quotes a passage from Benjamin's *Theses on the Philosophy of History* to challenge the contention that 'the past has its own order independently of its present enunciation';[97] but of course it all depends on what you mean by order and independence. McCabe is certainly right to insist that the past is a discursive construct of the present; but it is not, of course, merely an imaginary back-projection of it. Materialism must insist on the irreducibility of the real to discourse; it must also remind historical idealism that if the past itself—by definition— no longer exists; its *effects* certainly do. In the *Origin*, Benjamin issues a specific warning against any such idealism: 'just as a man lying sick with fever transforms all the words which he hears into the extravagant images

97 'On Discourse', *Economy and Society*, vol. 8, no. 3 (August 1979), p. 305, n. 4.

of delirium, so it is that the spirit of the present age seizes on the manifestations of past or distant spiritual worlds, in order to take possession of them and unfeelingly incorporate them into its own self-absorbed fantasizing'.[98] Such epistemological imperialism is no more than an inversion of the antiquarian impulse, pivoting all on some fetishized 'current conjuncture', reading off reality from that privileged point as empiricism reads off its discourse from the structure of the real. A fatal foreclosure of the historical sense is masked by a specious liberality, which can pull any historical object into its epistemological orbit because they are all its secret creations in the first place. The distance of the aura is abolished, while its intimacy is retained. 'When our theatres perform plays of other periods', complained Brecht, 'they like to annihilate distance, fill in the gap, gloss over the differences. But what comes then of our delight in comparisons, in distance, in dissimilarity—which is at the same time a delight in what is close and proper to ourselves?'[99] Benjamin had anticipated Brecht's protest in the *Origin*, writing of the 'fatal, patholo-gical susceptibility' of the age: 'there is no new style, no unknown popular heritage to be discovered which would not straight away appeal with the utmost clarity to the feelings of contemporaries'.[100] No historical tremor could shake this enclosure, for history is always already processed, neutralized, spatialized; it takes Marx literally, in posing only such questions to history as it can already answer. The left versions of this idealism in the realm of 'culture' are either a dogmatic rejection of any work that does not spontaneously 'appeal with the utmost clarity to the feelings of contemporaries', a perpetual fetishism of the present; or that other carnival of the conjuncture which believes that it can displace each and every work into its own ideological space. The *Trauerspiel*, by contrast, is at once relevant and resistant to Benjamin's own moment: it must be prised free from the past in all its exotic strangeness, by a movement of thought responsive to its faintly familiar resonance.

To speak of a dialectic between strangeness and familiarity is to evoke a quite different German legacy, that of hermeneutics; for it is precisely in the 'between' opened up by such a dialectic that Hans-Georg Gadamer situates hermeneutical thought.[101] If Gadamer's defence of the radical

98 O, p. 53.
99 *Brecht on Theatre: The Development of an Aesthetic*, John Willett, ed., London 1964, p. 276.
100 O, p. 53.
101 See *Truth and Method*, London 1975, passim.

historicity of interpretation is not far from Benjamin's own, his concept of 'tradition' certainly is. Gadamer's tradition is by no means mere repetition, since all acts of understanding are productive rather than mimetic; understanding is always understanding otherwise, creative misprision. But Gadamerian tradition in fact provides an exemplary illustration of Benjamin's 'aura'. The temporal distance that tradition establishes between subject and object is an enabling one: in eliminating inessentials and neutralizing prejudgments, it permits the true meaning of the object to emerge. The 'classical' artefact (as opposed, one takes it, to skin-flicks or the Sunday *People*) is the one that patiently survives the buffetings of the contingent, and is thus drawn by the cleansing operations of distance into the present. 'The deeper the remoteness which a glance has to overcome, the stronger will be the spell that is apt to emanate from the gaze'. Gadamer, like Heidegger before him, thinks that he has transcended the subject/object duality by positing the primordial givenness of *Dasein*, of which tradition is the privileged bearer; but he has done so only by covertly transforming the tradition into a subject in its own right. In a series of expressive homologies, Being speaks in *Sache* (subject matter), which in turn speaks through the language of literary texts, which in turn go to compose the tradition that speaks to and though the individual subject. That subject, conversely, listens attentively to this speaking and speaks back. Since the individual subject can respond appropriately only by virtue of inhabiting the tradition that speaks through it, what all this speaking amounts to is that the tradition is having an endless conversation with itself. It is not exactly *saying* anything, since this would entail the fallacy of linguistic instrumentalism into which we were dropped by the Greeks;[102] what it is saying is precisely the fact that it is in dialogue with itself. Individual texts, or for that matter individual subjects, become passing topics in the tradition's garrulous self-communing, but this, in fact, is no mean thing to be. For in being guided by tradition to interpret creatively a text created by the tradition, we are challenged, interrogated, taken out of ourselves, only to be returned to ourselves more thoroughly unified and 'at home' than we were in the first

---

102 Gadamer thinks that he has succeeded in transcending logocentrism by denouncing that instrumentalism of the sign which grasps it as a mere transmitter between subjects. Instead he would shift our attention so that we start from the subject matter and then move to the signs that are its 'medium'. Logocentrism is thus, as they say in Germany, simultaneously cancelled and preserved.

place. The point of the tradition, then, is to get us back to where we were, only more radically so.

It might seem natural in the light of Benjamin's work to ask Gadamer whose tradition exactly he has in mind, and whether we are allowed to opt out if we don't like it. Similar questions may occur to the reader of T.S. Eliot's *Tradition and the Individual Talent* (1919). In a famous passage, Eliot writes of a tradition of 'monuments' that 'form an ideal order among themselves, which is modified by the introduction of the new (the really new) work of art among them. The existing order is complete before the new work arrives; for order to persist after the supervention of novelty, the *whole* existing order must be, if ever so slightly, altered; and so the relations, proportions, values of each work of art towards the whole are readjusted; and this is conformity between the old and the new'.[103] 'Modified', 'if ever so slightly', 'readjusted', 'conformity': Eliot's tradition is a self-equilibrating organism extended in space and time, eternally replete but constantly absorptive, like a grazing cow or the Hegelian Idea. Perhaps it is most usefully visualized as a large, bulbous amoeba, whose pulsating body inflates and deflates, changes colours, relations and proportions, as it digests. Eliotic tradition is organicist but not progressive: its constant metonymic displacements are immediately recuperated into metaphorical stasis. It is not, however, an empirical concept, simply denoting all that has been produced: the apparently bottomless pit of its stomach is surmounted by a discriminating pair of eyes. Not every writer belongs to the tradition, nor even widely admired ones: 'the poet must be very conscious of the main current, which does not flow at all invariably through the most distinguished reputations'.[104] To believe that the 'main current' does indeed flow through the most distinguished reputations would be rather like believing that the main route from London to Swansea is the M4 motorway. Even though the M4 does pass through most of the major towns en route and is commonly judged to be the main thoroughfare between those points, it is perfectly possible that the main route from London to Swansea is in fact a network of B roads via Leeds and Glasgow. This could well be the genuine 'main current', since only those who are themselves part of that current, feel it in their bones, can tell us what it is, and there is consequently no objective way of judging between the

103 *Selected Essays*, p. 15.
104 Ibid., p. 16.

competing claims of M4 and B-road drivers.

Eliot's sense of a subterranean current that may skirt around 'the most distinguished reputations' has something in common with Benjamin's retrieval of repressed lineages; but the resemblance is purely formal. For the 'non-tragic' tradition that Benjamin invokes is, as we have seen, a *construct*: it is not a homogeneous given, the mystically intuitable essence of all authentic writing.[105] It is not the 'main current' masquerading as a minor one, but one filament among many which must be *fashioned* into major significance by politico-cultural practice. Such fashioning demands the kind of sideways slicing into history ('All the decisive blows are struck left-handed', Benjamin once remarked[106]) that the smooth surface of Eliot's amoeba is precisely designed to repel. If both men are akin in rejecting the vulgar teleologies of Marxist or liberal-humanist progressivism, it is because Eliot ends, this side of eternity at least, with the 'bad things' from which Benjamin begins.

'Depth', Brecht commented tartly to Benjamin, 'doesn't get you anywhere at all.' For Brecht, depth is 'just depth—and there's nothing whatsoever to be seen in it'.[107] If depth is delusion, then for Brecht there can be no real surfaces either; the space in which the negation unfurls is not beneath the object but alongside it, in difference, alterity, other possibilities. Benjamin retorted that penetration into depth was his way of travelling to the antipodes; he would reach the global antithesis of class society by burrowing within that formation and coming out on the other side. And of course his work is rife with images of excavation and disinterment, of grubbing among buried ruins and salvaging forgotten remains. We do not need to put a proper name to the 'children' who, as Benjamin tells us, 'are particularly fond of haunting any site where things are being visibly worked upon. They are irresistibly drawn by the detritus generated by building, gardening, housework, tailoring or carpentry. In waste products they recognize the face that the world of things turns directly and solely to them. In using these things they do not so much imitate the works of adults as bring together, in the artefact produced in play, materials of widely differing kinds in a new, intuitive relationship. Children thus produce their own small world of things within the greater

105 For F.R. Leavis, this essence is a rich and racy Englishness. The essence of all great English texts is that they are essentially *English*.
106 OWS, p. 49.
107 UB, p. 110.

one.'[108] Benjamin himself, the *bricoleur* whose texts violently yoke the most heterogeneous materials together while appearing blandly undisturbed by their own boldness, has a child's eye for the cast-off and contingent: Atget the photographer, whom he admires for by-passing the 'so-called landmarks' of Paris and lingering over a row of boot lasts,[109] is an image of the revolutionary who by-passes the Eliotic monument for the explosive power of the inconspicuous. In playfully reconstructing rather than imitating adult work, the child enacts criticism's relation to its object, which is similarly one of mimetic displacement rather than pure mimicry. So is the minature, to which the final sentence of the quotation alludes; indeed Benjamin's own fascination with the miniature strikingly condenses many of his dominant motifs. The miniature is a form of reproduction, but one that 'helps men to achieve a control over works of art',[110] thus facilitating different social relations of cultural production. It signifies a kind of 'estrangement' of the original object, a visual 'quoting out of context' that renders the latter politically portable; and it can assume the force of a talisman or hieroglyph, thus interlocking with the themes of the *Origin*. (Benjamin particularly admired two grains of wheat in the Musée Cluny on which a complete Judaic text was inscribed.) In its humble proportions, the minature has a political meaning, suggesting those 'inconspicuous and sober and inexhaustible' things with which the revolutionary must align; it is the heterogeneous chip that slips through the ideological net; and there is even about it a hint of the 'monad' or compacted field of forces of Benjamin's Messianic thought.

Benjamin's imagery of excavation is out to deconstruct the homogeneity of history into what we might now, after Michel Foucault, call an 'archaeology'. The analogy is necessarily loose, since Benjamin is not seeking to specify the rules for the formation of discourses or formalization of utterances; but there is a sense in which he is, nevertheless, an archaeologist *avant la lettre*. In his masterly essay on the collector and historian Eduard Fuchs, he rejects the historicism of the Second International for a method that 'breaks the epoch away from its reified *historical continuity*',[111] refusing the abstract gesture of a 'cultural history' that would subsume disparate discourses into unity. The dream of a

108 OWS, pp. 52–3.
109 OWS, p. 250.
110 OWS, p. 243.
111 OWS, p. 352.

dialectical 'history of culture' is absurd, 'since the continuum of history, blown apart by dialectics, is nowhere scattered over a wider area than in that part people call culture'.[112] Yet in blowing apart the continuum of history, dialectical thought does not thereby explode all continuities along with it. What it promises is 'a science of history whose subject matter is not a tangle of purely factual details, but consists rather of the numbered group of threads that represent the weft of the past as it feeds into the warp of the present'.[113] Such historical 'textuality' cannot be thought in historicist terms: 'It would be a mistake to equate this weft with the mere nexus of causation. Rather, it is thoroughly dialectical, and threads may have been lost for centuries that the present course of history erratically, inconspicuously picks up again'.[114] But there are, for all that, complexly recoverable continuities, and to this extent Benjamin's image is indeed 'historicist' for those for whom any breath of continuity whatsoever is inevitably tainted by the linear self-becoming of an essence—for whom, in short, 'history' and 'historicism' are unified by an ideological gesture.

Benjamin is unable to countenance such an identity because his engagements with history differ from those of a Foucault. The mark of a dialectical encounter with history is that it renounces 'a calm, contemplative attitude towards its subject to become aware of the critical constellation in which precisely this fragment of the past is found with precisely this present'.[115] History is not, then, simply a theoretical construct, but a political one too; when Benjamin contrasts historicism's 'eternal image of the past' with historical materialism's 'specific and unique engagement with it',[116] the engagement in question is practical as well as theoretical, entailing an emancipatory interest of proportions that present-day 'archaeology' can only find naive. To speak of a practical engagement with the past is of course in one sense meaningless, since the past does not exist; but it nevertheless 'feeds into the warp of the present', a fact which was for historical reasons perhaps rather clearer in the Europe of the 1930s than it has been in the Europe of the 1970s. For Benjamin, history discloses itself only to the agitated gaze, responds coherently only to urgent questioning: 'to articulate the past historically does not mean to recognize it "the way it

112 OWS, p. 360.
113 OWS, p. 362.
114 OWS, p. 362.
115 OWS, p. 351.
116 OWS, p. 352.

really was" (Ranke). It means to seize hold of a memory as it flashes up at a moment of danger. Historical materialism wishes to retain that image of the past which unexpectedly appears to a man singled out by history at a moment of danger. The danger affects both the content of the tradition and its receivers. The same threat hangs over both: that of becoming a tool of the ruling classes'.[117] And 'every image of the past that is not recognized by the present as one of its concerns threatens to disappear irretrievably'.[118] Such a moment of danger is recorded at the opening of *One-Way Street*, where Benjamin recounts a dream that violently disinters the image of a forgotten school-friend: 'in a night of despair I dreamed I was with my first friend from my school days, whom I had not seen for decades and had scarcely ever remembered in that time, tempestuously renewing our friendship and brotherhood. But when I awoke it became clear that what despair had brought to light like a detonation was the corpse of that boy, who had been immured as a warning: that whoever one day lives here may in no respect resemble him'.[119] The 'detonation' shatters the regressive impulse towards recovering a lost unity, dislocating the imaginary continuum of past and present in the symbolic figure of a corpse; but it is precisely through this irruption of difference that the past is turned upon its axis to speak to the present, as a warning that the present must not compulsively repeat it. In class society, the danger that flashes up from time to time in dream is a permanent condition; and it is perhaps this insight that finally distinguishes Benjamin from our foremost contemporary genealogist, who adopts a somewhat more judicious view of the class struggle.[120]

'Some pass things down to posterity', writes Benjamin in *The*

117 I, p. 257.
118 I, p. 257.
119 OWS, p. 46.
120 'There are not, immediately given, subjects of whom one would be the proletariat and the other the bourgeoisie. Who struggles against whom? We all struggle against each other. And there is always something in us which struggles against something else in us.' (Michel Foucault, cit. Peter Dews, 'The *Nouvelle Philosophie* and Foucault', *Economy and Society*, vol. 8, no. 2, May 1979.) 'Immediately given' and 'subjects' are acceptable reservations, but their effect is somewhat tempered by the subsequent three sentences, which would not be out of place in a bad French movie. Whatever the undoubted richness of Foucault's researches on power, from which Marxism can surely learn, it is glaringly obvious how the hasty Anglo-Saxon appropriation of his work provides a glamorous rationale for erstwhile revolutionaries unnerved into pessimism by the current problems of class struggle in the advanced capitalist societies.

Destructive Character, 'by making them untouchable and thus conserving them, others pass on situations, by making them practicable and thus liquidating them.'[121] What is transmitted by tradition is not 'things', and least of all 'monuments', but 'situations'—not solitary artefacts but the strategies that construct and mobilize them. It is not that we constantly revaluate a tradition; tradition *is* the practice of ceaselessly excavating, safeguarding, violating, discarding and reinscribing the past. There is no tradition other than this, no set of ideal landmarks that then suffer modification. Artefacts are inherently available for such reinscription, just as Benjamin's mystical theory of language sees 'translatability' as an essential quality of certain texts.[122] A passage in *A Berlin Chronicle* refers obliquely to this fact: 'true, for successful excavations a plan is needed. Yet no less indispensable is the cautious probing of the spade in the dark loam, and it is to cheat oneself of the richest prize to preserve as a record merely the inventory of one's discoveries, and not this dark joy of the place of the finding itself. Fruitless searching is as much a part of this as succeeding, and consequently remembrance must not proceed in the manner of a narrative or still less that of a report, but must, in the strictest epic and rhapsodic manner, assay its spade in ever-new places, and in the old ones delve to ever deeper layers.'[123] What is at stake is not merely the spoils of situations but the situations themselves, the practices of digging and discovery, sightings and oversightings, which trace through the exhumed objects so deeply as to constitute a major part of their meaning. It is a question of the process of production, not just of the product, a process that Brechtian 'epic' rescues from the concealments of 'Aristotelian' narrative. Mistakes—fruitless searchings—are for epic theatre and remembrance as much integral parts of the text as they are for scientific research programmes; history is not a fair copy but a palimpsest, whose deleted layers must be thrust to light, written together in their episodic rhythms rather than repressed to unruptured narrative.

In effecting 'a liquidation of tradition which thereby restores whatever liquidity it still has',[124] the destructive character, Benjamin tells us, 'stands in the front line of the traditionalists'.[125] To this extent he

121 OWS, p. 158.
122 See 'The Task of the Translator', I, p. 71.
123 OWS, p. 314.
124 The phrase is Irving Wohlfarth's (cf. n. 53 above).
125 'The Destructive Character', OWS, p. 158.

resembles his opposite number, the narrator, who transmits by preserving rather than by destroying. Benjamin's essay *The Story-teller*, written in the same year as *The Work of Art in the Age of Mechanical Reproduction*, is something of an embarrassment to those who would press him unequivocally into the service of an anti-narrational 'textuality', enlist him in the ranks of those modernists or post-modernists for whom narrativity is no more than the suspension and recuperation of an imaginary unity. For in *The Story-teller*, scandalously, Benjamin is out to celebrate the very aura he dismantles with his other hand. The story or folk tale is the radiant locus of such an aura, for in it glows the rich sagacity of remembrance, the ripely garnered 'experience' of an unbroken tradition. The essay, however, is more than a regrettable lapse into a nostalgia repudiated elsewhere; in its eminently dialectical uniting of the aura and its opposite, it stands as a mature warning to the fashionable Foucauldean and post-structuralist cult of the 'discontinuous'. The folk tale is indeed auratic, but it also has the anonymity and anti-psychologism of epic theatre; and because the hearer or reader, for want of such psychological connections, is left to construct the tale, the story is a kind of hybrid of the auratic and mechanically reproduced artefacts, redolent of mythological meaning yet amenable to the labour of interpretation. This is why the tersest, least elaborate tale is most likely to survive: its dry compactness resembles 'the seeds of grain which have lain for centuries in the chambers of the pyramids shut up air-tight and have retained their germinative power to this day'.[126] Texts patient of multiple readings have the greatest staying-power: the folk tale thus enables a new, 'democratic' redefinition of the 'classic', retaining auratic authority while inviting Brechtian *Umfunktionierung* or recycling. If it retains authority, it is nonetheless un-authored: traces of the storyteller cling to it as a potter's handprints cling to a clay vessel, but though the storyteller is in this sense an artisanal producer, his or her product is nevertheless a collective one. In this way, too, the image is fruitfully ambivalent: the traces in question are auratic, vibrations from mnemonic depths, but they also recall the traces of a 'practised hand' imprinted on a 'utilitarian object'.[127] The mnemonic depths from which the tale springs are counterposed by the mnemonic techniques necessary for its recounting, techniques that are, so to speak,

126 'The Story-teller', I, p. 90.
127 CB, p. 145.

mechanically reproducible: anybody can tell a story just as anybody can take a photograph,[128] and for Benjamin the listeners' most productive response will be an impulse to repeat the narrative themselves. In this sense the folk tale has something of the quality of Roland Barthes's 'writerly' sentences, which make you want to write sentences yourself.

Since the story, unlike the novel, is a collective genre, the storyteller is a kind of collector; and the collector is another recurrent figure in whom Benjamin ponders the dialectic between reconstruction and recuperation. In one sense, the collector is a preserver: his or her task is to safeguard the past by salvaging it, as the revolutionary salvages the dead from the oblivion to which fascism would consign them. But this preservation is also a form of destruction, for to redeem objects means to dig them loose from the historical strata in which they are embedded, purging them of the accreted cultural meanings with which they are encrusted. The collector releases things from the tyranny of traditional hierarchies into the free space of sheer contiguity, transforming a metaphorical relation between objects—this is valuable because it is like/unlike that—into one of simple metonymy.[129] Snatched into this space, the object is liberated from the drudgery of usefulness, stripped of its exchange-value and so rescued from the fate of the commodity. Yet though what remains is in one sense its use-value, the collected object is not in fact used; thus it emerges from the fetishism of the commodity only to dip back once again. Collectibility, like novelty, is a quality that does not depend upon the use-value of the object. The collector is a modernist in so far as he or she breaks with the suave schemas of the museum catalogue in the name of a fiercely idiosyncratic passion that fastens on the contingent and unregarded. Collecting is in this sense a kind of creative digression from classical narrative, a 'textualizing' of history that reclaims repressed and unmapped areas. So it is that Eduard Fuchs the collector 'taught the theoretician many things to which his time barred access. It was the collector who found his way into grey

128 For Benjamin, photography too is a hybrid of the auratic and the mechanical: 'the most precise technology can give its products a magical value, such as a painted picture can never have for us' (OWS, p. 243). If technology destroys the aura, it also reproduces it in different form. Significantly, both 'The Story-teller' and 'A Small History of Photography' end with (parallel) 'auratic' images.

129 Benjamin's own library reflected such a heterogeneous arrangement, as Scholem notes: 'the great works that meant so much to him were placed in bizarre patterns next to the most out-of-the-way writings and oddities' (*On Jews and Judaism in Crisis*, New York 1976, p. 175).

areas—caricature, pornography—where the models of conventional art history sooner or later came to grief. In the first place it should be noted that Fuchs broke right across the board with the classicist conception of art, whose traces can still be recognized even in Marx. The ideas employed by the bourgeoisie in developing this conception of art no longer operate in Fuchs: not beauty of appearance, not harmony, not unity in diversity'.[130] But this digressiveness also has something of the pretentious meanderings of the *flâneur*. 'O bliss of the collector, bliss of the man of leisure!' apostrophises Benjamin with self-parodic smugness, seriously doubting nonetheless whether public collections can retain the aura that clings to private ones such as his own. The collector, who levels things in one sense only to foreground their uniqueness in another, thus repeating the gesture of the very commodities he disdains, is a destroyer who himself offers a prime target for historical destruction. Like Karl Kraus in Benjamin's eyes, he appears to stand on the frontier of a new age only to stand in reality on the threshold of the Last Judgment.[131]

Kraus's own particular mode of collecting was the quotation, a pursuit that obsessed Benjamin too. Quoting in the Krausian mode is a form of collecting because it restores writing to its true significance by violently displacing it from context—a practice that in Kraus's own moral thunderings manifests 'the power not to preserve but to purify, to tear from context, to destroy'.[132] Quotation 'summons the word by its name, wrenches it destructively from its context, but precisely thereby calls it back to its origin. It appears, now with rhyme and reason, sonorously, congruously in the structure of a new text. As rhyme it gathers the similar into its aura; as name it stands alone and expressionless. In quotation the two realms—of origin and destruction—justify themselves before language. And conversely, only where they interpenetrate—in quotation—is language consummated. In it is mirrored the angelic tongue in which all words, startled from the idyllic context of meaning, have become mottoes in the book of Creation'.[133] Quotation is reproduction rather than repetition, an erasure of genesis that restores authentic meaning; if it has the imaginary force of similarity it also jars with the isolating shock of the symbolic, the brute expressionlessness of the *Trauerspiel* death's head or

130 OWS, p. 361.
131 See 'Karl Kraus', OWS, p. 271.
132 OWS, p. 287.
133 OWS, p. 286.

emblematic slogan. It is also a handy way of carrying writing around with you, a miniaturizing aid to remembrance, for as with political history what is most memorable is what is skewed out of context. In the mosaic of quotation as in the explications of baroque emblem, discourse is released from its reified environs into a conveniently portable kind of signifying practice, signifiers torn from their signified and then flexibly recomposed to weave fresh correspondences across language. The *Gestus* of Brechtian theatre is likewise a kind of writing—a detachable quotation that may be repeated in different contexts. The Brechtian actor 'must be able to space his gestures as the compositor produces spaced type'.[134] The *Gestus* is a kind of visual aphorism; for aphorism itself is a mode of *plumpes Denken* or crude thinking that distils complex discourse into practicable shape, a reach-me-down sloganeering of political theory. 'Because the earliest rude world was too crude and uncivilized,' writes the *Trauerspiel* dramatist Martin Opitz, 'and people could not therefore correctly grasp and understand the teachings of wisdom and heavenly things, wise men had to conceal and bury what they had discovered for the cultivation of the fear of God, morality, and good conduct, in rhymes and fables, to which the common people are disposed to listen.'[135] The moral tags of the *Trauerspiel* are an early technique of *plumpes Denken*, compacting mystical rather than political insight: the Brechtian maxim, which is at once wise and reproducible, pregnant with meaning yet humbly anonymous, has the quality of the baroque, as it has of Benjamin's folk tale. In William Empson's terms, it is a kind of 'pastoral'—a 'putting the complex into the simple' that is ironically aware of its own deliberate flattening, but which has about it a 'casualness and inclusiveness which allows it to collect into it things that had been floating in tradition'.[136]

Benjamin's vision of history raises questions for a contemporary Marxism once more pondering the 'alternatives' of continuity and rupture, caught as it is between a discredited historicism on the one side and an unacceptable synchronicity on the other. Perhaps we may approach these questions by asking baldly: to what extent is Marxism a *narrative*? At first glance, it would seem to take up its rank among the great narrative

134 UB, p. 19.
135 Cit. O, p. 172n.
136 *Some Versions of Pastoral*, Harmondsworth 1966, p. 159. Conveniently enough for our theme, Empson is here discussing Gay's *The Beggar's Opera*.

constructs of history. For what could be more truly fabular than the mighty world-historical plot of humankind's primordial unity, subsequent alienation, revolutionary redemption and ultimate self-recovery in the realm of communism? Revolutionary *peripeteia* as achieving a historical *eschaton* in the higher return of a lost genesis: it is certainly possible to write historical materialism in these terms, and indeed Marx himself more or less did so in his early writings. But one may contrast this 'narrative' version of Marxism with Marx's own well-known comments on the materialist method, in his Introduction to the *Grundrisse*:

'Bourgeois society is the most developed and the most complex historic organization of production. The categories which express its relations, the comprehension of its structure, thereby also allow insights into the structure and the relations of production of all the vanished social formations out of whose ruins and elements it built itself up, whose partly still unconquered remnants it carries along with it, whose mere nuances have developed explicit significance within it, etc. Human anatomy contains a key to the anatomy of the ape. The intimations of higher development among the subordinate animal species, however, can be understood only after the higher development is already known. . . .

'It would therefore be unfeasible and wrong to let the economic categories follow one another in the same sequence as that in which they were historically decisive. Their sequence is determined, rather, by their relation to one another in modern bourgeois society, which is precisely the opposite of that which seems to be their natural order or which corresponds to historical development. The point is not the historic position of the economic relations in the succession of different forms of society. . . . Rather, their order within modern bourgeois society.' [137]

With this passage, it might be claimed, Marx initiates a 'genealogical' break with any genetic-evolutionist conception of the historical materialist method, and, indeed, of its object—'history' itself. The constitutive elements of historical production—money, for example—may develop from simple to more complex forms, and the categories that 'express' them may shift accordingly from what Marx terms the more 'abstract' to the more 'concrete'. But this development cannot in itself provide us with the

137 *Grundrisse*, Harmondsworth 1973, pp. 105, 107–8.

key to an analysis of a specific mode of production. For (to continue the example) money in its simple form may occupy a *dominant* position in one historical mode of production, and in its more complex form a *subordinate* position within another. To put the point more succinctly: it is not 'history' that gives us the structure of the present. To quote Stuart Hall's gloss on Marx's text: 'what matters is not the mere appearance of (a) relation sequentially through time, but its *position* within the configuration of productive relations which makes each mode an *ensemble*. Modes of production form the discontinuous structural sets through which history articulates itself. History moves—but only as a *delayed and displaced trajectory*, through a series of social formations or ensembles. It develops by means of a series of *breaks*, engendered by the internal contradictions specific to each mode'.[138] The problem of Hall's figurative language— what is this unitary 'history' that moves through a set of discontinuous structures, this 'history' that is at once always deconstructed yet always self-identical?—is a symptom of the difficulty that any dialectical thought must confront in trying to think this fraught issue.

In writing of human anatomy as a key to the anatomy of the ape, Marx is suggesting a 'reversible' reading of the text of history. It is only by reading the historical narrative backwards that we can render it fully intelligible. But the organic-evolutionist metaphor he chooses has unfortunate effects: there is a symptomatic maladjustment here between figure and discourse, a shadowy fault-line along which Marx's text might be deconstructed. The thrust towards a full-bloodedly 'structural' reading of history remains in part the prisoner of an evolutionist problematic—as indeed do Marx's notorious remarks about the 'eternal charm' of ancient Greek art in the same text. For you do not escape a unilinear evolutionism merely by reversing its direction, any more than you escape a unilinear theory of narrative by insisting that chapter three can be fully understood only in the light of chapter sixty. The narrative of *Nostromo* cannot be persuaded to fall beautifully into place merely by opening the book at the wrong end. The human animal is a more complex development of the ape, but this genetic fact is precisely what determines its dominance over the ape in a given ecosystem; and it is exactly this identity of 'diachronic' and 'synchronic' that Marx is out to problematize in the case of history. The

---

138 'Marx's Notes on Method: A Reading of the "1857 Introduction",' *Cultural Studies*, no. 5 (Autumn 1974), p. 154.

image is deceptive in other ways too. The structure of a dominant mode of production is significantly determined by its relations of conflict and alliance with coexistent, 'residual' or 'emergent' modes of production; but it could hardly be claimed that human anatomy is thrown into conflict by the persistence within it of traits inherited from its pre-human past. Nor, of course, is the model of biological mutation in the least adequate for theorizing the transition from one historical mode of production to another. It is not that Marx *does* theorize in this way; it is just that one can detect within the crevices of his discourse the presence of an organicism at odds with 'structural' analysis.

For a full-blown presentation of such analysis, we may turn instead to Nietzsche. 'There is no set of maxims more important for an historian than this: that the actual causes of a thing's origins and its eventual uses, the manner of its incorporation into a system of purposes, are worlds apart; that everything that exists, no matter what its origin, is periodically reinterpreted by those in power in terms of fresh intentions; that all processes in the organic world are processes of outstripping and overcoming, and that, in turn, all outstripping and overcoming means reinterpretation, rearrangement, in the course of which the earlier meaning and purpose are necessarily either obscured or lost.'[139] Nietzsche presses Marx's transitional formulations to a boldly affirmative point, one which, moreover, was not lost on Walter Benjamin. For these sentences could well provide an epigraph to Benjamin's views of cultural revolution, his anti-historicist insistence on the ruptures, recyclings and re-insertions that underlie the bland ideology of 'cultural history'.[140] But Nietzsche's standpoint is equally ideological: by spurning all continuity as metaphysical, he threatens to subvert much of what Benjamin designates by 'tradition'. If Marx wishes to sublate the 'earlier meaning', Nietzsche desires to suppress it. Benjamin's writings are in a crucial sense post-Nietzschean, unthinkable without that astonishing iconoclasm; yet he knew also that there are traditions of political struggle, 'earlier meanings' that, if only they could be remembered, would blow Nietzsche's own crass politics into the historical rubble he had himself created.

When William Wordsworth writes that 'the Child is Father of the

139 *The Genealogy of Morals*, New York 1956, p. 201.
140 For a highly suggestive study of Benjamin, Nietzsche and Derrida, see Helmut Pfotenhauer, 'Benjamin und Nietzsche', in *Walter Benjamin im Kontext*, Burkhardt Lindner, ed., Frankfurt-am-Main 1978, pp. 100–126.

Man', he is accredited often enough with an intuitive anticipation of Freud. But Wordsworth has merely reversed the narrative: we still have fathers and children, origins and issue, openings and closures, only now the terms have been interchanged. Hierarchies of cause and effect persist, but in inverted form; evolutionism is preserved within a reversal of direction. For Freud, however, the transition from child to adult involves the disruption of this classical narrative structure. At the point of Oedipal crisis the child rejects the emplotments of genealogy, strikes against the authority of origins, and in wishing to oust one parent and possess the other desires nothing less than to become its own progenitor. This impossible conundrum, could it be realized, would naturally spell the death of all narrative—literally so, for since five-year-olds cannot fertilize their mothers or be fertilized by their fathers, the narrative of human genealogy would grind to a halt, and with it the production of narrative discourse. The child's wish to be self-originating threatens to burst through the narrational syntagm, in which it is invited to take up its place as one more subordinate signifier, and transforms that decorous lineage into the tangled skein of the Oedipal *text*, where narrative hierarchies of cause and effect, parent and child, self and other, past and present, are radically undermined. Edward Said has pointed to the Oedipal tangle as a sort of paradigm of modernist anti-narrational textuality; and he also informs us that in Arabic societies the novel proper does not exist because of the Koran.[141] The Koran is the *original* text that strikes all subsequent ones dead at birth, condemning them to the lowly status of mere repetitions or elaborations of its primordial authority. In Harold Bloom's terminology, we might say that it has a paternal status so unspeakably strong as to castrate those subsequent texts that seek anxiously to engage it in Oedipal rivalry. The child is certainly father of the man; but it is only by virtue of a repression of Oedipal 'textuality', a self-dividing submission to narrative logic, that he becomes so.

In his famous opening to *The Eighteenth Brumaire of Louis Bonaparte*, Marx comments with fine sardonism on the efforts of modern revolutionaries to assume the heroic insignia of their ancient counterparts. 'Among all relationships into which modernity entered,' Benjamin remarks in his Baudelaire study, 'its relationship to classical antiquity stands out.'[142] For Benjamin, this constellation of modern and archaic

141 *Beginnings*, New York 1975, p. 199.
142 CB, p. 81.

constitutes the dialectical or 'utopian' image, in which, when history is ruptured or arrested, dreams from chthonic depths flood into the present to configurate a future.[143] For Marx, of course, the bourgeois revolutions replay antiquity as farce. History repeats itself, but not exactly; no event quite repeats itself, precisely because it has happened once already. In striving to recuperate the past, to affirm the consoling continuities of narrative, the present finds reflected back to itself nothing less than its own ineradicable *difference* from that imaginary ideal ego. What we have in the opening of the *Brumaire*, despite the ambiguities I shall examine later, are the seeds of a theory of historical textuality that in challenging more entrenched notions of historical narrative lays bare their ideological basis. The bourgeois revolutions seek to place themselves within some privileged, primordial moment of authority; yet that placing is inevitably a displacing, a retextualizing of the revered origin, which is itself available only as text in the first place. It is in their pompous blindness to their own 'fictionality' that such revolutions betray the inauthenticity of their trust in simple historical linearity.

The socialist revolution, by contrast, does not for Marx derive its poetry from the past. It rejects the seductive tyrannies of parental authority, displacing the myth of origins for the practice of 'beginning'.[144] The socialist revolution takes its poetry from the future; but since that future, much more palpably than the past, does not exist, this amounts to saying that it derives its poetry from absence. For it seems that the future of which Marx speaks here is not to be grasped as a utopian model to which the present must be conformed, but is rather the space into which socialist transformation projects itself, the space *produced* by that projection. Like Benjamin's Messianic coming, it cannot be written now as a *telos*. To predict the future—an activity which, as Benjamin reminds us, is prohibited to the Jews—would merely be to reproduce in a different tense, so to speak, the mystifications of those who draw on the past for their utopias; like them, it would be permitting the 'phrase to go beyond the content', in Marx's significantly aesthetic image, subduing the heterogeneous movement of history to the enthralment of an *eschaton*. For

143 See Peter Krumme, 'Zur Konzeption der dialektischen Bilder', *Text und Kritik*, nos. 31–2 (October 1971), pp. 72–80.
144 I use the term in Edward Said's sense, to mean a thrust to transformation that is always already situated, and which will derive its authority from the unfolding of its own future rather than from a mythical past.

Marxism, however, the 'text' of revolutionary history is not foreclosed in this way: it lacks the symmetrical shape of narrative, dispersed as it is into a textual heterogeneity ('the content goes beyond the phrase') by the absence around which it turns—the absence of an *eschaton* present in each of its moments. The authority of socialist revolution, then, is not to be located in the past, least of all in the texts of Marx himself, but in the intentionality of its transformative practice, its ceaseless 'beginning'.

This is not to reduce socialist revolution to a form of liberal pluralism. The aim of such politics is to abolish commodity production by the institution of workers' self-government, an aim involving the planned, exclusive 'narratives' of revolutionary organization. But the consequent overriding of 'quantity' by 'quality', of the measured homogeneity of exchange-value by the 'measureless' heterogeneity of use-value, cannot be 'read off' from the social forms that will bring it into being. Marxism, as an inevitably 'limited' 'text', thus stands in ironic relation to the historical 'text' it exists to produce, and whose emergence will finally signify its own demise. Historical materialism stands to its object somewhat as a materialist criticism stands to its text. Its task is to refuse the phenomenal coherence of that text's narrative presence so as to expose the generative mechanisms that produce its repressed heterogeneity. This, precisely, is what Marx's *Capital* undertakes; it is of crucial importance that the founding economic document of Marxism, unlike that of Christianity, is not a narrative. Slicing sideways into historical development, it re-assembles it under the concept of mode of production.

The ironic relationship between Marxism and its object, or criticism and its text, is also evident in the relation between a literary text and the history that produces it. All such texts have beginnings and ends, and are consequently modelled in part on a narrative structure they may nonetheless refuse. But in what sense history itself has a beginning and an end is problematical. Empirically speaking, of course, history certainly had a beginning and will no doubt have an end; but we cannot speak of the moment of the origin of history, for to do so means that we are already subsequent to it—already in the midst of significations. We cannot think ourselves back beyond language, for we need language in order to do so in the first place. The origin of history can never be a presence: it is, rather, a moment continually displaced and absented by that play of textualization which signifies that we are always already posterior to it. An origin is nothing to speak of. Similarly, we cannot speak of the end of history because there is no imaginable end as long as we can still speak of it. 'The worst is not, So long as we can say "This is the worst",' as Shakespeare's Edgar comments. The end is perpetually deferred by the discourse that at once posits and denies it. There is a sense, of course, in which this might be claimed of literary discourse too. What is the 'beginning' of *The Rainbow*? It might be an answer to reply: *Jude the Obscure*. But in an obvious sense *The Rainbow* does have a beginning and an end, and this indeed is one of the problems with which it must grapple. For if the work itself opens and closes, the evolving genealogies with which it deals do not; and it is in this sense that the relation of every text to its object is ironic. The modernist text is simply one that has incorporated this irony into its very structure, and, like *Tristram Shandy* or *Finnegans Wake*, struggles to deconstruct closure into a textual heterogeneity forever impossible as long as books exist.

If, for Jacques Derrida, we are always already posterior to the luminous presence of the 'real', if there is always something given in advance, the same is true in a different sense for Marxism. What is always anterior for Marxism is material conditions; where consciousness is, there material conditions have been. Fredric Jameson has noted, perhaps a little too symmetrically, this parallel: 'in this context, [Derrida's] "trace" thus becomes a striking, symbolic way of conveying Marx's ever-scandalous discovery that "it is not the consciousness of men that determines their existence, but on the contrary their social existence determines their consciousness"'.[145] We cannot lift ourselves up by our bootstraps back behind 'material conditions' to an 'origin', for all we shall find will be yet more anterior conditions; we cannot project ourselves back beyond the materiality of discourse to the ghostly thought in which it originated, for that thought will be already inscribed in the material of a signification. And this is clearly one sense in which history is not a classical narrative: for what kind of narrative is it that has always already begun, that has an infinitely deferred end, and consequently can hardly be spoken of as having a middle?

There is another sense in which history figures for Marxism as 'text'. In *Reading Capital*, Louis Althusser speaks in a famous passage of that historicism for which historical time is 'continuous and homogeneous and contemporaneous with itself'[146]—that endless exfoliation in which, since

145 *The Prison-house of Language*, Princeton 1972, p. 184.
146 *Reading Capital*, London 1970, p. 98.

each moment teems with the burden of the whole, diachrony is no more than a kind of phenomenal appearance of a secret synchrony. Althusser's response to this conception is not to denounce all continuities as metaphysical, but to counterpose a deconstructed image of history: 'as a first examination, we can argue from the specific structure of the Marxist whole that it is no longer possible to think the process of the development of the different levels of the whole *in the same historical time*. Each of these different 'levels' does not have the same type of historical existence. On the contrary, we have to assign to each level a *peculiar time*, relatively autonomous, and hence relatively independent, even in its dependence, of the 'times' of the other levels. We can and must say: for each mode of production there is a peculiar time and history, punctuated in a specific way by the development of the productive forces; the relations of production have their peculiar time and history, punctuated in a specific way; the political superstructure has its own history . . .; philosophy has its own time and history. . . .'[147] And of course, as Althusser goes on to say, 'aesthetic' production as well. Althusser's concept (it is not, in fact, his own) is not without its severe problems;[148] but it has its consequences for a materialist theory of 'culture', whose first task, then, is not to offer materialist readings within the coherent narrative of 'literary history', but to deconstruct that ideological coherence and construct in its place a concept of the 'time of literary production'. That 'time'—which will allow us to identify the groupings and dispersals of 'literary' texts within a discursive formation itself articulated upon other formations—will have little in common with the 'Dickens to Hardy' chronology of bourgeois literary history.[149]

Althusser's concept of differential histories has a clear relation to the modernist notion of 'textuality'. As such, it sours the consolations of classical narrative, the ideological basis of which is well enough revealed in a sentence from Frank Kermode's *The Sense of an Ending*: 'peripeteia, which has been called the equivalent, in narrative, of irony in rhetoric, is present in every story of the least structural sophistication. Now peripeteia depends on our confidence of the end; it is a disconfirmation followed by a

---

147 Ibid., p. 99.
148 See Perry Anderson's discussion of this topic in his *Arguments Within English Marxism*, NLB 1980, pp. 73–7.
149 A literary history that, as Benjamin remarks, is a hydra with seven heads: 'creativity, empathy, timelessness, imitation, re-living, illusion and taste' ('Literaturgeschichte und Literaturwissenschaft', GS, 3, p. 286).

consonance; the interest of having our expectations falsified is obviously related to our wish to reach the discovery or recognition by an unexpected and instructive route.'[150] Reverse these formulations, speak of a consonance followed by a disconfirmation, and you have something of the formula for Brechtian theatre. 'Our confidence of the end', in Benjamin's view, was what led the German left to abandon the working class to the mercies of fascism. Not, of course, that all narratives end on a note of consonance. But whether they end well or badly, the fact is that they end; and not only that they *end*, but that *they* end—that the end, whether tragic or comic, arbitrary or predetermined, 'closed' or 'open', is the end of *this* piece of discourse, and so is part of its very shape. However open or arbitrary an ending may be, it still rounds off the text 'syntactically', even if it does not do so 'semantically'; and ideology is carried as much in syntax as in semantics. If George Eliot had decided in a fit of wild abandon to kill off all the characters of *Middlemarch* in the final paragraph, she would certainly have radically undermined Victorian ideological expectations and it is unlikely that the novel would ever have been published; but she would not have undermined such expectations as effectively as if she had finished the novel in mid-sentence.

It would be easy to conclude from all this that narrative is a mode to be abolished—that everything that happened from Defoe to Dostoevsky was a ghastly mistake. Indeed, amazing though it may seem, such a position has been hotly insinuated in our time. Narrative, however, far from constituting some ruling-class conspiracy, is a valid and perhaps in-eradicable mode of human experience. To quote Jameson once more: '. . . the ideological representation must . . . be seen as that indispensable mapping fantasy or narrative by which the individual subject invents a "lived" relationship with collective systems . . .'.[151] We cannot think, act or desire except in narrative; it is by narrative that the subject forges that 'sutured' chain of signifiers that grants its real condition of division sufficient imaginary cohesion to enable it to act. The insertion of the subject into an ideological formation is, simultaneously, its access to a repertoire of narrative devices and conventions that help to provide it with a stable self-identity through time. We know that the 'truth' of the subject

150 London 1966, p. 18.
151 'Imaginary and Symbolic in Lacan', *Yale French Studies*, nos. 55–6 (Spring 1978). Jameson's formulation seems to me too 'Althusserian' in its implicit reduction of ideology to social 'cement', but the general point remains valid.

has no such stable self-identity; the unconscious knows no narratives, even though it may instigate them. But this is not to argue that narrative is merely 'illusory', any more than we should chide the working-class movement for nurturing its mighty dramas of universal solidarity overcoming the evils of capitalism. Such motifs are the necessary inflections by which the theory of historical materialism 'lives itself out' in the practice of class struggle. And just as the individual subject is permitted to construct for itself a coherent biography, so a revolutionary or potentially revolutionary class creates, across the structurally discontinuous social formations identified by Marxism, that 'fiction' of a coherent, continuous struggle which is Benjamin's 'tradition'.

But that fiction is not a *lie*. Narrative continuities do not merely orchestrate into momentary cohesion a cacophony of historical noises. For there *are* real historical continuities, and it is a dismal index of our theoretical befuddlements that one needs to assert anything so obvious in the first place. The history of, say, the Fourth International is an extraordinarily tangled text, but it is not just grist to the mill of the latest discursive recycler. When Jacques Derrida writes of a 'continuous' tradition of Western logocentrism, it is not of course that there is in reality such an unflawed philosophical cohesion. The continuity in question is in part an imaginary self-image, how that Western tradition would *wish* to represent itself; it thus represses and expels awkward elements, cosmetically conceals disjunctures, constantly rewrites itself in the image of this desirable fiction. But only in part: that this very process of rewriting itself relies upon the sustaining of influences, the establishment of pacts and alliances, the elaboration of old themes, is also true. The same applies to Benjamin's 'tradition'. There is no unbroken lineage from the Lollards to Lenin; but within that dispersed history, more or less coherent, continuous forces and tendencies do indeed exist.

Frank Kermode speaks of the contrast between history as *chronos* and history as *kairos*—between the mere passing of time, and that dramatic moment in which time is suddenly 'seasonal', 'charged with a meaning derived from its relation to the end'.[152] In Benjamin's terms, these times are respectively those of historicism and of the *Jetztzeit*. It is not difficult to see how much classical narrative combines the two: one thing happens, and then another, and then something else that threatens or promises to transform everything. This is also a way of reading history—say, the history of the capitalist mode of production. For a while things slide along smoothly, and then there occurs a crisis, disruption or revolution. The normal condition is one of continuity, but a continuity punctuated by occasional breaks. It is important to recognize what truth this model contains—to reject the ultra-leftist catastrophism that would sniff out a world-historical recession in every fluctuation of the currency. But it is also important to grasp how the character of social reproduction under capitalism contributes to producing this viewpoint as an ideological misrecognition. For what it fails to see is that every such reproduction of the social relations of capitalism is the result of a *struggle*—a struggle conducted day by day, hour by hour, at the very point of production. Capitalism is a system of ceaseless transformations, in which a certain kind of *peripeteia* is not punctual but persistent. 'The fact that "everything just goes on" *is* the crisis,' Benjamin wrote.[153] And in so far as it is a *system of transformations*, in which the 'content' may go beyond the 'phrase', it can be encompassed as an object of study neither by a 'structuralist' narratology that expels all heterogeneity, nor by a cultic pluralism that dissolves it to sheer difference.

'Remembrance must not proceed in the manner of a narrative or still less that of a report, but must, in the strictest epic and rhapsodic manner, assay its spade in ever-new places, and in the old ones delve to ever deeper layers'. Nobody could accuse Walter Benjamin of classical narrative lucidity. Of the mere two books of his published in his lifetime, only one, the *Origin*, was in conventional book form, and that because it was his *Habilitationsschrift*; even then it could hardly be described as systematic, and encountered examiners who declared themselves unable to understand a single word of it. The other, *One-Way Street*, with its typographical experimentation and spasmodic structure, was a deliberate deconstruction of the traditionally unified text.[154] Susan Sontag has noticed that Benjamin's sentences 'do not seem to be generated in the usual way; they do not entail. Each sentence is written as if it were the first, or the last'.[155] This is true: his literary style is remarkable for its paucity of

153 GS, 1, p. 583.
154 For a valuable account of Benjamin's changing conceptions of critical production, and of the function and crisis of criticism in the 1920s in Germany, see Bernd Witte, *Walter Benjamin—Der Intellektuelle als Kritiker*, Stuttgart 1976, part 3.
155 'Introduction', OWS, p. 24.

connectives, so that sentences seem less to modify or elaborate upon one another than to stand cheek-by-jowl, apparently unconscious of each other's intimate presence, in a cunningly wrought patchwork or mosaic that reading seems able to slice into at almost any point. His writing, with its busily resourceful twists and turns, its crablike advances and sudden crystallizations, has the detailed intricacy of a tactic without the teleological thrust of a strategy. Its local leanness and economy, bracingly free of all excess, contrasts with the apparently shapeless eclecticism of the whole; items seem slackly collected but fanatically arranged, in a reversal of the *Trauerspiel* method. It is, surprisingly, a form of writing that effaces its own traces: the exotic boldness of the initial thought is instantly subdued to a kind of terse equability of tone, which casually passes itself off as humdrum truth. Each thought is wrenched from the tortured depths in which it germinated into a structure that seems to level it alongside others, preserving its angular discreteness while fitting it with technical precision into the entire discourse. In this sense, Benjamin's texts seem remarkably blind to their own brilliance: they have the idiosyncrasy of the baroque without its panache, at once daring and, as it were, inconspicuous. Every sentence is a crisis, none is a consummation, in a kind of stylistic equivalent to Benjamin's Messianic thought; each *aperçu* is woven by a capillary logic into the whole, yet has the air of being detachable. With an almost pathological vigilance to correspondences, the texts draw endless criss-cross tracks across their surface, meshing themselves into a mosaic so packed as to allow only hairsbreadth lines to appear between its fragments; yet since these webbings are so dense as to appear potentially infinite, they lend something of an arbitrary feel to the structure as a whole, the sense of a casual cross-sectioning of subtly imbricated strata.

Writing of Karl Kraus, Benjamin has the impudence to accuse him of indulging at one point in a 'mere analogy' between a movement in trade and a movement in sculpture. Such analogism— what might better be described as 'adjacentism', the unmediated juxtaposition of an infra-structural with a superstructural feature—is a notorious characteristic of Benjamin's own writing, and one that provoked a proper rebuke from Adorno. 'Throughout your texts', Adorno writes, 'there is a tendency to relate the pragmatic contents of Baudelaire's work directly to adjacent features in the social history of his time, preferably economic features. . . . I regard it as methodologically unfortunate to give conspicuous individual features from the realm of the superstructure a "materialistic" turn by relating them immediately and perhaps even causally to corresponding features of the infrastructure. Materialist determination of cultural traits is only possible if it is mediated through the *total social process*.'[156] Whatever Adorno's general standpoint, his particular criticisms of Benjamin's 'adjacentism' seem just. Nothing could be more quintessentially Benjaminesque than a passage from the Baudelaire study such as: 'In the performance of the clown, there is an obvious reference to economy. With his abrupt movements he imitates both the machines which push the material and the economic boom which pushes the merchandise'.[157] No other writer, surely, could have produced exactly these two sentences, with their mixture of audacious metaphorizing and casually 'factual' observation. Yet Adorno does not track this stylistic habit to its source. It springs from the deep-rooted problem—still unresolved today—of defining a relation between 'base' and 'superstructure' that avoids at once 'expressive', homologous or mechanical connotations.[158] In one sense, Benjamin 'solves' this problem by suspending it, forcing adjacentist parallels between the two realms that leave their true relations entirely unspoken. But if that method underscores a blunt separation, its implication of intimate, almost magical correspondence pulls the two structures rather too close for comfort. Like the Metaphysical conceit, Benjamin's metaphors yoke materials by violence together at the very moment when they gesture semi-ironically to their own artifice in doing so, to the essentially incongruous nature of the elements conjoined. They thus signify not just an individual theoretical lapse, but an objective lacuna within modern Marxism: the absence of a theory of the relations in question that would be at once non-mechanistic and non-historicist.

156 *Aesthetics and Politics*, p. 129.
157 CB, p. 53.
158 It is, of course, a problem one can solve at a stroke by ditching the metaphor altogether—either in the name of a mere discreteness of social practices, which has counter-revolutionary purposes, or, more interestingly, in the manner of Raymond Williams. In his superb set of interviews with *New Left Review*, Williams is constrained more than once to acknowledge the power of a 'sophisticated' version of the metaphor, only to revert to a cruder model which he can then dismiss (*Politics and Letters*, pp. 136–50ff.). It is also notable that Williams in his later work at once declares himself a 'cultural materialist' and suspects the materialism/idealism opposition as itself idealist. In his invaluable concern to return cultural practices to their material reality, he would seem to assume that this thereby invalidates the hypothesis of ultimate economic determination. By implicitly positing an idealist notion of the 'superstructure', he is then able to reject it with little trouble—as, indeed, he tends to counterpose the concept of 'hegemony' to that of 'ideology' in part because he posits an impoverished version of the latter, which then tends naturally to dismiss itself.

Style, in Benjamin, is what occupies that gap. Like the *Trauerspiel*, it seeks a suitable relation between materiality and meaning that alludes to their subtle complicity while stopping just short of conflation. Ceaselessly insinuating but never specifying relations, Benjamin's style hovers constantly between the 'symbolic' and the 'allegorical', between express-ive and homologous notions of the base/superstructure couple. It defines an indeterminacy out of which somebody—but not he—might conjure a theory. So it is that his style has the curious double-effect of seeming at once to paint thick the empirical object and hunt down its elusive essence, reproduce all the seething contingency of the superstructure with one hand, while exposing its secret infrastructural mechanisms with the other. His metaphorical 'disturbances' are thus sites of a more pervasive crisis: the crisis of an epoch in which the superstructure seems to have shattered into a thousand opaque pieces that obtrude themselves on the mind, but where the ruling logic of the base is day by day more discernible.

The process of Benjamin's writing, then, is a peculiar one. On the one hand it presents itself as a constant metonymic sliding, a potentially infinite succession of items that seems never to draw breath and recuperate itself. A mention of new technical means of identifying citizens leads on to the invention of photography, which in turn evokes the theme of the trace, which triumphantly gives us the invention of the detective story. Yet on the other hand the text recuperates itself all the time, as this unstoppable metonymic chain folds back into a set of synchronic metaphors. Through continual digressiveness we have in fact managed to stand still all the time; or we have progressed in such crabwise fashion that we were unaware of any motion. This problematizing of narrative in Benjamin's work is closely related to his theories of history. For he is constrained to reject both the 'empty, homogeneous' time of historicism, and that fetishism of the eternal conjuncture which would waste the resources of tradition. 'Experience', he writes of Henri Bergson, 'is indeed a matter of tradition, in collective existence as well as private life. It is less the product of facts firmly anchored in memory than of a convergence in memory of accumulated and frequently unconscious data. It is not, however, Bergson's intention to attach any specific historical label to memory. On the contrary, he rejects any historical determination of memory'.[159] The 'experience' of which Benjamin speaks here is that of the aura, the imaginary, the narrated tale; and Benjamin's prose style must yield a sense of such immanent meaning in the object while accumulating data rapidly enough to prise it loose from an imaginary paralysis, mobilize it within a 'narrative' that will not, however, reduce it to a mere passing moment.

Benjamin's criticism of Bergson is not that he harps on auratic 'experience', but that he dehistoricizes it. He differs in this way from those contemporary disciples of Lacan who will grudgingly insist that the imaginary is an indispensable moment of relation to any object, while implying by their tone that they would rather be shut of the whole thing. If Benjamin refuses any such facile denigration of the auratic, it is because he recognizes, as Bergson of course does not, its potentially revolutionary force. 'The utilization of dream-elements in waking,' he writes, 'is the textbook example of dialectical thought. Hence dialectical thought is the organ of historical awakening.'[160] The memory traces deposited by history are not only those of Proust's madeleine, that 'storm in a teacup' as Irving Wohlfarth has called it;[161] they are also those of the enslaved ancestors the memory of whom, as Benjamin reminds us, is more likely to rouse us to revolt than dreams of liberated grandchildren.[162] We repeat, as Freud taught us, what we cannot recollect; and we cannot recollect it because it is unpleasant. If we were able to recollect our ancestors, then in a moment of shock we might trigger the unpalatable memory trace at a ripe time, blast through the continuum of history and create the empty space in which the forces of tradition might congregate to shatter the present. That moment of shock is socialist revolution.

160 CB, p. 176.
161 'Walter Benjamin's Image of Interpretation', *New German Critique*, no. 17 (Spring 1979), p. 88.
162 I, p. 262.

TWO

Towards a Revolutionary Criticism

'The soothsayers who found out from time what it had in store certainly did not experience time as either homogeneous or empty. Anyone who keeps this in mind will perhaps get an idea of how past times were experienced in remembrance—namely, in just the same way. We know that the Jews were prohibited from investigating the future. The Torah and the prayers instruct them in remembrance, however. This stripped the future of its magic, to which all those succumb who turn to the soothsayers for enlightenment. This does not imply, however, that for the Jews the future turned into homogeneous, empty time. For every second of time was the strait gate through which the Messiah might enter.'[1]

For the historical materialist, the final proposition of this thesis is simply false. Not every moment is the strait gate through which the Messiah may enter; socialist revolution occurs only in particular material conditions, not in some transcendental gift or voluntarist seizing of the time. There is no way in which the apocalyptic aspects of Benjamin's historical imagination may be neatly harmonized with his Marxism, though the struggle to reconcile them, or to reduce him to either pole, will doubtless continue.[2] What matters, however, is not primarily an analytic

1 'Theses on the Philosophy of History', I, p. 266.
2 One of the most useful theological studies of the relations between Benjamin's Marxism and Messianism is Gerhard Kaiser's *Benjamin. Adorno, Zwei Studien*, Frankfurt 1974, esp. pp. 63–74. This provides a scrupulously detailed analysis of the 'Theses on the Philosophy of History', as also does Irving Wohlfarth's 'On the Messianic Structure of Benjamin's Last Reflections' (*Glyph*, no. 3, 1978, pp. 148–212). Scholem argues that since Benjamin's dialectical materialism was a 'heuristic principle' rather than a 'dogma', it left the door open to a metaphysics whose categories had often little or nothing to do with Marxism as such (*Walter Benjamin–Geschichte einer Freundschaft*, Frankfurt am Main 1975, p. 210). Scholem's point should, of course, be taken together with his general hostility to Benjamin's Marxism, and his belief that Brecht's influence on his friend was 'baneful'.

exercise that would seek to separate the materialist wheat from the idealist chaff within his work; it is rather a question of understanding the historical conditions that produced these strange blendings in the first place. When Benjamin himself remarked that the ambiguities of his writings could be blamed on the lack of a German Bolshevik revolution, he posed the essential materialist question to his own idealism.[3]

It is a question that can be posed to that entire lineage sometimes graced with the title of 'Marxist aesthetics'. For the problem of a 'revolutionary criticism' is not that it now risks incorporation into the bourgeois academy; it is that it was always already partly incorporated from the outset. Perry Anderson has noted how 'Western Marxism' swerved back to the idealist resources that nurtured it;[4] and this resort is perhaps nowhere more apparent than in that dominant strain of Western Marxism which is its theories of art. Nor is it a failure confined to Western Marxism as such. From Marx to Marcuse, Plekhanov to Della Volpe, 'Marxist aesthetics' has been for the most part an ambiguous amalgam of idealism and materialism; and that 'impurity', not least in its post-Bolshevik developments, has a historical ground. The vulnerability of Western Marxism to idealist deformations lies above all in its relative separation from mass revolutionary practice; and the fate of most 'Marxist aesthetics' has been to reproduce this condition at a specific level. It is only from within such a materialist political perspective that the meaning of much of what has passed for 'Marxist aesthetics' may be deciphered.

Marx and Engels's own occasional writings on aesthetics, illuminating though they usually are, display for the most part an anthropological humanism, an incipient 'sociology of culture', and a form of *Ideologiekritik* uncritically indebted to the aesthetics of Hegel. The one text of Marx from which we might learn something of a 'political aesthetics'—*The Eighteenth Brumaire of Louis Bonaparte*—is formally unconcerned with that topic; and though the seeds of a materialist theory of cultural practice are doubtless present in Marx and Engels, they are hardly there in much that they explicitly write of 'culture'. 'Marxist criticism' proper is datable from the work of Franz Mehring and Georgi Plekhanov, whose mechanistic determinism unites a reformist or Menshevik politics with a drastically reductive cultural theory. The crude historicism of much of their

3 B, 2, p. 530.
4 *Considerations on Western Marxism*, NLB 1976.

treatment of literature was at one with the evolutionism that indefinitely postpones socialist revolution. But since that historicism was plainly incapable of accounting for such concepts as 'beauty', Plekhanov in particular needed to have recourse to the aesthetics of a Kant. 'Aesthetic' questions, which in the case of Marx and Engels either went largely untheorized or were discussed in the language of Hegel, now required a considerably more conscious importation of bourgeois ideology. Indeed 'Marxist criticism' was launched as an uneasy alliance of two of the chief variants of that ideology dominant in the *fin de siècle*: sociologistic positivism and neo-Kantian idealism. Trotsky, a far finer literary critic than either Mehring or Plekhanov, found himself caught in such the same duality: historical materialism could account for the genesis and ideological content of art, but questions of form must to some extent be relegated to the aestheticians. The rift between Marxism and Formalism accordingly hardened, prolonged by the later Stalinist suppression of the so-called school of Bakhtin. 'Marxist criticism' queried the possibility of its own project from its very birth, and turned for aid to the bourgeoisie.

In 1926, Trotsky and the Left Opposition were expelled from the politbureau. In the same year Stalin made his first explicit formulation of the doctrine of 'socialism in one country', while Bukharin exhorted the kulaks to enrich themselves. Georg Lukács repudiated the idealism of *History and Class Consciousness* and grimly toed the Stalinist line. Michael Löwy has convincingly demonstrated the inner logic of Lukács's fraught alliance with Stalinism—how, despite the tragicomic frequency of his self-denunciations, it was less a question of Lukács's zigzagging than of Lukács's standing still and the Comintern zigzagging around him.[5] Lukács was regularly out of favour when the Comintern lurched to the left (the Third Period, the Nazi-Soviet pact—and again at the height of the Cold War), and was back at the lecture podium whenever it swung to alliance or *détente* with the international bourgeoisie. Lukács's later career, in fact, represents a sustained, internally consistent attempt to reconcile Stalinism and bourgeois humanism. Indeed what was Marxism itself for Lukács but the triumphant sublation of the bourgeois humanist heritage, the full flowering of an anthropological essence whose history could be tracked all the way from Sophocles to Solzhenitsyn? That such a project entailed grievous contradictions is clear enough: spiritually pained

5 See Michael Löwy, *Georg Lukács—From Romanticism to Bolshevism*, London 1979, ch. V.

beneath his perfunctory enthusiasm, Lukács gibbed at Stalinism's dreary philistinism and privately winced at its pathetic 'socialist realism'. A lonely, aloof Hegelian, he became the Idea that entered upon real, alienated existence—the heart of a heartless world, the soul of soulless conditions, and indeed, at base, the opium of the people. For at a deeper level, his pursuit of a desirable synthesis between Soviet Marxism and Thomas Mann had a real historical base. Neither party was in the least enamoured of international socialism. Lukács's task in the realm of aesthetics, then, was to sell bourgeois culture to the Stalinists while defending it from time to time on their behalf against an alarmingly 'plebeian' or 'modernist' Marxist art—against those, in short, whose attempted rupture with bourgeois cultural forms threatened the class collaborationism which the Soviet Union so desperately sought in order to protect its sovereignty from the violations of fascism.

The greatest, as generally judged, Marxist aesthetician of the century, then, is not the answer; he is part of the problem. If Lukács was in one sense a good revolutionary fallen among Stalinists, it is also vital to grasp the internal unity of his development, from an earlier ultra-leftism shaped by a whole repertoire of idealisms to a later Stalinist complicity with 'progressive' bourgeois values. These later issues emerge in his notable contentions of the 1930s with Bertolt Brecht, centring as they do on a conflict between 'realism' and experimentation. The experimental forms which for Brecht are an urgent imperative in the struggle against fascism are for Lukács precisely part of the 'irrationalist' heritage of which fascism is the grotesque culmination. Behind this antagonism, it would seem, lie opposing assumptions about the problem of 'rationality' itself. For Lukács, in his classic epistemological coupling of empiricism and idealism, the rational is what faithfully reflects the real. What is striking about Lukács's aesthetics is that they play upon some quite unexamined shift from 'fact' to 'value'. Throughout his extensive, well-nigh preternaturally self-consistent *oeuvre*, Lukács seems for the most part merely to assume that a correct epistemology and ontology will produce significant art—given, of course, the appropriate mastery of 'technique', which for Lukács sometimes seems little more important than acquiring the knack of riding a bicycle. The question which his work leaves in suspension—a question so enormous and banal as to be effectively invisible—is simply: why *should* accurate cognition and representation of the real afford aesthetic gratification? What is the unargued nexus here between description and evaluation? It is no doubt possible for *us* to supply some answer to this question—along the lines, perhaps, of the regressive pleasure to be afforded by that fixing of the object which is the 'imaginary'. But it is surely revealing that Lukács himself feels on the whole no need to confront this issue, just as the Romantic poet feels no need to argue why living among mountains should make you morally purer. It just is the case that art which gives us the 'real' is superior art.

Now there is a sense in which Brecht would agree; but his sense of 'rationality' surely differs in important respects from Lukács's. For Brecht, it is not quite that art can 'give us the real' only by a ceaseless activity of dislocating and demystifying; it is rather that this *is*, precisely, its yielding of the real, not a mere prelude to the dramatic moment when the transcendental signified will emerge in all its glory. Brecht's practice is not to dispel the miasma of 'false consciousness' so that we may 'fix' the object as it really is; it is to persuade us into living a new discursive and practical relation to the real. 'Rationality' for Brecht is thus indissociable from scepticism, experiment, refusal and subversion. It is not a matter, as with Lukács, of delving through ideological deformations of the object in order to foreclose all upon the reassuring embrace of the 'real', the artistic or theoretical reproduction of which is then 'rational'. It is rather for Brecht a question of rationality as practice and production, a flexing and redoubling of consciousness that must cannily beware of resting finally in the bosom of even the most apparently plausible 'representation of the real'.

For Lukács, there is an internal bond between the object and a proper (theoretical or aesthetic) knowledge of it; 'essences' have the force they do in his system because they are flushed with all the heady Hegelian potency of the rational itself, and will transmit something of that power to any text that succeeds (for what remain largely mysterious reasons) in suspending its active ideological prejudices. The discourse of the text unrolls alongside the world and transparently gives us its truth; but then, as with the early Wittgenstein, that same discourse cannot possibly let us in on the secret of how on earth it comes to do anything as mysterious as that. It is that question, precisely, which plagues and delights the 'modernist' work. Brecht's cunning of reason, however, is no property of the object, but that cunning of dialectical thought within which the object is endlessly constructed and deconstructed, conjured up and torn apart. The aesthetic pleasure his art affords, then, is that of the 'symbolic' rather than the 'imaginary'—although it certainly (how could it not?) includes the latter too.

Now both of these notions of rationality are in some sense at odds with Stalinism. Lukács, in striving to preserve the power of 'critical reason', fought what compromised rearguard action he could against the Comintern's more 'irrational' excesses; but by the same token his stand upon that concept of reason, inherited as it was from bourgeois aesthetics and philosophy, rejoined at crucial points the counter-revolutionary betrayals of Stalinism itself. Brecht, for his part, sustained in his artistic practice a version of rationality which, in its critical, concrete, agnostic interrogating, ran counter to the whole weight of Stalinist orthodoxy, but which, in its associated prudence, could find a certain nervous accommodation within it. (It sometimes faintly surprises me, on reading the transcript of Brecht's appearance before the McCarthy Committee, that on being asked 'Is your name Bertolt Brecht?' he did not instantly reply 'No'.) Not only accommodation, indeed, but shabby complicity: for those among the Western Left for whom Brecht is now a revolutionary cult-figure and Lukács a tedious humanist, it is salutary to remember the contrast between Lukács's courageous, clear-eyed participation in the Hungarian workers' uprising, and the 'mixture of truculent bluff and sentimental pathos' with which Brecht responded to the 1953 struggles in the DDR.[6]

What we are trying to comprehend, in seeking to define the difference between two kinds of rationality, is perhaps nothing less than the Marxist concept of contradiction. For Brecht, social reality was contradictory in its very being; but then consider what strange tricks language plays if, like Lukács, you replace the word 'being' there with 'essence'. In his reply to Bloch's defence of Expressionism, Lukács speaks in one sentence of the artefact having a 'surface of life sufficiently transparent to allow the underlying essence to shine through', and writes a few lines later of art 'grasp[ing] hold of the living contradictions of life and society'.[7] But it is surely very strange to think at once in terms of essence and contradiction. For one meaning of 'contradiction' simply cancels the whole notion of 'essence'; it is only the reifying ploys of Hegelian parlance that allow us to conceptualize contradiction as unity. That Lukács, like the rest of us but more than some, remains the prisoner of a metaphysical problematic is perhaps nowhere better demonstrated than in this. The capitalist social formation is a totality of contradictions; what therefore determines each contradiction is the unity it forms with others; the truth of contradiction is accordingly unity. It would be hard to think up a more flagrant contradiction. One has only to ponder the nuanced distinction between arguing that 'contradiction is essential to capitalism', and that 'the essence of capitalism is contradiction', to recognize how extraordinarily difficult it is for any of us to think ourselves outside that crippling essence/phenomenon 'model' which is for Lukács the very key to historical truth. For we certainly do not erase that dichotomy by rendering a substantive as an epithet. And it sometimes seems the case that Lukács tries to unpick this knot in our thinking by conceiving of contradiction as the diachronic putting-into-motion of a synchronic essence. But if Lukács employs the essence/phenomenon model in ways from which we all find it difficult to extricate outselves, it is also true that some of the uses to which he puts this duality, in his polemic with Bloch, are nothing but blatantly disreputable. The artist, for Lukács, must first abstract the essence of reality, then 'conceal' that essence in his text by recreating it in all its 'immediacy'. Successful texts, in short, 'know the truth', but a function of that is their capacity to pretend that they do not. The effective text is like the circus acrobat whose spontaneous mid-air cavortings are meant to conceal from us the fact that he is all the time suspended from the high wire.

For Lukács, 'immediate' experience is inescapably 'opaque, fragmentary, chaotic and uncomprehended';[8] it is only by the good offices of the 'totality' that we can see life steadily and see it whole. So art that merely reflects immediate experience is accordingly doomed to distortion. Bloch retorts that Expressionism, by reflecting the immediacy of a particular capitalist crisis, performed a progressive role; but in failing to seize an opportunity to shift the very terms of the debate, he remains here an unwilling captive of the Lukácsian problematic. For what is at stake is not whether this or that art-form, in reflecting 'immediate' experience, can lay claim to 'progressive' status; it is rather a matter of challenging that Lukácsian empiricism (the logical bedfellow of his idealism) which would believe that there is ever anything called 'immediate experience' in the first

8 Ibid., p. 39.

place. Expressionist and surrealist art, need it be said, are every bit as much constructed as Balzac; we are judging (if we need to) between two different products of ideological labour, not between 'experience' and the 'real'. It is only because Bloch fatally places himself on the ground of 'reflection' theory that this point is damagingly conceded to Lukácsian doctrine. For Lukács, true knowledge is a knowledge of the whole; ideology is the sensuous empirical which distracts you from that insight, too close to the eyeball to be proficiently mediated. It is difficult to see that this adequately represents the difference between Marx and Ricardo.

Brecht's achievement, unlike this particular contribution of Bloch, was precisely to have shifted the very terms of the 'realism' disputation. Caught though Brecht was from time to time within much the same epistemology as Lukács (he writes, for example, of artefacts 'making possible the concrete, and making possible abstraction from it'),[9] it is true even so that, for Brecht, realism can only be, so to speak, retrospective. You thus cannot determine the realism of a text merely by inspecting its intrinsic properties. On the contrary, you can never know whether a text is realist or not until you have established its effects—and since those effects belong to a particular conjuncture, a text may be realist in June and anti-realist in December. So although I have just indicated a certain parallelism between the epistemologies of Brecht and Lukács, it is nonetheless crucial to take the force of that verb 'making possible'. A text may well 'potentialize' realism, but it can never coincide with it; to speak in this way of 'text' and 'realism' is in an important sense a category mistake. Texts are no more than the enabling or disabling occasions for realist effectivity. If you want to know whether your play was realist, why not ask the audience? Did it, in their estimation, 'discover the causal complexes of society / unmask the prevailing view of things as the view of those who are in power / write from the standpoint of the class which offers the broadest solutions for the pressing difficulties in which human society is caught up / emphasize the element of development / make possible the concrete, and make possible abstraction from it?'[10] And if not, is it audience or text that needs to be rewritten? A difficult question, for sure: a question on the qualification of which the whole of Brecht's dramaturgy turns. One of the

9 Ibid., p. 82.
10 Ibid., p. 82. In the interests of grammatical consistency, I have altered the aspect of this quotation from present participle to present tense.

most important of Brecht's achievements is to have replaced the aesthetic and ontological definitions of realism proffered by Lukács with political and philosophical ones. One might say quite simply of his practice, to adapt one of his own adages: realism is as realism does.

On this as on other issues, Brecht currently seems to have won the day. But Western Marxism's debt to bourgeois idealism was never merely loss, and the current fashionable dismissal of Lukács in certain quarters as some latter-day Quixote who mistook the working class for the World Spirit is over-ripe for interrogation. If Lukács's championship of realism belongs in part to a reactionary thrust, it also crystallizes concepts of enduring value; and it is precisely the *contradictory* nature of his *oeuvre*, whose neo-Hegelian categories now challenge, now ratify the Stalinist closure, that is repressed by his anti-realist opponents. Realism for them, in so far as it aims at the fixing of a naturalized representation whose traces of production have been repressed, is by that token intrinsically reactionary: it can form no more than the imaginary space within which the subject sutures the gapings of those diacritical discourses which then cunningly permit the illusion of authorship. The ideological has been reduced to the naturalizing, in a way against which Althusser has specifically warned. In a comical inversion of the aesthetics of Lukács, realism is now the ontological enemy; the problematic has been stood on its head, with all the defiant ferocity of one who was out to abolish its very terms in the first place. And that this should be so is hardly surprising. For there is no 'modernism' without its attendant 'realism'; historically positioned as we are, we cannot possibly identify a 'modernist' text without automatically thinking up the 'realist' canon from which it deviates. Realism and modernism, like signifier and signified, are the binary terms of an imaginary opposition; we are as yet quite unable to pick ourselves up by our philosophical bootstraps out of that metaphysical enclosure into some realm beyond it.

But we might be able, nonetheless, to prise open a little that ideological encirclement in order to allow a whiff of history to enter and contaminate the aesthetic purity of its premises. It might be argued, for example, that in an earlier stage of industrial capitalist accumulation, where the dominant ideological experience was one of fragmentation and nuclearity, literary realism fulfilled a progressive role in revealing covert interconnections—in demonstrating, in short, the power and character of something like a system. It might then be argued that, once that system was indeed fleshed within ideological experience—once industrial capitalism had passed into its monopoly forms—modernism in art arrived upon the agenda as a resistance to precisely all that, exploiting the fragment, the private and the unspeakable, the agonized and irreducible moment, as the lone necessary negation of the apparently 'monolithic' society it confronted. Whether or not that is true I do not know; and any such case must beware of lapsing into that despairing, privileged myopia as to the contradictions of late capitalism which marks some of the wilder enunciations of the late Frankfurt School. But some such approach would seem to offer a more fertile mode of inquiry into the realism/modernism debate than those contending dogmatisms which, in ontologizing aesthetic categories, fall directly under the deflating judgments of a Brecht. The tedious predictability with which Lukács produces Thomas Mann from his sleeve (a writer whose very existence, one sometimes feels, is for Lukács no more than the felicitous embodiment of a necessary essence) is matched only by the automatism with which the erstwhile 'materialists' of *Tel Quel* reach for their Mallarmé, Lautréamont and Joyce.

Beneath the contradictory nature of Lukács's work lies that more fundamental contradiction which is Stalinism. Stalinism preserves the material basis of a socialism that it simultaneously frustrates; and Stalinist theory is thus a radical deformation of Marxism from which valuable materialist concepts may nevertheless from time to time be salvaged. So much is clear from the most ferociously anti-Lukácsian of contemporary Marxist schools, that of Althusserianism. In a different inflection of the Stalinist closure, Louis Althusser and Pierre Macherey adopt a version of the social formation difficult at times to distinguish from structural-functionalism, and then proceed to rescue something from the shame of this set-up. For the early Althusser it is Theory; for the early Macherey it is Art. In a new twist to the old Russian Formalist notion, art so distantiates and embarrasses the ideological as to enable us to 'perceive' it more clearly.[11] This, shorn of its dogmatic universalism, is an un-doubtedly suggestive notion; but it is also rather relieving to learn that art may embarrass a dominant ideology, since little else seems to. As the masses are spontaneously anti-scientific, labouring in the grip of an ideology that (in its 'expansionist' Althusserian definition) has become coextensive with the 'lived' as such, it is probable that such ideologies are

11 See Pierre Macherey, *A Theory of Literary Production*, London 1978.

to be unhinged by theory and literature somewhat sooner than by such traditional devices as class struggle. Aesthetic contemplation provides a lonely enclave of estrangement within the tyrannically closed, self-reproducing 'eternity' of late monopoly capitalism.

Seen in this light, such aesthetics find a surprising resonance in that strain of Western Marxism which from the outset refused all truck with Stalinism: the Frankfurt school. For if Althusserian aesthetics posit at their gloomiest an all-pervasive hegemony that only silence, negation and estrangement seem able to subvert, exactly the same is true of that marooned group of German intellectuals who, theoretically and practically divorced from the working-class movement, either sank into disillusion, veered to ultra-leftism, or collapsed ignominiously into the arms of the bourgeoisie. Georg Lukács and Theodor Adorno might be said to represent between them the 'positive' and 'negative' moments of Hegelian Marxism, as the difference between their literary styles well enough indicates—between the measured, mouth-filling, Olympian pronouncements of a Lukács, and the dense, devious enigmas of an Adorno. If Lukács seeks to correct ideological error with the full blast of the 'real', Adorno aims more and more to outflank and embarrass it by the guerrilla tactics of a discourse that deconstructs the rash positivity of another's speech into a negativity so dire as to threaten to vanish into its own dialectical elegance. As Adorno sinks steadily into disillusion, his language becomes little more than a temporary agitation, inscribing across itself the trace of a resistance to that which evoked it into being in the first place. *Minima Moralia*, in its bizarre mixture of probing insight and patrician grousing, reveals the trajectory that will lead to *Negative Dialectics*—a text which, for all its verbose presence, is finally clinched on the silence that supposedly follows from Auschwitz.

It is, then, with a certain historical irony that we now read the Adorno of the thirties taking Benjamin to task for his neglect of historical materialism—the Adorno who must inevitably figure for us as the man who, along with Max Horkheimer, delivered to the world the doleful news that the Volkswagen had spelt the death of metaphysics. Yet there is, perhaps, a certain unity between the earlier critic of Benjamin and the later upbraider of Lukács, Brecht and Sartre. Almost all of Adorno's penetrating criticisms of Benjamin's *Passagenarbeit* come down to a question of dialectics: the unity of his particular chidings of Benjamin is that his texts are in one way or the other undialectical, or indeed correct one violation of dialectics only to fall foul of another. Either Benjamin spirits away historical fidelity in his theoretical zeal, or he topples over into a theoretically unmediated positivism.

That much of this is true seems clear; but the two-prongedness of Adorno's critique seems oddly to presage some of the difficulties in which he found himself later. For the later Adorno refuses at once the 'positivist' tyranny of the self-identical object, and the obverse tyranny of that totalizing thought which threatens to swallow it up. Dialectics dig the object free from its illusory self-identity, but threaten thereby to liquidate it within some ghastly concentration camp of the Absolute Idea. For the later Adorno, then, the merest trace of 'positivity' becomes a peril, just as any hint of resisting the stubborn presence of the real poses a totalitarian menace. For discourse to *refer*, even protestingly, is for it to become instantly complicit with what it criticizes; in a familiar linguistic and psychoanalytic paradox, negation negates itself because it cannot help but posit the object it desires to destroy. Any enunciation is fatally compromised by the very fact of being such; and it follows that what one is left with is the purest imprint of the gesture of negation itself, the prototype of which, for Adorno, is modernist and post-modernist art.

It is surely not difficult to see how this pessimism is implicit in the very premisses of Hegelian Marxism. For if you rewrite Hegel in terms of Marx, the proletariat will play the role of the 'negation'. But it will never be quite as pure a negation as you want: rather than present itself as the absolute other of the system, it will reveal itself, not least at times when the class struggle has been tranquillized, as part of the system itself, as an effect of the process of capital. The political reality of the proletariat will fail to live up to its philosophical idea; and it is then always possible to abandon the proletariat and shift the idea somewhere else, into art or the third-world peasantry, philosophy or the student movement. The theoretical achievements of the 'neo-Hegelians' will stand, in many cases, as enduring monuments within Marxism; but it is true, nevertheless, that the general political destiny of the Frankfurt School (and, indeed, of Lucien Goldmann) was always to some degree written into its founding assumptions.

If Adorno's aesthetics are in one sense the polar opposite of the oppressively 'positive' assertions of a Lukács, there is another sense in which they are their mirror-image. The Hegelian tradition, of which Adorno, despite himself, is an inheritor, could always move either way—

into an affirmation of those positive essences that underlie the 'negativity' of immediate experience, or into an insistence on those essences' sheer negating force. Adorno and Lukács to that extent share the same problematic, as indeed the former's dazzlingly caustic review of the latter's discreditable *Meaning of Contemporary Realism* would suggest.[12] 'Art is the negative knowledge of the actual world': wholly opposed though Adorno and Lukács are on so many central aesthetic issues, they nonetheless link hands in the assumption that art enables a cognition of essences. Lukács had from the outset fetishized the 'totality'; Adorno will end up by fetishizing the particular (and, it might be added, by fetishizing the 'fetishism of commodities'—almost the only item of classical Marxism, one feels, that he seems able to rescue from the rubble). If for Adorno art is something like what it is for Brecht—critical, subversive—it criticizes and subverts in an essentialist way not far removed from Lukácsian orthodoxy. It is just that, for Adorno, art *becomes* the negative essence of the real, carries those contradictions on its head, rather than (as for Lukács) reflecting those contradictions in its content but repulsing them in its form.

The problem of a 'Marxist aesthetics' is above all the problem of a Marxist politics. The profundity of Lukács's work on the historical novel and the brilliance of Adorno's insights into modernism are inestimable gains for Marxist theory as a whole; but they cannot be dissociated from their impoverishing political moments. Much the same can be said of Sartre. If Sartre's elephantine study of Flaubert is in one sense a masterly contribution to historical materialism, it is in another sense a political retreat—a tacit acknowledgment that, in a period of relative political deadlock within the imperialist homelands, the question urgently posed by *Qu'est-ce que la littérature?*—how is one to write, bereft of an adequate political base?—is incapable of positive resolution.

There is, however, an alternative narrative to Caudwell on Donne and Kristeva on Mallarmé—to that academicist project, encircled by strange cross-currents of Stalinism and idealism, that has passed for a 'Marxist aesthetics'. There are also those astonishing moments in post-revolutionary Russia when at the Moscow State Theatre you might find Meyerhold at work on a play with music by Shostakovitch, script by Shklovsky, Mayakovsky or Tretyakov, film-effects by Eisenstein, stage

12 See *Aesthetics and Politics*, pp. 151–76.

designs by Tatlin. Or the moment of Rodchenko, El Lissitsky and the other Constructivists, men and women who went into the factories to harness design to 'social need'. Or Meyerhold once more, occupying a whole town to produce a play to celebrate the third anniversary of the Bolshevik revolution, with a cast of 15,000, real guns and a real battleship. Or the moment of Erwin Piscator in the 1920s at the SPD theatre in Berlin, where you might find him directing a play in which Brecht had a hand, with music by Eisler or Weill, film-effects by Grosz, stage designs by Moholy-Nagy, Otto Dix or John Heartfield. In a quite different register, there is the moment of the imprisoned Antonio Gramsci, for whom 'Marxist criticism' signified not primarily the interpretation of literary texts but the cultural emancipation of the masses.

To think of Meyerhold and Piscator is to consider what one might call a 'revolutionary modernism', and its project for transforming the subject's position within ideology under the guidance of revolutionary theory. It is to ponder the fact that if we look back to Weimar and the Bolsheviks we do indeed have, right behind us, a revolutionary culture, contaminated as it always was by aspects of bourgeois ideology. For one has only to glance at certain central aspects of such modernism, all the way from Futurism to surrealism, to avoid the temptation to fetishize that mixed phenomenon to intrinsically revolutionary status, in yet another tiresome cat-and-mouse game that feeds off that equally imaginary position which is 'realism'. Pragmatist and dogmatic, ultra-leftist and utilitarian by turns, 're-volutionary modernism' bore the scars of its turbulent emergence from pre-revolutionary ideologies as surely as did Georg Lukács, and there is, as we have seen, nothing politically innocent about a Bertolt Brecht. But Brecht was to a great extent made possible only by the existence of a mass socialist movement, however politically ambiguous; and the fact of a Brecht in turn helped to make possible the fact of a Walter Benjamin. Revolutionary cultural practice, as with the fertile liaison between Mayakovsky and Osip Brik, furnished in part the conditions for revolutionary cultural theory; the Owl of Minerva flew at night.

To those who inquire what was happening in England while the European *avant-garde* was at its height, it might be suggestive to reply that we had E.M. Forster. The English surrealist movement, which appears to have flourished and died somewhere around summer 1936, is one index of English culture's relative impermeability to such trends. While Meyer-hold and Piscator were at their peak, English theatre was dominated by the grandfather of all naturalists, George Bernard Shaw. The oldest capitalist nation in the world, provincial and deeply empiricist, ruled by a strongly hegemonic bourgeois class, was peculiarly unable to effect the 'modernist' break, as opposed to providing some of its avatars with a borrowed or temporary home. Not that bourgeois political hegemony went in the least unchallenged in this period. In 1910, waves of syndicalist strikes embroiled docks and coalfields. In 1911, troops were despatched throughout the country with orders to fire if necessary on militant workers, and gunboats entered the river Mersey with their guns trained on Liverpool. In 1912, the mineworkers launched the greatest strike in British history, and one year later a miner's son published a novel entitled *Sons and Lovers*, portraying the miners as mute, passive, 'female' creatures. There is, naturally, no mechanical connection between political and cultural upheaval; but in Europe they showed complex interrelations that on the whole failed to materialize in Britain. In the region of aesthetic ideology, the reign of realism and naturalism remained relatively unshaken. There was, of course, an English modernism, but it was mostly a foreign implantation. Joyce and Beckett left Ireland for Europe, by-passing the imperialist homeland for the cradle of the *avant-garde*. Lawrence spurned England likewise; Pound passed through; Eliot arrived to import Europe into it. The modernist moment occurred, but in peculiarly ephemeral, marginalized and reactionary form. The heavy sway of artistic realism and naturalism, with their correlative liberal or social-democratic ideologies, coupled with the entrenched hegemony of an empiricist bourgeoisie and the relative absence of a revolutionary inheritance, conspired to ensure that what modernism managed to flower or implant itself was overwhelmingly that of the extreme political right. By the same token, however, such 'extremist', starkly reactionary forms could not easily survive within the sedate, tepid milieu of the dominant culture, and typically conducted a brief, precarious existence in conflict with it. By the 1930s, with Auden and Orwell, realism was firmly back in the saddle. What Marxist criticism England could produce occurred in this period following the missed moment of modernism, when the heights of criticism had already largely been captured by the political right or liberal centre. As far as the latter position went, there was the moment of *Scrutiny*, whose ambivalent attitude towards the *avant-garde* was profoundly symptomatic of the English condition. Pioneering in its championship of Eliot and Lawrence, thoroughly grudging about Pound, primly closed to Joyce and

Beckett, *Scrutiny* represented the best, one might claim, that a provincial, empiricist culture could produce, at once courageously open to certain experiments and deeply mortgaged to a traditional 'Englishness'. (It would not be difficult to conclude from the work of F.R. Leavis that *Anna Karenina* was the only novel not written in English that he ever read with enjoyment.) There was thus from the outset no possibility of a 'modernist Marxism' to resist the imposition of socialist realism or challenge the inroads of *Scrutiny*. The Marxist writers and critics of the 1930s were on the whole Marxist *Englishmen*, whose historical materialism remained deeply entwined with the Romantic, empiricist and liberal humanist motifs of the dominant culture. Much the same may be said of the only major British socialist critic to emerge in the following decades, Raymond Williams. But to mention Williams is to quell at once any temptation to regard the materialist inheritance of dominant ideological motifs as merely contaminating. For without Williams's necessary rejection of Zhdanovite orthodoxy, and his cognate transformation of native English themes into work of unparalleled richness, little of subsequent merit could have been achieved. Precisely the same is true, in a related field, of the magnificent work of the historian E.P. Thompson. At the same time, however, it must be said that empiricism and Romantic humanism wreak their damage in the materialist critics of the 1930s. Taken together with Williams for this purpose alone, these writers may be described in a rough sense as the English equivalent of Lukács; but there is no English Brecht.

Let us review some of the names of the major Marxist aestheticians of the century to date: Lukács, Goldmann, Sartre, Caudwell, Adorno, Marcuse, Della Volpe, Macherey, Jameson, Eagleton. What is notable about all of these writers, in contrast to Lenin, Trotsky, Brecht, Benjamin and the Left Front in Art, is that they produce their work at a time when the class struggle is effectively on the downturn, temporarily quiescent or brutally suppressed. This generalization must, of course, be qualified. Caudwell's work coincides with France 1936 and the Spanish crisis; Lukács's *The Meaning of Contemporary Realism* belongs to the period of Hungarian insurgency; and no neat homology can be posited between Brecht's cultural criticism and the tides of twentieth-century class struggle. By and large, however, 'Marxist criticism' springs from periods of proletarian defeat and partial incorporation. For all the undoubtedly productive concepts that may be disengaged from the work of the writers listed, it remains work which bears the visible scars of this political fact.

My own earlier work, while certainly critical of Althusserian theory at key points, remained theoretically limited by that problematic and culpably blind to its political implications. Though I would still for the most part defend its essential critique of the work of Williams, its own residual idealism and academicism compare unfavourably with Williams's bold efforts to shift attention from the analysis of an object named 'literature' to the social relations of cultural practice. That tendency, too, can easily become fetishized in less adroit hands, as a coy or cavalier disregard for the partial 'givenness' of a literary text licenses a newly fashionable dissolution of products to processes. But it is, nevertheless, an historically requisite shifting of emphasis, blandly ignored by the greater body of traditional 'Marxist criticism'. The only major corpuses of such cultural theory to have definitively transcended their politically unpropitious moments remain the work of Bakhtin and the writings of Antonio Gramsci.

'Correct revolutionary theory,' wrote Lenin, 'assumes final shape only in close connection with the practical activity of a truly mass and truly revolutionary movement.' That this is as true of culture as it is of politics is clear enough from the history I have schematically sketched. Given the relative absence of a revolutionary cultural practice, in what sense can there be an adequate revolutionary cultural theory? It is certainly possible to produce Marxist analyses of George Eliot. It is even necessary. But any 'Marxist criticism' that defines itself in terms of such analyses has once again failed to effect a decisive break with bourgeois ideology. Such a criticism, far from staking out a new theoretical space that may make a practical difference, merely addresses new answers to the same object. The production of Marxist analyses of traditional artefacts is an indispensable project: such artefacts, after all, are one of the grounds on which the ruling class has elected to impose its hegemony, and thus one of the grounds on which it must be contested. But such contestation cannot be the primary object of a 'Marxist criticism'. If that primary object is difficult to define, it is largely because it does not as yet properly exist. The primary task of the 'Marxist critic' is to actively participate in and help direct the cultural emancipation of the masses. The organizing of writers' workshops, artists' studios and popular theatre; the transformation of the cultural and educational apparatuses; the business of public design and architecture; a concern with the quality of quotidian life all the way from public discourse to domestic 'consumption': in short, all of the projects on which Lenin, Trotsky, Krupskaya, Lunacharsky and others of the Bolsheviks were intensively engaged remain, for all the differences of historical situation, the chief responsibilities of a revolutionary cultural theory that has refused, other than tactically and provisionally, that division of intellectual labour which gives birth to a 'Marxist literary criticism'.

Lenin's pronouncement is not to be taken as a recipe for inertia. *Correct* revolutionary theory assumes *final* shape only in relation to a mass political movement; but though this is to claim that theory, deprived of that context, will inevitably suffer deformations, it is not to plead that without such a movement there can be no theory or practice at all. Lenin's statement needs to be taken dialectically with another of his well-known declarations: 'without revolutionary theory, no revolutionary politics'. Marxist cultural theory will have its tasks set for it by politics; and until that moment is ripe, it will not know exactly what it is about. The 'Marxist critic' will have no sure identity, since he or she takes his poetry from the future. But there remain, meanwhile, tasks to be performed, and even now they are not entirely confined to the academy. Let us briefly imagine what shape a 'revolutionary literary criticism' would assume. It would dismantle the ruling concepts of 'literature', reinserting 'literary' texts into the whole field of cultural practices. It would strive to relate such 'cultural' practices to other forms of social activity, and to transform the cultural apparatuses themselves. It would articulate its 'cultural' analyses with a consistent political intervention. It would deconstruct the received hierarchies of 'literature' and transvaluate received judgments and assumptions; engage with the language and 'unconscious' of literary texts, to reveal their role in the ideological construction of the subject; and mobilize such texts, if necessary by hermeneutic 'violence', in a struggle to transform those subjects within a wider political context.

If one wanted a paradigm for such criticism, already established within the present, there is a name for it: feminist criticism. No other form of criticism over the past decade has fought so fiercely and consistently to unite all of these objectives. While Marxist criticism has been largely enshrined within the academy, feminist criticism, though often actually produced there, transgresses those boundaries and takes its primary impulse from a political movement. It is unlikely that feminist criticism should detach itself from that movement; it is less possible therefore for it to attend to a 'science of the text' at the expense of such texts' material ideological effects. Feminist criticism is spontaneously aware of the ideological nature of received literary hierarchies, and struggles for their reconstruction; conscious as it is of language and the unconscious as sites of oppression, it is unlikely to lapse wholly into a mere extrinsic sociologism of literature. Since it must inevitably engage with 'literature' as an institution—with questions of the position and destiny of the woman writer—it is constantly warned against a mere idealism of its object. Its concerns cut through ideological divisions between literary and other practices, and challenge the separation of cultural criticism from cultural production. If 'literature' itself is posed at the conjuncture of power and desire, experience and the real, the production of subjects and the reproduction of social relations, feminist criticism itself in principle occupies precisely this position.

Three reservations must immediately be made. First, we are speaking of an intention rather than an achievement. Feminist criticism is still notably undeveloped, and much of it so far has been empiricist, unsubtle and theoretically thin. Second, it remains to be seen what a 'feminist literary theory' as such might mean. Current feminist criticism divides on the whole into two main kinds: on the one hand, the essential empirical tasks of exposing patriarchal power within literature, examining representations of gender and retrieving repressed areas of writing; on the other hand, a more ambitious, uneasy theoretical project that engages with questions of form, language and psychoanalysis. The first kind of criticism is politically crucial but theoretically limited, easily prey to the mere reproduction of 'practical-critical' techniques. The second kind is undoubtedly more adventurous and sophisticated, but is only in a dubious sense *specifically* feminist. Its feminism consists rather in the concrete political application to literary texts of certain general theories—most notably, Marxism, semiotics and psychoanalysis—that are in themselves by no means confined to feminism. There is, then, a theoretical problem about the meaning of an autonomous 'feminist literary theory' of any developed kind.

The third reservation is the most important. Much feminist criticism to date has arisen from within what in Britain is termed a 'radical-feminist' problematic; this must be unswervingly opposed. Anti-theoretical, rampantly idealist and frequently sectarian, such 'radicalism' represents the presence within the women's movement of a familiar brand of petty-bourgeois ideology. The facility with which a callous middle-class indifference to the political fate of the global masses may be tricked out as a jealous defence of feminist 'autonomy'—*separatism*, in fact—is a scandal that any revolutionary, woman or man, must surely denounce. Marxism is now reaping the whirlwind of its own frequently callous insensitivity to the oppression of women, and it is to be hoped that the lesson is deep and enduring. By virtue of its own partially sexist history, Marxism has lowered its moral and political credibility in the eyes of one of the most potentially vital of all mass movements, at just that moment of global crisis when such disunity may have tragic effects. It is clear at any rate that any attempt now on the part of Marxism cynically to cash in on the sufferings of women will be fiercely and rightly repulsed. But it is clear, too, as Fredric Jameson has remarked, that any left politics that refuses Marxism—that historical horizon which, in Sartre's phrase, may be ignored but not as yet transcended—is condemned to rehearse one or another variety of pre-Marxist radicalism.[13] Nowhere is this plainer than with 'radical feminism'. In England, indeed, a certain theoretical strain in feminism has provided one of the major impulses for the most thorough-going assault on revolutionary socialism to have been witnessed for some time, launched from the standpoint of a post-Althusserian left whose representatives, even in their orthodox Marxist days, were sometimes little more than petty-bourgeois theoreticists in materialist clothing. Nothing of this can be blamed on the women's struggle as such; but the ease with which even the most tight-lipped Althusserianism can disappear via its own symptomatic silences into a trenchant, abrasive, theoretically glamorous defence of reformism is one index of a political loss of nerve of which we can expect to see future expressions.

13 'Reflections in Conclusion', *Aesthetics and Politics*, p. 196.

2

A political literary criticism is not the invention of Marxists. On the contrary, it is one of the oldest, most venerable forms of literary criticism we know. The most widespread early criticism on historical record was not, in our sense, 'aesthetic': it was a mode of what we would now call 'discourse theory', devoted to analysing the material effects of particular uses of language in particular social conjunctures. It was a highly elaborate theory of specific signifying practices—above all, of the discursive practices of the juridical, political and religious apparatuses of the state. Its intention, quite consciously, was systematically to theorize the articulations of discourse and power, and to do so in the name of political practice: to enrich the political effectivity of signification.

The name of this form of criticism was rhetoric. From its earliest formulations by Corax of Syracuse in fifth-century Greece, rhetoric came in Roman schools to be practically equivalent to higher education as such. It constituted the paramount study in such schools down to the fourth century, providing a whole course in the humanities, incorporating the art of speaking and writing well in any discourse whatsoever. Throughout late antiquity and the middle ages, 'criticism' was, in effect, rhetoric; and in its later history rhetoric remained a textual training of the ruling class in the techniques of political hegemony. Textual analysis was seen as preparatory to textual composition: the point of studying literary felicities and stylistic devices was to train oneself to use them effectively in one's own ideological practice. The textbooks of rhetoric were the densely codified manuals of such politico-discursive education; they were handbooks of ruling-class power. Born in antiquity as a supremely pragmatic discourse—how to litigate, prosecute, politically persuade—rhetoric emerged as a discourse theory utterly inseparable from the social relations of exploitation. Cleric and litigant, politician and prosecutor, military leader and popular tribune would naturally have recourse to the prescriptions of rhetorical theory; for how absurd to imagine that the business of politically effective discourse could be left to the vagaries of individual inspiration. Specialists in the theory of signifying practices—rhetoricians—would thus be at hand, to offer systematic instruction in such matters. Their theoretical meditations—born often enough, as with Cicero, out of their own political practice—would then be encoded by the pedagogical apparatuses of later ruling classes, for their own political purposes. Textual 'beauties' were not first of all to be aesthetically savoured; they were ideological weapons whose practical deployment was to be learnt. The term 'rhetoric' today means both the theory of effective discourse and the practice of it.

It is, indeed, in the rhetorical theories of antiquity that many of the questions that have never ceased to dog 'literary criticism' have their root. Is rhetoric/criticism confined to particular discourses, or can it embrace any use of language whatsoever? Does it have a definitive object—juridical, aesthetic—or is it rather a 'portable' analytic method independent of any particular object? Does 'literary criticism' study 'literary' texts, or is it a branch of semiotics, and thus part of the study of any signifying practice from girning[14] to geological writing? Beneath this difficulty lies an ideological problem by which ancient rhetoric was already beset. Is rhetoric purely a question of 'technique', or does it engage substantive ethical matters? Can an immoral person efficiently persuade? How far does the 'content' of discourse, as opposed to its 'embellishments', fall under the aegis of rhetoric? For Quintilian, there was no doubt that rhetoric concerned truth as well as tropes; Socrates was a good deal more suspicious of the dangers of sophistry. In the *Phaedrus*, the good rhetorician must also be a philosopher; the gap between the technical and the veridical was already worryingly open. Though the ancients of course recognized a special variety of discourse known as 'poetry', there was no hard-and-fast distinction between this and other discursive modes: rhetoric was the science of them all. Poetry was in part discussed under the heading of the 'aesthetic', but more readily in terms of its discursively effective devices, and so as a sub-branch of rhetoric. If 'poetics' was

14 A signifying practice confined to the proletariat of certain more northerly regions of the British social formation, the point of which is to pull the ugliest possible face.

dedicated to the 'beauties' of certain fictional uses of language, rhetoric subsumed such discussion in a transdiscursive gesture, indifferently engaged with the written and spoken, text and practice, 'poetic' and 'factual'. For Quintilian, historiography could certainly be just as much a proper object of rhetorical theory as fiction.

But such a general theory of discourse, radically prior to the later divisions of theoretical labour between 'fact' and 'fiction', spoken and written, poetic and pragmatic, might then come to threaten certain ideological values. Abstracted from the practical political contexts which gave it birth, rhetoric could harden into a set of self-regarding procedures indifferent to the truth-value of particular discourses, a 'sophistical' declension that posed a latent threat to the state. Once the techniques of persuasion were fetishized as a form of meta-discourse, anyone was in principle open to be persuaded of anything. The masses must be suitably gullible, but not the dupe of any passing sophist. It was, then, largely in the political context of ancient rhetorical theory that later critical disputes between 'form' and 'content', 'technique' and 'morality', were to emerge—disputes that would come to be mystified to the level of the purely 'aesthetic'. The ancient rhetorician needed to know whether 'form' and 'content' were separable or inseparable because he needed to know whether you could achieve 'different' effects in discourse with the 'same' thought. An 'aesthetic' error could lead to a political miscalculation. All discourse must underwrite the political and ethical values of the state: the earliest piece of Western 'literary criticism' we have, a debate in Aristophanes's *The Frogs*, set the standards of 'literary' practice as skill in art and 'wise counsel for the state'. Plato in the *Laws* would admit only 'hymns to the gods and praises of famous men' as permissible 'literary' acts. But such an emphasis was in incipient contradiction with the full flowering of rhetoric, which Aristotle defined as the discovery of possible means of persuasion with regard to any subject whatever. Rhetorical theory, in a historical context prior to any highly specialist division of discursive labour, was inevitably to some extent autonomous of particular objects; yet it seemed only a short step from such autonomy to a dangerously self-regulating set of meta-linguistic devices. Beneath this whole debate, in turn, lay a deeper ideological crisis in the ancient Greek state. Did 'moral' discourse specify modes of behaviour appropriate for a member of a particular *polis*, thus requiring as its basis a specific 'science' of that *polis*; or was it a universal language that could specify the nature of 'moral' action in any *polis* at all? It is the shape of this racking dissonance—one symptomatic of historical changes that have thrown the definition of traditional 'social roles' into question—that one can perhaps glimpse between the lines of the rhetoricians' wrangling.[15]

The effects of this wrangling on later 'criticism' were severe. For if criticism was merely a matter of 'technique', indifferent to the truth-value and moral substance of the text, then it courted triviality; if, however, it was a question of such 'moral truths', then—not least in ideologically fraught epochs when such truths were themselves fiercely contested—it risked either unacceptable didacticism or embarrassing vagueness. The history of 'criticism' is among other things the vexed narrative of this dilemma, torn as it continually is between a rebarbative 'technicism' on the one hand, and a nebulous or insipid 'humanism' on the other. Almost every major critical 'school' has been characterized by an attempt to resolve this embarrassment anew. In the very cradle of ancient rhetoric, however, such a dilemma could not fully arise. Debating within a political assembly, arguing the merits of a law-suit or urging a government to war were forms of discourse whose devices were closely determined by the pragmatic situation to hand, techniques of persuasion indissociable from the substantive issues and audiences involved.

The ancient quarrel between 'form' and 'content' recurs in our own time in the shape of a controversy between 'ideology' and 'science'. Rhetoric, in some models, is an articulation of knowledge with power; but what proportionate role does each element play within it? For most classical rhetoricians, the cognitive and affective must be closely combined: *dialectic* (philosophy) must govern the production of ideological effects, *inventio* (substance of argument) must lay the groundwork for *dispositio* (structure of discourse) and *elocutio*. With the rise of Ramist logic in the seventeenth century, however, rhetoric and dialectic became increasingly disjoined. Cicero was already complaining in the *De Oratore* that Socrates had damagingly divided philosophy from rhetoric, thinking wisely from speaking gracefully; and under the impact of bourgeois rationalism and empiricism, that division was to become entrenched to the point where rhetoric would come to mean what it popularly means now: specious, filigree or bombastic language. The grounds for such a divorce had already been prepared by the fate of rhetoric in the middle ages. In

15 See my *Criticism and Ideology*, NLB 1976, for a brief account of this debate.

that era, rhetoric retained its hegemony over 'poetics': poetry was seen in effect as versified rhetoric, poets and orators imitated one another, and George Puttenham could remark that the poet was the best rhetorician of all. But with the change of material conditions from antiquity to the medieval period, rhetoric fell into a sterile formalism, a mere repertoire or museum of exotic verbal devices. What had happened in part was a severance of rhetorical theory from rhetorical practice, with the notable exception of the pulpit: the Greek city-state, with its partially phonocentric, oratorical political practices, had yielded decisively to government by script. Rhetoric was now a predominantly textual rather than political activity, a scholastic rather than civic pursuit. Though it retained high authority throughout the Renaissance, the rise of rationalist and empiricist philosophies of language spelled its ultimate demise. A rigorous division of labour was gradually instituted between thought and speech, theory and persuasion, language and discourse, science and poetry. By 1667, Thomas Sprat, historian of the Royal Society, was clamouring for the banishment of 'Eloquence' from all civil societies, 'as a thing fatal to Peace and good Manners'. Ramus, as Walter Ong has pointed out, appeared upon the scene when dialectic was slowly shifting from the (Ciceronian) art of discourse to the art of reasoning; 'theory' now had its specialist protocols remote from the market-place and public forum, untainted by truck with the masses, a privatized and elitist mode of production that had rejected the 'dialogism' of ancient rhetoric for a resolutely monologic cast. Reasoning, Ong remarks, wanted to dispense with words, since 'these annoyingly hint that in some mysterious way thinking itself is always carried on in the presence—at least implicit—of another'.[16]

It is not, of course, a question of nostalgically resurrecting some Bakhtinian carnival of the word from the ancient *polis*. It does not seem that Roman slaves had much chance of answering Cicero back. If Sprat and Ramus wished to expel the materiality of the sign, halting its dangerous dance of connotations, ancient rhetoric threatened to repress that materiality in another direction, by its full-blooded logocentrism. For Cicero, rhetoric could encompass everything, precisely because everything was based upon the word. Plato's objections to rhetoric were closely allied to his unease at the 'artifice' of writing. A distinction between voice

---

16 'Ramus and the Transit to the Modern Mind', *The Modern Schoolman*, no. 32 (May 1955), p. 308.

and script was already apparent in the ancient world in the assigning of the former to rhetoric and the latter to grammar. Only in the Renaissance, after the birth of printing, would rhetoric be fully applied to written texts. The decline of rhetoric, then, was the overdetermined effect of a number of factors: the dwindling of the 'public sphere'[17] of political life with the growing power of a complex, bureaucratized 'civil society'; the correlative power of script in the exercise of class rule; the puritan, rationalist and empiricist distrust of verbal 'ornamentation' in the name of rigorous denotation; the bourgeois-democratic suspicion of rhetoric as 'aristocratic' manipulation and discursive authoritarianism; the emergence of a political science relatively sealed from the turmoil of political practice.

In the English eighteenth century, rhetoric retained something of its traditional force. It was apparent to much eighteenth-century theory, for example, that rhetorical figures were by no means confined to 'poetic' uses of discourse but inhabited other forms of language too; and to this extent the transdiscursive stress of rhetoric remained active, subsuming all such signifying practices to the domain of 'polite letters', rather than to the distinctive region of 'imaginative literature'. With the advent of Romanticism, however, a deep transmutation of discourses was witnessed. From the standpoint of linguistic rationalism, both rhetoric and poetry were highly suspect modes, akin in their fictional spuriousness and emotive infection; but the Preface to the *Lyrical Ballads* was to pit poetry *against* rhetoric, demotically disowning the lying figures of eighteenth-century poetic diction for the emotionally charged language of common life. In a curiously circular movement, an initially logocentric rhetoric had passed into the pernicious falsities of print, to be opposed by an equally logicentric anti-rhetoric. Poetry was now a counter-force to those dominative discourses that, in Keats's phrase, had a 'palpable design' upon us. It did not cease to lay claim to the 'public sphere', as Blake and Shelley well enough attest, but against a public rhetoric now firmly identified as ideological it proffered the non-authoritarian values of feeling, creativity and imagination—of, in a word, the 'aesthetic'. Poetry was Nature, as opposed to the artifice of rhetoric, but in an adroit manoeuvre it strove at the same time to appropriate the 'special' status with which rhetoric had become identified, its intense and heightened

17 A sphere of open, participatory communication whose recovery such thinkers as Jürgen Habermas see as crucial to the establishment of socialism. See his *Strukturwandel der Öffentlichkeit*, Neuwied 1962.

style. 'Literature'—a privileged, 'creative' use of language—was accordingly brought to birth, with all the resonance and panoply attendant upon traditional rhetoric, but without either its 'authoritarianism' or its audience. The former was countered by the 'aesthetic'; the latter compensated for by the Author. Emotive effects, particularly in early Romanticism, continued to work within the context of public political persuasion; but the cultivation of the spontaneous and intuitive, the eccentric and transcendental, came to produce a quasi-political language of its own, whose source was a specialized 'aesthetic' or 'imaginative' faculty as loftily remote from the 'public sphere' as the increasingly redundant rhetoric it strove to oust. In the absence of that known audience that was in a strict sense a material condition of rhetoric, the creative authorial subject was duly enthroned, source or medium of a trancendental discourse that spurned rather than wooed 'the public'. Language was less public medium than unique individual expression; rhetorical analysis would be gradually outflanked by 'stylistics'. The social conditions of the Romantic poet—at once ideally 'representative' and historically marginalized, prophetic visionary and commodity-producer—were encoded in a form of writing that could still retain the urgent public inflections of rhetoric while almost wholly lacking its pragmatic context. By the later nineteenth century, Matthew Arnold was anxiously demanding of poetry a recovery of rhetoric's tonal authority (the 'grand style'), precisely as John Stuart Mill struck an historically more realistic emphasis: poetry was now that which is 'overheard', the exact opposite of the rhetorical.

With the rise of the great idealist schools of aesthetics of late-eighteenth-century revolutionary Europe, 'feeling' was displaced from the material effects of pragmatic discourse to become the crux of a higher, contemplative mode of cognition. 'Sensibility' was at war with rhetoric, symbolic synchrony with the pompously discursive. The 'special' yet social discourse of classical rhetoric, intensifying common verbal effects for concrete political aims, had now become the esoteric, ontologically unique language of poetry, whose intuitions were in revolt against all such politics. The very form of the 'aesthetic' provided imaginary resolution of real contradictions: for where could one find a more perfect integration of the conflicts that seemed to have riven ideological history apart— universal/particular, rational/sensuous, order/spontaneity, transformative will/wise passiveness, Nature/Art—than in the poem itself? What else was the Romantic symbol but a full-blooded ideology of its own, the last great idealist totalization before the birth of historical materialism?

But rhetoric had not been defeated; it merely shifted its ground. For Nietzsche, in his notes on rhetoric, a concern with techniques of eloquence and persuasion was to be subordinated to a study of figures and tropes— tropes that were the 'truest nature' of language as such. By exposing the covertly rhetorical nature of all discourse, Nietzsche took the 'technical' aspects of rhetoric and turned them sceptically against its traditionally social, cognitive and communicative functions. Rhetoric was undermined on its own ground: if all language worked by figure and trope, all language was consequently a form of fiction, and its cognitive or representational power problematized at a stroke. Nietzsche retrieved the rhetoric written off by rationalism as a dangerously abnormal device, and with the same suspecting glance universalized it to the structure of all discourse; both bourgeois rationalism and its materialist-scientific opponents were thus triumphantly out-manoeuvred. Even the most apparently cognitive or colloquial of languages was ambiguously infiltrated by deceit; the final 'exposure' of rhetoric was one that detected its ineradicable presence everywhere. Mocked and berated for centuries by an abrasive rationalism, rhetoric took its terrible belated revenge—a revenge that consisted not in any last-ditch claim to dignity, but in showing the self-righteous enemy that he himself was contaminated, even unto death, by its own leprous disease, its own flaking and seepage of meaning. Rhetoric was the foul-mouthed beggar in whom even the king would find himself echoed.

The ultimate reversal had thus been effected. Born at the juncture of politics and discourse, rhetoric now had the Fool's function of unmasking all power as self-rationalization, all knowledge as a mere fumbling with metaphor. In retreat from market-place to study, politics to philology, social practice to semiotics, rhetoric was to end up as that vigorous demystifier of all ideology that itself provided the final ideological rationale for political inertia. Mischievously radical, it delighted in confronting the bourgeoisie with the truth that its own ideologies had spread wider than it wished, sunk into the very fabric of its sciences, undermined the very structures of its communication. But since it was itself, after all, 'mere rhetoric', it could do little more than bear witness to this fact, and even then was not to be trusted. Nietzsche's emancipatory enterprise had as its other face a gross failure of ideological nerve—one which, as his present-day acolytes testify, is still with us. 'Rhetoric,' writes Paul de Man, 'radically suspends logic and opens up vertiginous possibilities of referential aberration . . . poetry gains a maximum of convincing power at the very moment that it abdicates any claim to truth.'[18] All communications mar themselves, presenting us at the very crisis of persuasion with the reasons why they should be suspected. The liberal academic, marooned in a brash world of manipulative messages, may now discover in the very body of rhetoric itself the reasons why such vulgar commercial and political hectorings may be blandly mistrusted.

That the nurturing of verbal ambiguity is at once source of critical insight and ideological evasion is surely as obvious in the new Yale school as it was in the old. Encircled by a presumed ideological monolith, 'literature', or discourse in general, is once more fetishized as the last place to play, the sole surviving antechamber of liberal hesitancy. If the materialists can get their grubby hands even on *that*, then the game is almost certainly up. This is not, naturally, to dismiss such work as nugatory—least of all the penetrating insights of a de Man. The present book, for example, is a text that such work can do much to illuminate. For it is intended as revolutionary rhetoric aimed at certain political effects, yet speaks a tropical language far removed from those in whose name it intervenes. In one sense this should not be taken as unduly worrying: slogans and aesthetic treatises are both workable genres provided neither is mistaken for the other. In another sense, however, the rhetorical tropes and figures of my own discourse could be accused of undoing my rhetorical intentions, constructing a reader whose political clarity and resoluteness may be threatened by the very play of language that hopes to produce them. What distinguishes the materialist from the deconstructionist *tout court* is that he or she understands such self-molesting discourse by referring it back to a more fundamental realm, that of historical contradictions themselves. For there can be no doubt that such a text as this, produced within an academy it also challenges, will inscribe such contradictions in its very letter—will figure at once as political act and as libidinal substitute for those more deep-seated actions that are in any full sense presently denied us. Universities are now precisely such sites of contradiction: the conditions required for them to reproduce ruling–class skills and ideologies are also in part those which allow them to produce a socialist critique. It is unlikely that texts generated from this point will escape unscathed by these ironies. But this is a different kind of

18 *Allegories of Reading*, New Haven and London 1979, pp. 10 and 50.

ambiguity altogether from that which at a certain point in modern criticism becomes a wholesale ideological assault, a fresh strategy necessitated by the decline of traditional rhetoric itself. Ambiguity, to put it bluntly, is wheeled onstage when the ruling class realizes that its official rhetoric is going unheeded. Arnold wrote *Literature and Dogma* as a last-ditch attempt to salvage a well-tried rhetorical discourse—religion—that was failing to convince the proletariat. The trick was to 'poeticize' such language, retaining its authoritative images while blurring its unacceptable terms to grandiloquent vacuities. Linguistic indeterminacies were absolutized, and the name for them all was God.[19]

Arnold's strategy failed, of course, but another was to hand: England was just entering upon its epoch of high imperialism, and a more palpable rhetoric—that of chauvinism—was accordingly available. On the other side of the First World War, however, with its carnage of ruling-class eloquence, this strategy looked none too lively either: by 1919 T.S. Eliot was writing of an English drama that had 'grown away from the rhetorical expression, the bombastic speeches, of Kyd and Marlowe to the subtle and dispersed utterance of Shakespeare and Webster'.[20] Eliot did not write rhetoric off, but he 'introjected' it, removing it from the bombastic sphere of a merely public discourse to the inner territory of the emotions. That for him was the positive sense of rhetoric; but it might also be taken to signify 'any adornment or inflation of speech which is *not done for a particular effect* but for a general impressiveness'.[21] Rhetoric, in other words, was now permissibly synonymous with 'bad rhetoric', and was countered by certain concrete intentional tactics that it was the very function of classical rhetoric to fulfil. In a similar way, I.A. Richards wrote in his *The Philosophy of Rhetoric*, published in an era when there was indeed much of it about, that the study of classical rhetoric could be advantageous at least 'until man changes his nature, debates and disputes, incites, tricks, bullies and cajoles his fellows less'.[22]

A supreme ideological pragmatist in his working methods, T.S. Eliot ravaged language and ransacked world literature to penetrate what had

---

19 There is a certain logic in the critical development of J. Hillis Miller, ideologue of this trend in *The Disappearance of God*, Cambridge, Mass., 1963, and now propagating a more acceptable, 'secularized' version of such indeterminacies as an enthusiast of Jacques Derrida.
20 'Rhetoric and Poetic Drama', *Selected Essays*, pp. 38–9.
21 Ibid., p. 42.
22 New York 1936, p. 24.

now become a general weariness with ideological rhetoric. Beneath that disillusioned anti-rhetorical guard, by every device of verbal indirection, he cultivated those effects that engaged with the ideological on its very homeland—the organs of 'lived experience' themselves, the 'cerebral cortex, the nervous system, and the digestive tracts'. By selecting words with 'a network of tentacular roots reaching down to the deepest terrors and desires'.[23] thus achieving 'direct communication through the nerves',[24] poetry would make it appear natural that fertility cults might hold a clue to the salvation of capitalism. This enterprise, of course, was as absurd as Arnold's: Eliot's erudite primitivism, his belief that if the lower classes were grabbed by their visceral regions then their minds would follow, foundered on the minor difficulty that they didn't read his poetry—something that his notoriously olympian public bearing effect-ively conceded in advance. Even so, Eliot's anti-rhetoric was at least in the service of 'belief-effects', which is more than can be said for our contemporary (anti-) rhetoricians. Since it now seems less possible for bourgeois ideology outside of Northrop Frye's Toronto to pass off fertility cults as plausible, the one lame rhetoric remaining is the rhetoric of anti-rhetoric. In the place of the rhetorical deceits of language we are offered—the rhetorical deceits of language. This does not bode well for the future of critical ideology. It may therefore emerge that what will prove more productive in the future will be that partial return to traditional rhetoric now promised by 'speech-act theory', which reinterprets the literary text in terms of subject-positions and conjunctural discourse. Any such theory, however, will need at once to confront the valuable insights of the contemporary (anti-)rhetoricians, and the challenge of historical materialism.

The early career of a professional rhetorician like the German Marxist theatre director Erwin Piscator suggests a problem of revolutionary rhetoric that may be focused in the somewhat oxymoronic term *agit-prop*. Is socialist art primarily affective (*agit*) or informative (*prop*)? And what is the relation between theatre as ideological transformation and theatre as laboratory of dialectical theory? In strikingly new guise, some familiar problems of classical rhetoric are raised once more. In one sense, it might

---

23 'Ben Jonson', *Selected Essays*, p. 155.
24 'Philip Massinger', ibid., p. 215.

be claimed, these are in fact pseudo-problems. For any socialist involved in teaching knows that nothing is more 'ideologically' effective than knowledge, and that any exclusive epistemological carve-up of consciousness between the two is itself a theoreticist fantasy. It is perhaps not surprising, given the political effects of reliable knowledge, that much current ideology is devoted to questioning its very possibility. Nevertheless, the difficulty is not entirely factitious. Historical materialism is itself a 'rhetoric', in the fundamental sense that it is unthinkable outside those suasive interests which, through trope and figure, project the world in a certain controvertible (falsifiable) way. There is in the end no 'rational' ground for committing oneself to this view: it is theoretically possible to be persuaded of the truth of historical materialism without feeling the least compunction to act upon it. Nobody becomes a socialist simply because he or she is convinced by the materialist theory of history or moved by the persuasive elegance of Marx's economic equations. Ultimately, the only reason for being a socialist is that one objects to the fact that the great majority of men and women in history have lived lives of suffering and degradation, and believes that this may conceivably be altered in the future. There is nothing at all 'rational' about that (though rationality does indeed play its part in the transition from moralistic or utopian socialism to historical materialism). There is no 'rational' riposte to one who, having acknowledged this truth, remains unmoved by it. It is, if you like, a question of the cortical and visceral regions. But this is not to say that Marxism has the cognitive status of a scream. All scientific theory is perhaps 'metaphorical', but it does not follow that any old trope will do, nor, as pragmatism would have it, that any old trope that 'does' will do. 'Black is beautiful' is paradigmatically rhetorical, since it deploys a figure of equivalence to produce particular discursive and extra-discursive effects without direct regard for truth or falsity. It is not 'literally' true. Yet neither is it 'mere' rhetoric, since it is an utterance of a piece with certain falsifiable hypotheses concerning the racial structure of contemporary societies.[25] In this sense, 'black is beautiful' is a 'literary' text, a piece of language which, seized 'non-pragmatically', nonetheless produces certain particular effects. To say that the slogan is 'true' is not to claim that it represents a real state of affairs. It is to claim that the text so fictionalizes

25 I am grateful to my friend Denys Turner of the University of Bristol, who first suggested this slogan to me as paradigmatic of 'moral' discourse.

the 'real' as to intend a set of effects conducive to certain practices that are deemed, in the light of a particular set of falsifiable hypotheses about the nature of society, to be desirable. It could be, of course, that the utterance 'black is beautiful' is fatally self-molesting. You could show how subtly its structural symmetry and utopian impulse belie the political inequality it challenges, or how the reversible reading it unconsciously holds open might inhibit the political practice it intends. On the other hand, it is possible that the deconstruction of the ghettoes might outstrip the deconstruction of the phrase.

As far as rhetoric is concerned, then, a Marxist must be in a certain sense a Platonist. Rhetorical effects are calculated in the light of a theory of the *polis* as a whole, not merely in the light of the pragmatic conjuncture fetishized by post-Marxism. Rhetoric and dialectic, agitation and propaganda, are closely articulated; what unites them for Plato is justice, a moral concept itself only calculable on the basis of social knowledge, as opposed to *doxa* or ideological opinion. Since all art is rhetorical, the tasks of the revolutionary cultural worker are essentially threefold. First, to participate in the production of works and events which, within transformed 'cultural' media, so fictionalize the 'real' as to intend those effects conducive to the victory of socialism. Second, as 'critic', to expose the rhetorical structures by which non-socialist works produce politically undesirable effects, as a way of combating what it is now unfashionable to call false consciousness. Third, to interpret such works where possible 'against the grain', so as to appropriate from them whatever may be valuable for socialism. The practice of the socialist cultural worker, in brief, is projective, polemical and appropriative. Such activity may from time to time include such things as encouraging others to reap pleasure from the beauty of religious imagery, encouraging the production of works with no overt political content whatsoever, and arguing in particular times and places for the 'greatness', 'truth', 'profoundly moving', 'joyful', 'wonderful' qualities of particular works. . . .

3

The cross-breedings of materialism and idealism within Marxist cultural theory could not be more dramatically exemplified than in the work of Walter Benjamin. Lukács may be idealist, but at least he does not solemnly discuss the Messiah; Adorno is much bound by high culture, but he nowhere speculates that all languages are inflections of a single Adamic essence. Benjamin's mixture of the elements, by contrast, is so flamboyant and unabashed as to be faintly comic. Yet one of the poignant aspects of the man is surely the courage with which he strove to dispossess himself of what he saw as the more disabling features of *haut-bourgeois* culture. Benjamin was of course a formidably cultivated intellectual in the high German tradition, meditative, courteous and unworldly, temperamentally unfitted for the public rancour of class politics. He remarks in *A Berlin Childhood* that he would have been incapable of building a front with his own mother. Yet he was prepared, in his own self-apologetic phrase to the disapproving Gershom Scholem, to 'hang the red flag out of the window', even if it was 'nothing but a scrap of rag',[26] and prepared moreover to court the ludicrous and pathetic corollaries of that, the *mauvaise foi* and loss of solidarity on all sides that such an action might involve. Being himself most rich, Benjamin became poor for the revolution; he viewed his own life as a kind of *kenosis*, a suffering self-abandonment that culminated, appropriately, in his being severed by the class enemy from his cherished library. That such self-emptying entailed more than a degree of guilty self-castigation is clear enough: his admiration for the Brechtian 'destructive character', brashly willing to let himself be hollowed by winds of history, has a marked quality of fantasy or compensatory wish-fulfilment about it,

26 B, 2, p. 531.

just as his celebrated essays on the productive basis of art risk technologism and ultra-leftism in their anxious desire to appear impeccably materialist. What we have lost, however, with *Krisis und Kritik*—the journal of revolutionary criticism that Benjamin planned with Brecht, never to appear—is probably grievous. In it, no doubt, we would have found the full fruits of Benjamin's bold readiness to shatter and reforge the whole apparatus of 'cultural criticism', all the way from styles of writing to the revolutionary recycling of the critic him/herself. Benjamin's deeply idiosyncratic Marxism displays the traces of his never-jettisoned idealisms; but by the same token it detaches him from Marxist 'orthodoxy' to catapult him to a point that we have in some senses yet to arrive at. Caught between the brusque pragmatism of a Brecht and the patrician esotericism of an Adorno, he stood in the cross-fire of contradictions that no revolutionary intellectual can today escape; indeed that he incarnated such contradictions so exotically is a major part of his political meaning. For no revolutionary intellectual can today escape the following dilemma: that in the teeth of all forms of *ouvriérisme* and iconoclasm he or she must exploit the resources of traditional culture to the full, while living in the perpetual readiness to lose absolutely everything of that should it become historically necessary. The intensity with which Benjamin lived this aporia distinguishes him just as much from the sanguine teleology of a Lukács as it does from the occasional facile philistinism of a Brecht. The Messianic idea in Judaism compels a life lived in radical deferment, in which nothing can be definitively performed, nothing irrevocably accomplished. If this was Benjamin's belief, it is also the condition of his modern-day inheritors.

Benjamin's Messianism is at once the clearest evidence of his idealism and one of the most powerful sources of his revolutionary thought. For the Jewish theology that concerned him, scriptural revelation is the voice of God, but one not instantly meaningful: this obscure original text must be ceaselessly reinterpreted by tradition, which represents 'an attempt to render the word of God utterable and usable'.[27] The revealed text is generative of meaning but in itself meaningless; for Kabbalistic Judaism, the original name of God rests in an Ur-Torah which, infinitely remote as it is from all human language, is all-embracing and inexhaustibly interpretable. Indeed for Messianism the written Torah itself will take on new meanings in the transfigurative light of the Messianic age, yielding

27 Gershom Scholem, *The Messianic Idea in Judaism*, London 1971, p. 50.

itself to entirely original interpretations. When the Jewish mystic encounters the sacred scriptures of tradition, the sacred text is smelted down and new dimensions discovered within it. Mysticism involves a 'revolutionary' reading of scripture, scandalous in its almost unlimited exegetical freedom; St Paul, Scholem considers, practised 'incredible violence' on the Old Testament, reading it 'against the grain'.[28] Such mysticism is thus always in danger of 'ultra-leftist' deviations from the traditions it exists to conserve. For certain Jewish mystics, indeed, there is no written Torah: the controlling text is radically decentred, grasped as always already mediated through oral tradition, viewed as no more than one crystallization of meanings that the tradition always holds in solution. For some Kabbalists, the scroll of the Torah used in synagogues, without vowels or punctuation, is an allusion to the original Torah as it existed in the sight of God before the creation—no more than a heap of unorganized letters. When the Messiah comes, God will annul the existing Torah and compose its letters into other words; the text itself will not materially change, but God will teach us to read it in accordance with another scriptive arrangement. For the anonymous author of the Kabbalistic *Book of Configuration* (c. 1250), in every *shemittah* (cosmic cycle) men and women will read something entirely different in the Torah, as its letters ceaselessly exchange and combine. One view holds that one of the letters of the Torah alphabet is missing in the present *shemittah*, but will be restored in the next to transform our reading of the text. Alternatively, the problem of squaring the 'new' Torah of the Messianic age with the doctrine that not a letter of the existing Torah can be changed may be resolved by claiming that the white spaces between the letters of the existing Torah are in fact invisible letters that we shall finally be able to read.

It seems a far cry from the Asiatic mode of production. But if these are the features of Benjamin's thought that prove for us the most intractable, there is surely no doubt that they are integral to his cultural materialism. That the task of criticism is 'not merely to transmit cultural information about a literary phenomenon, but to stimulate the reader to reflection on his own political situation';[29] that cultural artefacts are not immutable revelations but projects to be strategically reconstructed in changing historical conditions; that literary texts are to be violated, smelted down,

28 Idem, *On the Kabbala and Its Symbolism*, London 1965, p. 14.
29 Witte, p. 157.

read against the grain and so reinscribed in new social practices; that the tyranny of Scripture is for the revolutionary reader the dissemination of polyvalence: all of this refers at once to Benjamin's mystical and materialist interests. All texts are sacred for Benjamin because they are autonomous—autonomous not of history but, like the Bible, of authorial intention ('Truth', he writes, 'is the death of intention'[30]), and so of a single exhaustive interpretation. They figure for him less as expressive media than as material ceremonies, scriptive fields of force to be negotiated, dense dispositions of signs less to be 'read' than meditatively engaged, incanted and ritually re-made.[31] As non-intentional constellations, texts may be deciphered only by the equally 'sacred' pursuits of critique and commentary, in which a language similarly unleashed from intention into its material fullness may catch in its net of mutual resonances something of the 'idea', the pattern of diverse significations, of the text it studies. Such sacred criticism involves an 'aesthetic' responsiveness to the particularity of its object alien to the dominative rationality of the Enlightenment; but it does not thereby become the object's obedient ghost. For to be 'redeemed' into the 'truth' of criticism or philosophy, the empirical phenomena must be dismantled, redispersed and rearticulated, drawn into an objective constellation of concrete relations that cuts through the literary and historical categories of conventional theory. Already present in the tortuously idealist Prologue to the *Trauerspiel* book, this notion will find its materialist significance in Benjamin's later work. For the activity of 'constellating' demands a submission to the inner logic of the material object that rejects the subjectivist vagaries of idealism, even as that object is then 'magically' transmuted by the power of creative naming, verbally articulated and so rendered non-identical with its isolated empirical appearance. The 'idea', far from constituting some Platonic essence into which the sordidly material evaporates, is nothing more than a unique configuration of conceptualized particulars, a creation of the subject that is at the same time a revelation of objective structures. The constellation is neither the 'law' nor 'deep structure' of the phenomena:

30 O, p. 36.
31 For an excellent discussion of this topic, and of the relations between Benjamin and French symbolism, see Charles Rosen, 'The Origins of Walter Benjamin', *New York Review of Books*, vol. 24, no. 18 (1977), pp. 30–38. Benjamin writes in 'A Berlin Chronicle' that as a child 'you did not read books through; you dwelt, abided between their lines, and, reopening them after an interval, surprised yourself at the spot you had halted' (OWS, pp. 341–2).

instead, 'ideas are to objects as constellations are to stars'.[32] Clinging with Husserlian tenacity to the things themselves, while granting the conceptual its proper status in a refusal of all intuitionism, Benjamin will nevertheless coax from these phenomena a truth of which they are themselves ignorant. 'The *phenomenal* realm [is] made to yield *noumenal* knowledge':[33] Kant is turned against himself.

Benjamin's 'non-metaphysical metaphysics'[34] thus represent an ingenious response to the problem which, as we have seen, obsessed Adorno too, and to which we have as little satisfactory answer today: how are we to think totality and specificity together, steadfastly avoiding a self-indulgent sport of the fragment even as we undo tyrannical unities? What can be said, at least, is that if Benjamin is a proto-deconstructionist in his microscopic devotion to those odds and ends that slip their conceptual anchor, he does not stop here: for it is precisely from these wayward, extreme and contradictory elements that a positive configuration is to be constructed. The 'idea' is a kind of structuralist *combinatoire* of phenomena, 'the sum total of all possible meaningful juxtapositions of such opposites', [35] which shows up best on its outer limits: it is in the shocking montage of extremities, not in the Hegelian trust in the typical, that the shape of the 'general' is to be deciphered. Yet if such a notion promises to transcend at a stroke both pure contingency and closed system, it is not clear on the other hand that it escapes in practice a mere mingling of positivism and metaphysics, as indeed Adorno was quick to point out about the Baudelaire study. The 'answer', according to Adorno, is dialectical mediation; but if this is not to lapse back into Hegelian closure, it must be (as Adorno recognized) a fraught, agonized dialectic forever unresolved; and how does this not then leave us with the same tense confrontation of phenomenon and essence that Benjamin's 'idea' or 'monad' seeks to surpass? It is surely clear, as Adorno himself again recognized, that the intractability of this issue is the sign not of shoddy thinking but of social contradiction – that we are here forced up against the very limits of our ability to think straight in the midst of commodity production.

The 'timeless' constellations of the *Origin*, untainted in Kantian style

32 O, p. 34.

33 The phrase is Susan Buck-Morss's, in *The Origin of Negative Dialectics*, Hassocks 1977, p. 74. This splendid book is indispensable to an understanding of Benjamin.

34 Ibid., p. 34.

35 O, p. 47.

by historical contingency, will become in the Baudelaire study a strange, alchemical or occultist form of historical materialism. The magical runes of the *Trauerspiel*, able to unlock the secrets of a reified Nature, will reappear as Benjamin's own sacred critique, which transmutes Baudelaire's script into allegories of material history, signs mutely resonant with crowds, cityscapes, technological shocks. It is not that Baudelaire's texts are expressive instruments that *speak* of such things: 'the masses had become so much a part of Baudelaire that it is rare to find a description of them in his works. His most important subjects are hardly ever encountered in descriptive form'.[36] The last thing Benjamin's commentary does is 'reflect' its object: it becomes rather an immanent critique of the Baudelairean image, displacing it (over-hastily, to be sure) into its historical conditions. In the alchemical transactions of Benjamin's own 'naming', creating letters, the letter of Baudelaire and the history from which it has been wrenched are reunited. Achievement of this entails redeeming Baudelaire in the truth of idea—smashing the 'literary-historical' constellation of his texts as a moment between Romanticism and Rimbaud, and reconstellating them in a discursive formation that includes the records of the Parisian secret police, documentary evidence on the behaviour of shop-girls, the history of Parisian gas-lighting and the detective story. In Kabbalistic fashion, the minute crevices of Baudelaire's texts are made to yield up startling truths of which they seem entirely innocent.

It is perhaps worth noting here, in parenthesis, how similar this Marxist-Kabbalistic method is to psychoanalysis. In listening to the speech of the analysand, the analyst must search its most casual crevices for significance, suspending any prejudgments of 'centrality' and 'contingency'. But the other face of this dogged, wide-eyed attention to detail is an immense scepticism, a 'hermeneutic of suspicion' that refuses the self-identity of the discourse it examines and reads into it the most scandalously implausible meanings. Resolutely bowed to the materiality of its text, psychoanalysis, like Benjamin, nevertheless rewrites it with breathtaking boldness; and its focus, like the Kabbala, is on the intersection of meaning and force. The drive, for Freudianism, lies on the border of the somatic and the ideational; it is thus that Paul Ricoeur's great essay on Freud turns on the conjoining of the economic and the

36 CB, p. 122.

hermeneutic, on that double marking whereby psychical phenomena are for Freud at once power and signification, somatic and semiotic.[37] Meanings for Freudianism are certainly meanings, not the mere imprints or reflexes of drives; but once this whole textual process is so to speak flipped over, focused through a different optic, viewed another way up, it can be read as nothing less than a mighty warring of somatic forces, a semantic field in which desire achieves, or fails to achieve, speech. For the Jewish tradition too, discourse is power, utterances are forces; and for Benjamin in his Baudelaire book, the Baudelairean image becomes the *Darstellung* or psychical representation in which force and meaning, technology and word, history and writing, may be conjoined. The image is therefore also the place where 'outside' and 'inside' meet—where an immanent critique may also be a materialist one. If this, as Adorno indicates, is not really achieved, then it may be because what is lacking is nothing less than an 'Einsteinian' criticism, in which every direction leads us at once 'out' and 'in', every point becomes a problematizing of 'surface' and 'depth', every historical commentary is continually in the process of being transformed into a textual critique and *vice versa*. And to mention Einstein is to look back to Freud: if for the former objects are configurations of force, so, for the latter, are signs.

If the Kantian constellation has been historicized, it will become in the *Theses on the Philosophy of History* nothing less than a whole theory of history in itself.[38] Concepts, Benjamin tells us in the *Origin*, group and subsume phenomena, whilst as 'ideas' such phenomena display themselves in their extreme, contradictory patterns of particularity. Historicism, one might argue, is thus the final triumphant tyranny of the concept, the relentless sublation of discrete particulars to a system radically closed in its very dreary infinity. What will blast such closure to bits then, is the constellation of *Jetztzeit*, in which a particular present reaches out a redemptive hand to a particular piece of the past about to go under. As with the *Trauerspiel* constellation, such a syncopated reading of history demands the vigilant, even violent activity of the subject at the same time as it manifests an objective structure, a logic of historical content that is more than the subject's creation.

---

37 *Freud and Philosophy: An Essay on Interpretation*, New Haven and London 1970.
38 The 'Theses' were intended as the methodological introduction to the Baudelaire study: see GS, 1/3, p. 1223.

Origin, Benjamin insists in the book whose title contains that term, has nothing to do with genesis: 'the term origin is not intended to describe the process by which the existent came into being, but rather to describe that which emerges from the process of becoming and disappearance . . . Origin is not, therefore, discovered by the examination of actual findings, but it is related to their history and their subsequent development'.[39] The historicist imprisoning of an artefact within its moment of genesis is to be rejected: the Benjamin of the *Trauerspiel* book instead grasps origin teleologically, as an unfolding dynamic structure within the work that is thoroughly caught up in the work's history, and of which that complete history is the only full account. By the time of his essay on Eduard Fuchs, however, that teleological thrust, itself an historicist residue, has effectively vanished: 'for a dialectical historian, these works ['works of art'] incorporate both their pre-history and their after-history—an after-history by virtue of which their pre-history, too, can be seen to undergo constant change. They teach him how their function can outlast their creator, can leave his intentions behind; how its reception by the artist's contemporaries forms part of the effect that the work of art has on us ourselves today, and how this effect derives not just from our encounter with the work, but with the history that has brought the work down to us . . . The past for (the historical materialist) becomes the subject of a construction whose locus is not empty time, but the particular epoch, the particular life, the particular work. He breaks the epoch away from its reified *historical continuity*, and the life from the epoch, and the work from the life's work. But the result of his construction is that *in* the work the life's work, *in* the life's work the epoch, and *in* the epoch the course of history are suspended and preserved.'[40] Deconstruction precedes reconstruction, but the former would be unintelligible if the latter, despite Benjamin's Hegelian terminology, were merely the recuperation of an expressive totality. Inseparable from this radical anti-historicism is an emphasis on the constitutive role of cultural reception: 'historical materialism conceives historical understanding as an after-life of that which is understood, whose pulse can still be felt in the present. This understanding has its place in Fuchs's scheme, but by no means an undisputed one. An old, dogmatic and naive notion of "reception"

39 O, pp. 45 and 46.
40 OWS, p. 351.

coexists in him with the new and more critical one. The former consists essentially in the assertion that what should count for most in our reception of a work is the way it was received at the hands of the artist's contemporaries. It forms an exact analogy to Ranke's "what it was actually like", which is "after all the only thing that matters". Cheek by jowl with this, however, we find a dialectical insight into the significance of a history of reception – an insight that opens the widest horizons.'[41] It is significant that Benjamin does not deny the *capacity* to reconstruct the terms of a work's reception by its contemporaries; he simply queries its central importance. Nor does his scorn for Ranke suggest that, say, whether the European middle ages were feudalist or neolithic is a matter of which way you care to construct the object within discourse. His concern with consumptional production, in other words, differs from that vein of scepticism now sometimes fashionable on the intellectual left, which posits the 'text itself' as an unknowable *Ding-an-sich*, dissolving it into the *ensemble* of its reading conjunctures. Such thoroughgoing neo-Kantian constructivism or 'extreme' reception theory forgets that the text, like any product, exerts a certain determinacy over its modes of consumption; and its political effects, as Stephen Heath has pointed out in the case of film, can be as drastically negative as the reification of the text to an ideological constant: 'debate around particular films often stumbles over the issue of effectivity, "the real effect of a film", deadlocks on notions of—on a choice between—either "the text itself", its meanings "in it", or else the text as non-existent other than "outside itself", in the various responses it derives from any individual or audience; the text "closed" or "open". The terms are weak on both sides: to hold that a given text is "different for everybody" is as much the end of any consequent political analysis and practice as to hold that it is "the same for everybody"; the implication of the latter is the possibility of a definitive analysis able to determine the use-value of a film in abstraction from the actual historical situations of its use; that of the former is a malleable transparency of the particular film to the determinations of the particular individual or audience, thus removing in the end all real basis for supporting through political-cultural analysis any film or films against any other or others.'[42] A 'knowledge' of the text—one able to reconstruct the conflicts and dispositions of its specific historical codes—is often possible; it is just that it is not necessarily the most important thing to do. For what will not be possible will be to 'read off' from such analysis the multiple destinations of the text, the ways it will be constructed in particular conjunctures; and these, precisely, are the primary sites of political intervention. In his lengthy study of Goethe's *Elective Affinities*, Benjamin names historical analysis 'commentary' and contemporary reconstruction 'criticism'; each, he considers, is empty without the other.

It could be claimed, indeed, that what constitutes a product as 'literary' is exactly this contextual mobility. Pieces of writing became 'literary' not chiefly by virtue of their inherent properties, for much that is called 'literature' lacks the estranging devices characteristic of 'poetic' discourse, and there is no piece of writing on which such estranging operations are not in principle possible. The 'literary', rather, is whatever is detached by a certain hermeneutic practice from its pragmatic context and subjected to a generalizing reinscription. Since such reinscription is always a particular gesture within determinate ideologies, 'literature' itself is always an ideological construct. What counts as a 'literary' text is a matter of ideological definition; it is perfectly possible for a piece of writing to move from a 'literary' to a non-literary' register and back in the course of its historical career. Some texts are born literary, some achieve literariness, and others have literariness thrust upon them. Breeding may in this respect count for a good deal more than birth. 'Seventeenth-century English literature', for example, customarily includes the theatre scripts of Shakespeare and Jonson, the essays of Bacon, the sermons of Donne, the historiography of Clarendon, perhaps the philosophy of Locke, the poetry of Marvell, the spiritual autobiography of Bunyan, and whatever it was that Sir Thomas Browne wrote. It would defy the best-trained taxonomist to say what all of these pieces of writing have in common. For it is certainly not a question of an 'objective' classification such as a 'fact/fiction' dichotomy. What all of these writings have in common is that they are *written*. 'Written', of course, in the sense of *well* written: 'fine writing'. 'Fine', that is to say, for anyone acquainted with what constitutes 'fine writing'. Which is to say, those who write 'finely' of such writing. But there remains the problem of what happens when few people or none find any of the writings just listed fine any more. Do they continue to be 'literature', only, as it were, 'bad fine writing'? Could such an event occur in any case, short of some utter spiritual catastrophe? Will Shakespeare continue to be 'great' if, given a radical enough historical mutation, people cease in Brecht's fine crude phrase to 'get anything out of him'? Is it possible that if we discovered a little more of what ancient Greek tragedy was 'really' about, we would stop liking it? Marx asks himself in the Introduction to the *Grundrisse* why it is that such ancient art continues to exercise an 'eternal charm'; but how do we know that it will? In what sense was it 'art' for the ancient Greeks in the first place?

If 'literature' is that writing which in some sense generalizes its propositions beyond a pragmatic context, or which is induced to do so by the operations of a particular reading, then we have an instant clue to its undeniable ideological power. For in the very act of such generalizing, 'literature' invests its propositions with peculiarly 'concrete' force; and there is no more effective ideological device than such a coupling. If the very form of a Burns poem intimates that it is of supreme indifference whether the author did indeed have a love who struck him as resembling a red rose, then it must be that all women are a little like that. One might risk saying, indeed, that in this sense the 'aesthetic' is the starkest paradigm of the ideological that we possess. For what is perhaps most slippery about ideological discourse is that, while appearing to describe a real object, it leads us inexorably back to the 'emotive'. Ideological propositions seem to be referential, descriptive of states of affairs, and indeed frequently are so; but it is possible to decode their 'pseudo-' or 'virtual' propositions into certain more fundamental 'emotive' enunciations. Ideological language is the language of wishing, cursing, fearing, denigrating, celebrating and so on. Any apparently 'constative' enunciation, such as 'The Irish are inferior to the English', is fully intelligible only in the light of some such 'performative' as 'I wish they would go back home'. This is not to claim that *every* proposition of ideological discourse has its emotive equivalent, any more than every piece of a dream-text may be unravelled to its attendant referent. There will be statements in the discourse that genuinely are referential, that may be either verified or falsified, and to do so is politically important. What should be recognized, however, is that the cognitive structure of ideological discourse is subordinate to its emotive structure—that such cognitions or miscognitions as it contains are on the whole articulated in accordance with the demands, the field of discursive play, of the emotive 'intentionality' it embodies. I say 'on the whole', because to say otherwise would be to mistake the homogenizing impulse of ideology for an achieved homogeneity—to ignore, in short, its contradictions, the points at which, for example, a contradiction between the cognitive and the emotive may provide a fissure for the levers of deconstruction.

If what is in question, then, is a form of discourse that while always apparently referential and sometimes genuinely so, nevertheless reveals itself to theoretical inquiry as a complex encodement of certain 'lived' relations to the real that may be neither verified nor falsified, what more exemplary model could there be to hand than 'literary' discourse itself? Like all ideology, literary texts frequently involve cognitive propositions, but they are not in business for that. When a novel tells us what the capital of France is, it is not of course to enforce a geographical truth; it is either to obliquely signal a fact about the nature of its discourse ('this is realism'), or to marshal a local 'support' for a particular set of emotive enunciations. If that local unit of discourse is falsifiable, the enunciation as a whole is not. In realist literature, the emotive level is slid under the pseudo-referential; and to this extent such literature resembles nothing quite so much as the workings of more quotidian forms of ideological language.

What they say of jokes is true of literature too: it's the way you tell it that matters. Indeed the fact that such speech-acts as jokes do, epistemologi-cally speaking, precisely what I have described 'literature' as doing warns us that such operations are not exclusively definitive of the 'literary'—that the 'literary' cannot be exclusively epistemologically defined. Since jokes are not primarily intended to communicate information, they have leisure to flaunt and foreground their 'form'—a fictionalizing crucial to their pleasurable effects. Such foregrounding may draw us libidinally deeper into the joke, endorsing its ideological 'world'; but it may also raise the joke's own freedom from direct reference to the second power, liberating us in turn into a pleasurable appreciation of its flagrant constructedness, its emancipatory powers to digress, embroider and self-proliferate. In this, it can be seen to resemble the 'modernist' text. If all 'literary' texts are parodies of speech-acts, then the modernist text might be said to be a parody of a parody. When Samuel Beckett concludes *Molloy* by telling us: 'It is midnight. The rain is beating on the windows. It was not midnight. It was not raining', he brazenly reveals the virtuality of his enunciation, exposes the text as a machine for producing pseudo-statements. It is in such doubling of the text, such raising of the parody to the second power, that 'literary' works may perform productive operations upon the ideological. For if an English chauvinist were able to say: 'The Irish are inferior to the English. The Irish are not inferior to the English', it would not merely be a matter of adopting another position: it would be a question of discovering something of the nature of positionality itself, its production of a closure constantly threatened by the heterogeneity of language.[43]

The aesthetic as contextually mobile: Benjamin is fully aware that the appropriation of artefacts is a process of struggle—that texts are arenas where battle is engaged, products to be wrested if possible from the grip of history and inserted instead into the matrix of tradition. To do so will mean contesting those productions of the artefact that are the work of bourgeois ideology. Let us take, as an example of such ideological production, the critical treatment of Thomas Hardy.

The name 'Thomas Hardy', like that of any other literary producer, signifies a particular ideological and biographical formation; but it also signifies the process whereby a certain set of texts are grouped, constructed, and endowed with the 'coherency' of a 'readable' *oeuvre*. 'Thomas Hardy' denotes that set of ideological practices through which certain texts, by virtue of their changing, contradictory modes of insertion into the dominant 'cultural' and pedagogical apparatuses, are processed, 'corrected' and reconstituted so that a home may be found for them within a literary 'tradition' that is always the 'imaginary' unity of the present. But this, in Hardy's case, has been a process of struggle, outrage and exasperation. He is a major realist, the creator of 'memorable' scenes and characters; yet he can be scandalously nonchalant about the 'purity' of orthodox verisimilitude, risking 'coincidence' and 'improbability'. With blunt disregard for formal consistency, he is ready to articulate form upon form—to mingle realist narration, classical tragedy, folk-fable, melodrama, 'philosophical' discourse, social commentary, and by doing so to betray the laborious constructedness of literary production. He is, acceptably enough for a Victorian, something of a 'sage'; yet his fictional meditations assume the offensively palpable form of 'ideas', obtrusive notions too little 'naturalized' by fictional device. He seems, gratifyingly

43 It would, however, be a purely formalist account of the ideological to see it merely in terms of 'closure' against 'heterogeneity', 'work' against 'text'. For 'textual' devices of slippage, displacement, condensation and so on are themselves vital to the operations of ideological discourse. See my 'Text, Ideology, Realism', in *Literature and Society*, Edward W. Said, ed., Baltimore and London 1980, pp. 149–73.

enough, a novelist of the 'human condition'; yet the supposedly dour, fatalistic bent of his art, its refusal to repress the tragic, has had a profoundly unnerving effect upon the dominant critical ideologies, which must be rationalized as 'temperamental gloom' or a home-spun *fin-de-siècle* pessimism. His 'clumsy' provincialism and 'bucolic' quaintness are tolerable features of a 'peasant' novelist; but these elements are too subtly intertwined with a more sophisticated artistry and lack of rustic 'geniality' to permit a confident placing of him as a literary Hodge.

A predominant critical strategy has therefore been simply to write him out. Henry James's elegant patronage ('the good little Thomas Hardy') finds its echo in F.R. Leavis and *Scrutiny*, who expel Hardy from the 'great tradition' of nineteenth-century realism. More generally, Hardy criticism may be seen to have developed through four distinct stages, all of which may be permuted in the work of any particular critic. Hegemonic in Hardy's own lifetime was the image of him as anthropologist of Wessex— the charming supplier of rural idylls who sometimes grew a little too big for his literary boots. After the publication of *The Dynasts*, a new critical phase was initiated: Hardy was now, in G.K. Chesterton's notorious comment, 'the village atheist brooding and blaspheming over the village idiot', the melancholic purveyor of late nineteenth-century nihilism. This view, conveniently distancing as it was, on the whole dominated the earlier decades of the century; but throughout the forties and fifties, Hardy's reputation was more or less in decline. An Anglo-Saxon criticism increasingly controlled by formalist, organicist and anti-theoretical assumptions ('New Criticism' in the United States, *Scrutiny* in England) could make no accommodation for Hardy's texts; R.P. Blackmur insisted in 1940 that Hardy's sensibility was irreparably violated by ideas.[44] From the late forties onwards, however, there was a notable shift towards a more 'sociological' reading of Hardy. In 1954, an influential study by Douglas Brown focused sentimentally upon the conflict between rural 'warmth' and urban invasion;[45] and four years later John Holloway was reflecting upon Hardy's 'vision of the passing of the old rhythmic order of rural England'.[46] Safely defused by such mythologies, Hardy could now for the first time merit the attention of critics more preoccupied with colour

44 *Southern Review*, VI, Summer 1940.
45 *Thomas Hardy*, London 1954.
46 *The Charted Mirror*, London 1960.

imagery than with the Corn Laws or the Immanent Will; and the sixties and seventies witnessed a stealthy recuperation of his texts by formalist criticism. Hardy has been phenomenologized, Freudianized, biographized, and claimed as the true guardian of 'English' liberal-democratic decencies against the primitivist extremism of emigré modernists.

From the beginning, however, the true scandal of Hardy has been his *language*. If there is one point on which bourgeois criticism has been virtually unanimous, it is that Hardy, regrettably, was really unable to *write*. Since this is rather a major disadvantage for a novelist, it is not surprising that criticism has found such difficulties with his work. Confronted with the 'unrealistic' utterances of his 'rustics' and his irritating 'oddities of style', criticism has been able to do little more than inscribe a 'Could do better' in the margins of Hardy's texts. The *Athenaeum* of 1874, reviewing *Far From the Madding Crowd*, complained that Hardy inserted into the mouths of his labourers 'expressions which we simply cannot believe possible from the illiterate clods whom he describes'. A reviewer of *The Return of the Native*, who protested *en passant* about the 'low social position of the characters', found that Hardy's characters talked as no people had ever talked before: 'The language of his peasants may be Elizabethan, but it can hardly be Victorian'. If the language of the 'peasants' was odd, that of their author was even odder. Again and again, Hardy has been berated for his maladroit, 'pretentious' use of latinisms, neologisms, 'clumsy and inelegant metaphors', technical 'jargon' and philosophical terms. On the one hand, criticism is exasperated by Hardy's apparent inability to write *properly*; on the other hand, it sneers at such attempts as the bumptiousness of a low-bred literary upstart. *Scrutiny* in 1934 bemoaned his 'clumsy aiming at impressiveness'; a doughty defender like Douglas Brown nonetheless finds his prose 'unserviceable, even shoddy'; and David Lodge informs us that 'we are, while reading him, tantalized by a sense of greatness not quite achieved'.

The ideological secret of these irritabilities is clear. Early Hardy criticism passionately desires that he should be a categorizable chronicler of bumpkins, and protests when such 'rustic realism' is vitiated; later criticism desires to take Hardy seriously as a major novelist, but is forced to acknowledge that, as an 'autodidact', he was never quite up to it. What is repressed in both cases is the fact that the significance of Hardy's writing lies precisely in the *contradictory* constitution of his linguistic practice. The ideological effectivity of his fiction inheres neither in 'rustic' nor 'educated' writing, but in the ceaseless play and tension between the two modes. In this sense, he is a peculiarly interesting illustration of that literary-ideological process that has been analysed in the work of Renée Balibar.[47] 'Literature', Balibar argues, is a crucial part of that process whereby, within the 'cultural' and pedagogical apparatuses, ideologically potent contradictions within a common language (in the case of post-revolutionary France, '*français ordinaire*' and '*français littéraire*') are constituted and reproduced. The 'literary' is an ensemble of linguistic practices, inscribed in certain institutions, that produce appropriate 'fictional' and ideological effects, and in doing so contribute to the maintenance of linguistic class-divisions. Limited though such an analysis is by its residual 'sociologism', and fragile though it may be when exported from the specific pedagogical conditions of bourgeois France, it nevertheless has a marked applicability to Hardy. It is not a question of whether Hardy wrote 'well' or 'badly'; it is rather a question of the ideological disarray that his fictions, consciously or not, are bound to produce within a criticism implacably committed to the 'literary' as yardstick of maturely civilized consciousness. This is not to suggest that the question of the aesthetic effects of Hardy's texts can be reduced to the question of their ideological impact; that a text may embarrass a dominant ideology is by no means the criterion of its aesthetic effectivity, though it may be a component of it. But in Hardy's case, these two issues are imbricated with a peculiar closeness.

The only critic who has understood this fact is, characteristically, Raymond Williams, who finds in the very letter of Hardy's texts the social and ideological crisis that they are constructed to negotiate.[48] Williams, indeed, has been one of the most powerfully demystifying of Hardy critics, brilliantly demolishing the banal mythology of a 'timeless peasantry' dislocated by 'external' social change. But his text, symptomatically, has had little general influence; and the same may be said of Roy Morrell's masterly study,[49] which tackled and defeated several decades of belief that Hardy was a 'fatalist'. Despite these interventions, criticism remains worried by the precise status of Hardy's 'realism'; and it is not difficult to see why. For the contradictory nature of his textual practice cannot but

47 Balibar, G. Merlin and G. Tret, *Les Français fictifs*, Paris 1974; and Balibar and D, Laporte, *Le Français national*, Paris 1974.
48 *The English Novel From Dickens to Lawrence*, London 1970, p. 106f.
49 *Thomas Hardy: The Will and the Way*, Oxford 1965.

throw into embarrassing relief those ideologically diverse constituents of fiction that it is precisely fiction's task to conceal; it is by 'not writing properly' that he lays bare the device.

Whether Thomas Hardy can be wrested from history and inserted into tradition—whether it is *worth* doing so—is not a question that can be historically preempted. It remains to be seen. 'Much of the greatness of [Proust's] work', writes Benjamin, 'will remain inaccessible or undiscovered until the [bourgeois] class has revealed its most pronounced features in the final struggle'.[50] For Benjamin, we are not yet capable of reading Proust; only the final political combat will produce the conditions for his significant reception. It is the proletariat who will render Proust readable, even if they may later find no use for him. Benjamin's antihistoricism is equally hostile to the teleology of a Lukács and the cultural ultra-leftism of some of the Futurists and Proletkultists. It is neither the case that Sophocles will inevitably be valuable for socialism, nor that he will inevitably not be; such opposed dogmatic idealisms merely suppress the complex practice of cultural revolution. Benjamin, to be sure, is the voracious snapper-up of unconsidered trifles who believes that 'nothing that has ever happened should be regarded as lost for history';[51] Sophocles must be collected, because he may always come in handy when you least expect it. But he always may not: for 'only a redeemed mankind receives the fullness of its past—which is to say, only for a redeemed mankind has its past become citable in all its moments'.[52] Only on Judgment Day will Sophocles and Sholokov be narratable within a single text; until then, which is to say forever, a proletarian criticism will reject, rewrite, forget and retrieve. And the Proust whose texts socialism shall recompose will not be the Proust consumed in the salons; no value is extended to the masses without being thereby transformed.

50 'The Image of Proust', I, p. 212.
51 'Theses on the Philosophy of History', I, p. 256.
52 I, p. 256.

4

Der der, deary didi! Der? I? Da! Deary? da!
Der I, didida; da dada, dididearyda.
Dadareder, didireader. Dare I die
deary da? Da dare die didi. Die derider!
Didiwriter. Dadadididididada.
Aaaaaaaaa! Der i da.

OEDIPAL FRAGMENT

As a collector of the contingent, of that which escapes the censoring glance of history in its sober yet potent unremarkability, Benjamin in some sense prefigures the contemporary critical practice of deconstruction. Yet he was clearly more than a 'textual' revolutionary; and the encounter within his work between Marxism and deconstruction is thus an intriguing one from our own standpoint.

In discovering that 'men make history',[53] the nineteenth-century bourgeoisie kicked out from under themselves the very transcendental signifiers they needed to legitimate that history ideologically. But this damage could be contained by a simple fact: in pulling the metaphysical carpet out from under themselves, they pulled it out in the same stroke from under their opponents. Do we find the latest rehearsal of this manoeuvre in the confrontation between deconstructionism and Marxism?

Consider the following epistemological option. Either the subject is wholly on the 'inside' of its world of discourse, locked into its philosophico-grammatical forms, its very struggles to distantiate them 'theoretically' themselves the mere ruses of power and desire; or it can catapult itself free from this formation to a point of transcendental leverage from which it can discern absolute truth. In other words: when did you stop beating your grandfather? For that this option is itself an ideological double-bind is surely obvious. How then does deconstruction negotiate it? Everybody rejects transcendental subjects, but some reject

---

53 An ideological 'discovery': if history has a subject then it is not, as Louis Althusser points out, 'men' or 'men and women' or even 'classes' but the *class struggle*. One does not escape a bourgeois problematic of 'the subject' simply by collectivizing that subject, as much Hegelian Marxism would appear to believe.

them more than others: deconstruction leans heavily towards the first option, but qualifies it with a curious form of catapulting—or perhaps, more precisely, a modest backward flip—characteristic of the second. We move on the inside of the discourses that constitute us, but there are vertiginous moments, moments when the signifier floats and falters and the whole top-heavy system swims and trembles before our eyes, when it is almost possible to believe that what we have perceived, through some figurative fissure in the smooth wall of meaning, is nothing less than the inconceivable shape of some non-metaphysical 'outside'. By pressing semiosis to its 'full' potential, by reading at once with and against the grain of a text that denegates its deep wounding with all the cheerful plausibility of a West Point war casualty, we can know a kind of liberation from the terrorism of meaning without having for a moment—how could we?—burst through to an 'outside' that could only be one more metaphysical delusion.

It is not, then, *really* a question of 'outside' and 'inside': that opposition, as an ex-student of mine was told of Marxism on arriving at Columbia, we deconstructed a few years back. Or did we? Let us consider a case where the metaphysical opposition 'inside/outside' seems to be in practice alive and well. Social democracy believes in working on the 'inside' of the capitalist system: persuaded of its omnipotent, all-pervasive, as it were 'metaphysical' presence, it seeks nonetheless in humble fashion to locate and prise open those symptomatic points of 'hesitancy', negativity and incompletion within the system into which the thin end of a slim-looking reformist wedge may be inserted. The forms of political theory and practice known to Marxism as 'ultra-leftism', by contrast, will have no truck with this feeble complicity. Equally convinced of the monolithic substance of the system as a whole, they dream, like the anarchist professor of Conrad's *The Secret Agent*, of some unutterably radical enterprise which would blow a black hole in the whole set-up and forcibly induce its self-transcendence into some condition beyond all current discourse.

The familiar deadlock between these two positions (Italian left politics might provide an interesting example) is one that Marxism is able historically to understand. Social democracy and ultra-leftism (anarchism, adventurism, putschism and so on) are among other things antithetical responses to the failure or absence of a mass revolutionary movement. As such, they may parasitically interbreed: the prudent reformist may conceal a scandalous utopian, enamoured of some ultimate negation that must nonetheless be kept clear of *Realpolitik*. 'Inside' and 'outside' may thus form strange permutations: in the figure of an Adorno, for example, a 'negative dialectics' allergic to the slightest trace of positivity can combine at times with an objectively reactionary stance. For traditional Marxism, the epistemological problems of 'inside/outside', transcendental subjects and subjects who are the mere play of power and desire, Althusserian scientisms and Foucauldean relativisms, subjects who seem unhealthily replete and subjects of an alarming Lacanian leanness—these problems cannot possibly be understood, let alone resolved, outside of the historical epoch, the specific modalities of class struggle, of which they are at once product and ideological instrument. (Nor, for that matter, can any 'theory of the subject' hope to succeed if it has repressed from the outset that familiar mode of existence of the *object* known to Marxism as 'commodity fetishism'.) What deconstructs the 'inside/outside' antithesis for Marxism is not the Parisian left intelligensia but the revolutionary working class. The working class is the agent of historical revolution not because of its potential 'consciousness' (Lukács), but because of that location within the capitalist mode of production ironically assigned to it by capitalism itself. Installed in the interior of that system, as one product of the process of capital, it is at the same time the class that can potentially destroy it. Capitalism gives birth to its own gravedigger, nurturing the acolyte who will one day stab the high priest in the back. It is capitalism, not Marxism, which has decreed that the prime agent of its own transformation will be, not peasants, guerrillas, blacks, women or intellectuals, but the industrial proletariat.

Hardly anybody *believes* this nowadays, of course, at least in the academies, and deconstructionism is among other things an effect of this despair, scepticism, indifference, privilege or plain lack of historical imagination. But it has not, for all that, abandoned trying to think through and beyond the 'inside/outside' polarity, even if it is fatally unable to deconstruct itself to the point where it could become aware of the historical determinants of its own aporia. Deconstruction is in one sense an ideology of left reformism: it reproduces, at the elaborate level of textual 'theory', the material conditions in which Western hegemony has managed partially to incorporate its antagonists—in which, at the level of empirical 'consciousness', collusion and subversion are so tightly imbricated that all talk of 'contradictions' falls spontaneously into the metaphysical slot. Because it can only imagine contradiction as the external warring of two monistic essences, it fails to comprehend class dialectics and turns instead to *difference*, that familiar ideological motif of the petty bourgeoisie. Deconstruction is in one sense an extraordinarily modest proposal: a sort of patient, probing reformism of the text, which is not, so to speak, to be confronted over the barricades but cunningly waylaid in the corridors and suavely chivvied into revealing its ideological hand. Stoically convinced of the unbreakable grip of the metaphysical closure, the deconstructionist, like any responsible trade union bureaucrat confronting management, must settle for that and negotiate what he or she can within the left-overs and stray contingencies casually unabsorbed by the textual power system. But to say no more than this is to do deconstruction a severe injustice. For it ignores that other face of deconstruction which is its hair-raising *radicalism*—the nerve and daring with which it knocks the stuffing out of every smug concept and leaves the well-groomed text shamefully dishevelled. It ignores, in short, the *madness* and violence of deconstruction, its scandalous urge to think the unthinkable, the flamboyance with which it poses itself on the very brink of meaning and dances there, pounding away at the crumbling cliff-edge beneath its feet and prepared to fall with it into the sea of unlimited semiosis or schizophrenia.

In short, deconstruction is not only reformist but ultra-leftist too. Nor is this a fortuitous conjuncture. Minute tenacity and mad 'transcendence' are structurally related moments, since the latter is the only conceivable 'outside' of the closure presumed by the former. Only the wholesale dissolution of meaning could possibly offer a satisfactory alternative to a problematic that tends to see *meaning itself* as terroristic. Of course, these are not the practical, working options for the deconstructionist. It is precisely because texts are power systems that ceaselessly disrupt themselves, sense imbricated with non-sense, civilized enunciations cursing under their breath, that the critic must track a cat-and-mouse game within and across them without ever settling quite for either signifier or signified. That, anyway, is the ideology; but whoever heard of a deconstructionist as enthralled by sense as by its disruption? What *would* such criticism do with a piece of agit-prop? Not that such 'literature' doesn't positively bulge with metaphysical notions, to an embarrassingly unambiguous degree. Characters are continually stomping upon stage and talking about justice.[54] Feminist theatre today is distressingly rife with

---

54 This notation alludes to Derrida's practice of placing a concept *sous rature*, cancelling and preserving it simultaneously, in order to indicate its unusable yet indispensable character.

plenary notions of oppression, domination, exploitation. Brecht, it is true, deconstructed himself a bit from time to time, but only got as far as dialectics; pre-Derridean that he was, he failed to advance beyond rudimentary metaphysical oppositions, such as the proposition that some social classes exploit others. He failed, consequently, to grasp the heterogeneity into which such antinomies can be dissolved, known to Marxism as bourgeois ideology. Viewing such dramas, the deconstructionist would no doubt wait, pen in hand, for the moments when literal and figurative discourses glided into one another to produce a passing indeterminacy. He or she would do so because we *know*, in *a priori* fashion, that these are the most important elements of a text. We just do know that, as surely as previous critics have known that the most important textual elements are plot or mythological structure or linguistic estrangement. Indeed we have been told by Paul de Man himself that unless such moments occur, we are not dealing with *literature*. It is not, of course, that there is any 'essence' called literature—merely that there is something called literature which always and everywhere manifests this particular rhetorical effect. Deconstruction does indeed attend to both sense and non-sense, signified and signifier, meaning and language: but it attends to them at those points of conjuncture whose effect is a liberation from the 'tyranny' of sense.

Deconstruction is not, of course, a system, or a theory, or even a method. It disowns anything one might call a 'programme'. It is, admittedly, a little difficult to appreciate this fact when confronted with de Man's assertion that the deconstruction of a certain 'naive metaphorical mystification' in literary texts 'will in fact be the task of literary criticism in the coming years'[55]—one could wish that he had been a little more indeterminate—but one should not rush to convict deconstruction of a method. The fact that, in its analyses of literary texts, it consistently focuses upon certain moments of indeterminacy and consistently discovers that the most significant point about the text is that it does not know what it is saying should be taken as a set of coincidences—perhaps a matter of 'style' or 'idiom'—rather than as anything so shabbily positive as a 'method'. Perhaps deconstruction is not a method in the sense that you cannot read off from its techniques exactly what it is going to do with them at any given point, unlike, say, Marxist criticism, where you can of course deduce the whole content of its discourse on a text, every detailed twist and turn, from its founding presuppositions about the historical mode of production. Nor is deconstruction concerned with blaming anybody, since this would presumably entail the kind of transcendental vantage-point from which definitive judgments could be delivered. In discussing those critical approaches deluded enough to believe that literary texts have relations to something other than themselves, de Man tells us that he wishes to consider this tendency 'without regard for its truth or falseness or for its value as desirable or pernicious'.[56] 'It is a fact that this sort of thing happens again and again in literary studies', he informs us, with the weary resignation of a Victorian headmaster commenting on the incorrigible sexual proclivities of his boys. A symptomatic reading of de Man's text might discern a certain suggestive indeterminacy between the wise neutrality of his disownment and the tone in which he discusses historical, biographical and other 'referential' forms of criticism, a tone which might certainly convey to the odd reader that he regards such methods as irritatingly irrelevant and just plain wrong. But since we deconstructed the 'truth/falsity' opposition some years ago, it is unlikely that the tone, in any actual or positive sense, can in fact be 'present'.

The mad anarchist professor of *The Secret Agent* has achieved the ultimate transcendence: he is prepared to blow himself up in the act of destroying others. Thoroughly implicated in the general holocaust, he nevertheless transcends it by having set it in motion himself. The deconstructionist, similarly, is prepared to bring him/herself down with the piece of cliff (s)he perches on. Deconstruction practises a mode of self-destruction that leaves it as invulnerable as an empty page. As such, it merely rehearses in different terms a gesture common to all ideology: it attempts to vanquish its antagonist while leaving itself unscathed. The price it has to pay for such invulnerability, however, is the highest of all: death. The collapse of classical epistemology has discredited those victories over the object that presuppose an untouched transcendental subject; now the one surviving mode of security is to be contaminated by the object even unto death. Deconstruction is the death drive at the level of theory: in dismembering a text, it turns its violence masochistically upon itself and goes down with it, locked with its object in a lethal complicity that permits it the final inviolability of pure negation. Nobody can 'out-left' or out-manoeuvre a Derrida because there is nothing to out-left or out-manoeuvre; he is simply the dwarf who will entangle the giant in his own ungainly strength and bring him toppling to the earth. The deconstructionist nothing lieth because he nothing affirmeth. Like Polonius, he is at once fool and state-lackey, eccentrically digressive yet a dispenser of metaphysical discourse. Either way you disown a 'position': by putting the skids under others, or by being—unlike Polonius—a *reluctant* metaphysician, acknowledging the ineluctability of that discourse, 'blaming' the very system you impudently subvert for your inability to produce a positive standpoint. It is possible to spend quite a long time crossing from one of these fronts to the other, depending on the direction of the fire.

Yet it is not, of course, anything as final as death. Metaphysics will live on, bloody but unbowed; and deconstruction, as a 'living' death, will regroup its forces to assault anew. Each agonist is ever-slain and ever-resurrected; the compulsion to repeat, to refight a battle in which the antagonist can never be destroyed because he is always everywhere and nowhere, to struggle towards a (self-) killing that will never quite come, is the dynamic of deconstruction. Because there is neither outside nor inside, because the metaphysical enemy is always already within the gates, deconstruction is kept alive by what contaminates it, and can therefore reap the pleasures of a possible self-dissolution which, as one form of invulnerability, is mirrored by another, the fact that it can never die because the enemy is within and unkillable. The nonsense of 'I killed myself' is the nonsense of deconstruction. If the metaphysical enemy is everywhere and nowhere, so too is deconstruction, which is to say that it can never die and has always died already, can never die because it has always died already and has always died already because it can never die. And the moment in which all of this occurs is of course the moment of *jouissance* or *petite mort*.

But it is not, speaking historically, the moment when it occurs. Many of the vauntedly novel themes of deconstructionism do little more than reproduce some of the most commonplace topics of bourgeois liberalism. The modest disownment of theory, method and system; the revulsion from the dominative, totalizing and unequivocally denotative; the privileging of plurality and heterogeneity, the recurrent gestures of hesitation and indeterminacy; the devotion to gliding and process, slippage and movement; the distaste for the definitive—it is not difficult to see why such an idiom should become so quickly absorbed within the

Anglo-Saxon academies. From De Quincey to deconstruction is not, after all, a very long way, and it is doubtless pleasant to find one's spontaneous bourgeois-liberal responses shorn of their embarrassing eclecticism and tricked out as the most explosive stuff around. It is not that these focuses of attention—to the contingent and marginalized, to the duplicitous and undecidable—are in the least to be despised; one has only to think of the productive ways in which, in the hands of feminism, they can be used to deconstruct a paranoid, patriarchal Marxism that reaches for its totality when it hears the word 'residue'. It is just that one can no longer doubt, watching the remorseless *centralizing* of the contingent, the dogmatic privileging of what escapes over what does not, the constant dissolution of dialectics, that one is in the presence of a full-blooded ideology. In some ways it is not far from traditional bourgeois liberalism: there is much in common, for example, between deconstruction's well-bred shuddering at 'totality' and the shy distaste of a traditional liberal critic like John Bayley for the high-roads of history. In other ways, however, deconstructionism signifies a radical mutation of the bourgeois-liberal problematic, one forced upon it by historical developments. If traditional bourgeois liberalism is humanistic, deconstructionism is vehemently anti-humanist; it is, if you like, a liberalism without the subject, or at least without any subject that would be recognized by John Bayley. For that privileging of the unitary bourgeois subject characteristic of the traditional liberalism of Bayley or Trilling will clearly no longer do: that inviolable private space, those strenuous ethical responsibilities and individualist autonomies, begin to ring more and more hollow, to appear more and more politically rearguard and implausible, in the claustrophobic arena of late monopoly capitalism. Nicos Poulantzas has reminded us that the 'private' is always a juridically demarcated space, produced by the very public structures it is thought to delimit;[57] and this fact is now more and more palpable in quotidian experience. Deconstructionism, then, can salvage some of the dominant themes of traditional bourgeois liberalism by a desperate, last-ditch strategy: by sacrificing the subject itself, at least in any of its customary modes. Political quietism and compromise are preserved, not by a Forsterian affirmation of the 'personal', but by a dispersal of the subject so radical as to render it impotent as any kind of agent at all, least of all a revolutionary one. If the proletariat can be reduced to text, trace,

57 See *State, Power, Socialism*, NLB 1978, p. 70.

symptom or effect, many tedious wrangles can be overcome at a stroke. Traditional liberalism, of course, contained this contradiction from the outset, between the impulse to shore up an eroded individual substance and a joyful yet disorienting self-abandonment; the fictions of Eliot, James and Forster are among other things strategic 'solutions' to this ambivalently crippling and energizing conflict. And one can observe the same tension today within the 'Yale school' itself, between those boldly prepared to erase the last traces of traditional humanism, and those wishing to preserve its residues in suitably Freudianized or deconstructed form. But it is, on the whole, Forster's Mrs Moore, not his Fielding, who has won the day. The liberal pleasure-principle is vanquishing the liberal reality-principle, the logic of multiplicity ousting the homogeneous self who was traditionally there to enjoy it. Deconstruction is as disorienting in North America as it was for Mrs Moore in India; it thus provides you with all the risks of a radical politics while cancelling the subject who might be summoned to become an agent of them. It is in one sense the suicide of liberalism, but then suicide and liberalism were never total strangers. The dispersed subject will not be recuperated—it always might not return—but this hardly matters, since the dispersal was purely textual in the first place; there was never any question of displacing the material conditions that permitted the textual dispersal in the first place, and thus nothing really to be recuperated, since the subject must have been always-already securely in place for the dispersal to have occurred. 'Irony', Geoffrey Hartman tells us, 'prevents the dissolution of art into positive and exploitable truth'.[58] Yes indeed: for if art were to tell anything as metaphysical as the truth then it might speak exploitably of exploitation, and then where would be the infrastructure that for deconstruction is not de(con)structible?

'Something always escapes, but it has to pay a heavy toll', Jacques Derrida once remarked in a seminar. Of nothing is this more true than of deconstructionism itself. Bourgeois liberalism, in its deconstructionist inflection, is now prepared—forced?—to sacrifice truth itself to freedom, a move that John Stuart Mill would have found unintelligible. The deconstruction of the traditional autonomous subject now seems more and more the condition of the preservation of that bourgeois-liberal freedom of which such a subject was once thought to be the source. The freedom that

58 *Deconstruction and Criticism*, New York 1979, p. viii.

was traditionally that of responsible action has become the spasmodic freedom of the deconstruction of such action. Objectivity is suspect, for we know, do we not, that it must rest upon metaphysical notions of absolute truth? (At least we know if we have not read Lenin.) The classical form of 'moral' questioning—what are we to do, *given the facts*?—is no longer articulable, for what could be less deconstructed than 'the facts'? And what, in monopoly-capitalist society, could be more revolutionary?

That we cannot lift ourselves up by our bootstraps outside the metaphysical closure of Western philosophy is surely true. That there are nonetheless ways of interrogating texts, floating the signifier, reading against the grain, that may prove to shake academic-ideological discourse to its roots is an insight of profound value. That deconstruction, as a particular set of textual procedures, can operate as a radical force is surely undeniable. What is at question is the appropriation of such insights and procedures in ways that objectively legitimate bourgeois hegemony. There is little doubt that Derrida's dismantling of the speech/writing opposition is richly resourceful; there is little doubt either that the retrieval of writing also provides a much-needed ideological boost for an increasingly marooned and discredited academy. (One could say the same of 'semantic materialism', that important emphasis which brought to birth a whole new generation of armchair materialists and lexical Maoists.) Derrida's own relative silence about historical materialism could perhaps be taken as strategic—the silence, say, of a socialist feminist, who bears witness to the 'imaginary' position that Marxism too often is by refusing premature, appropriative alliance. It is not certain that Marxists should be too tolerant of this stance: in a world groaning in agony, where the very future of humankind hangs by a hair, there is something objectionably luxurious about it. But it is certainly to be respected a good deal more than that modish jargon which hopes, pathetically, to shift the very ground beneath our feet by tropology.

In the deep night of metaphysics, all cats look black. Marx is a metaphysician, and so is Schopenhauer, and so is Ronald Reagan. Has anything been gained by this manoeuvre? If it is true, is it informative? What is ideologically at stake in such homogenizing? What differences does it exist to suppress? Would it make Reagan feel comfortable or depressed? If what is in question for deconstructionism is metaphysical discourse, and if this is all-pervasive, then there is a sense in which in reading against the grain we are subverting everything and nothing. If metaphysics is the outer limit or inner structure of all ideology, then our inability to deconstruct it has some very interesting ideological consequences indeed. It is notable that, one year before Derrida's *annus mirabilis* of 1967, a fully-fledged piece of deconstructionist theory made its appearance on the Parisian scene. Violently dismembering literary texts, the author spoke of the need to discern within them certain symptomatic absences and aporia, those points at which texts began to unravel themselves in ambiguous encounter with their deceptively homogeneous power systems. This book was Pierre Macherey's *Pour une théorie de la production littéraire*, and the splash it made, compared to Derrida, was that of a pebble compared to a rock. It could be, of course, that this was because Macherey's book was less ambitious or boring or just bad. But it might also be that Macherey is a Communist, a known ally of Louis Althusser, and that the discourses he saw texts as unravelling were 'ideological' rather than 'metaphysical'. In writing of property as well as presence, Macherey brought the whole affair a little nearer home. Its effects on the Anglo-Saxon academy are still, as they say, somewhat dispersed, not to say sparse.

Both Macherey and Althusser would seem to believe that ideology is monolithic: a seamless web enmeshing all lived practice, a homogeneous structure to subject the subject. If ideology is not grasped as a heterogeneous, contradictory formation, a question of constant struggle at the level of signifying practices, then this misrecognition may have something to do with a certain view of the class struggle: most simply, that it has disappeared. What you are then left with, as the 'outside' of that monolith, is Theory, or Literature, or perhaps the Third World. Deconstructionism raises this view of reality to the second power: ideologies may come and go, but the essential structure of all such significations—metaphysics—is massively immovable, operative all the way from Plato to NATO. What you then have to pit against it is the labour of the negative. It is remarkable how parallel deconstructionism is in this way to the later Frankfurt school.[59] The rage against positivity, the suspicion of determinate meaning *as such*, the fear that to propose is to be

59 The parallels between deconstruction and Adorno are particularly striking. Long before the current fashion, Adorno was insisting on the power of those heterogeneous fragments that slip through the conceptual net, rejecting all philosophy of identity, refusing class consciousness as objectionably 'positive', and denying the intentionality of signification. Indeed there is hardly a theme in contemporary deconstruction that is not richly elaborated in his work—a pointer, perhaps, to the mutual insularity of French and German culture, which now, ironically, converge more and more only in the Anglo-Saxon world.

complicit: historically distanced as we are, we can see fairly clearly how all this in the case of the Frankfurt school represented one extreme quietistic response to that series of defeats and partial incorporations of the proletariat that is the narrative of twentieth-century class struggle. If deconstruction never had much belief in the class struggle in the first place, it nevertheless strikingly reproduces just those gestures.

The power of the negative is by no means to be denied. It constitutes an essential moment of Marxism itself. But only a powerless petty-bourgeois intelligentsia would raise it to the solemn dignity of a philosophy. There is a real sense in which Marx's operations on the texts of bourgeois political economy may be said to be deconstructionist; but there is also an internal relation between those operations and the theoretical-political necessities that bring Marx to construct into 'presence' the absence that scars his opponents' texts, the concept of labour-power. That textual activity, moreover, brings into the clearest focus the relations, for Marxism, between 'theory' and 'interests'. To oppose 'objectivity' and 'interests', to reduce the cognitive status of propositions to the play of power and desire, is perfectly possible for the Parisian petty bourgeoisie, and is indeed the merest commonplace of late-nineteenth-century bourgeois philosophy. But it was not possible for the nineteenth-century proletariat. For that proletariat had an interest—amounting to its very physical survival—in getting to know the situation 'as it was'. Unless it knew whether there was a real theoretical distinction between 'labour' and 'labour-power' it was likely to go on seeing its sons and daughters abused by the bestialities of capitalism. There are some, even in Paris and Yale and Oxford, who still believe that today.

5

I have never found anybody without a
sense of humour who could understand
dialectics.

BERTOLT BRECHT,
Flüchtlingsgespräche

'The class struggle, which is always present to a historian influenced by
Marx, is a fight for the crude and material things without which no refined
and spiritual things could exist. Nevertheless, it is not in the form of the
spoils which fall to the victor that the latter make their presence felt in the
class struggle. They manifest themselves in this struggle as courage,
humour, cunning, and fortitude.'[60]

'Humour' is hardly a familiar concept in Marxism, least of all in the
work of the melancholic Benjamin. Indeed the suffering, Saturnine
aspects of Benjamin, the wreckage of ironic debacles and disasters that was
his life, have been seized upon with suspicious alacrity by those
commentators anxious to detach him from the vulgar cheerfulness of
social hope. Since political pessimism is a mark of spiritual maturity, the
gloomier side of Benjamin says much for his sensitivity; as the last
European, the shy, superannuated servant of *Geist* washed up on the
barren shores of materialism, Benjamin offers a consolingly familiar image
to disinherited intellectuals everywhere, downcast as they are by the
cultural dreariness of a bourgeoisie whose property rights many of them
would doubtless defend to the death.

It is salutary, then, to read that reference to humour, even though there
is no denying its untypicality. The 'classical sadness' that Perry Anderson
discerns in the work of Sebastiano Timpanaro, and which he sees as
pervading Western Marxism all the way from Gramsci to Adorno, is
nowhere bleaker than in Benjamin's often tortured meditations. It is true,
however, that in this as in much else he progresses by his bad side. The
very sluggishness and *gravitas* of his Saturnism place a time-bomb

60 I, pp. 256–7.

beneath glib historicist mythologies, just as his doleful nostalgia fastens upon images of the past only to pull them roughly through the empty spaces of the present. It is, then, a dangerous, peculiarly robust kind of inertia, that of the perpetually insurbordinate rather than the successfully pacified, just as his very shyness is somehow subversive. For if it consists in a kind of defence mechanism whereby he seems nervously to evade the public high-roads of history, dipping into concealed cul-de-sacs to linger over some stray architectural feature, it soon appears that this gesture has, so to speak, turned the whole landscape boldly upon its axis, so that we are no longer quite so confident that its centre was exactly where we thought it was. As the stray feature is gradually focused, it comes to deconstruct and reorganize the context that dominated it. Benjamin's very idiosyncrasies, his private obsessions and arcane pursuits, thus become a sign of that most historically public figure of all, the Messiah who for one strain of Judaic thought will transform the world not by shifting its foundations but by making slight adjustments.

Nevertheless, the melancholy of Western Marxism, bred largely by a history of proletarian defeat, represents the massive loss of an essential dimension of historical materialism. No greater contrast in the annals of Marxist writing could be provided than that between Benjamin's *Theses on the Philosophy of History* and another text written in the same year: Mikhail Bakhtin's *Rabelais and his World*. Produced in the darkest era of Stalinism, a period during which Bakhtin himself ominously disappeared from public view, the book is a precise enactment of Benjamin's own political aesthetic: it blasts Rabelais's work out of the homogeneous continuum of literary history, creating a lethal constellation between that redeemed Renaissance moment and the trajectory of the Soviet state. Courage, to adopt Benjamin's terms, works cunningly for the reclamation of humour; in what is perhaps the boldest, most devious gesture in the history of 'Marxist criticism', Bakhtin pits against that 'official, formalistic and logical authoritarianism' whose unspoken name is Stalinism the explosive politics of the body, the erotic, the licentious and semiotic. Rabelais is the memory that Bakhtin seizes hold of as it flashes up at a moment of danger; he is 'that image of the past which unexpectedly appears to a man singled out by history at a moment of danger'.[61] Not even Rabelais will be safe from the enemy if he wins, and this enemy has not ceased to be victorious; accordingly Bakhtin, by an 'inconspicuous transformation', charts that 'secret heliotropism' by dint of which 'the past strives to turn toward that sun which is rising in the sky of history'.[62] In the dialectical flash of a correspondence, the sterile landscape of Stalinism is transfigured into the 'state of emergency' that it truly is. A storm is blowing from the paradisal past towards which Bakhtin's horror-struck face is turned, a storm that may propel him beyond the mounting wreckage of the present to the archaic utopia of the future.[63] For Benjamin himself, this very method of raising the dead is incipiently comic, since it opposes that 'process of [historicist] empathy' with the past 'whose origin is the indolence of the heart, *acedia*, which despairs of grasping and holding the genuine historical image as it flares up briefly. Among medieval theologians it was regarded as the root cause of sadness'.[64]

Benjamin prises images loose from the authority of the past so that they may plurally interbreed; and this liberation of the image into polyvalence has for Bakhtin the name of carnival. In a riot of semiosis, carnival unhinges all transcendental signifiers and submits them to ridicule and relativism; by the 'radicalism of humour' (Jean Paul), power structures are estranged through grotesque parody, 'necessity' thrown into satirical question and objects displaced or negated into their opposites. A ceaseless practice of travesty and inversion (nose/phallus, face/buttocks, sacred/profane) rampages throughout social life, deconstructing images, misreading texts and collapsing binary oppositions into a mounting groundswell of ambiguity into which all articulate discourse finally stutters and slides. Birth and death, high and low, destruction and renewal are sent packing with their tails in each other's mouths. Absolutely nothing escapes this great spasm of satire: no signifier is too solemn to be blasphemously invaded, dismantled and turned against itself. The grotesque is intrinsically double-faced, an immense semiotic switchboard through which codes are read backwards and messages scrambled into their antitheses.

Through this crude cackling of an ambivalently destructive and liberatory laughter emerges the shape of an equally negative and positive phenomenon: utopia. Carnival is more than deconstruction: in rendering

62 I, p. 257.
63 Cf. Thesis IX (I, pp. 259–60).
64 I, p. 258.

existing power structures alien and arbitrary, it releases the potential for a golden age, a friendly world of 'carnival truth' in which 'man returns to himself'. Like Brecht's, its estrangement effects are reconstructive as well as deconstructive, dialectical images in which the parodic dissolution of the object presumes and provokes its 'normal' representation, reassembling it in the figure of that which it denies. The laughter of carnival is both plebeian derision and plebeian solidarity, an empty semiotic flow which in decomposing significance nonetheless courses with the impulse of comradeship. As such, it offers a notable contrast to the Messianic utopia of a Benjamin. For Benjamin's utopia is projected not out of present laughter but out of its reverse: the sounds of the coming kingdom, for Judaic as against classical thought, are to be heard in a misery which cries out to heaven for vengeance. The *Jetztzeit* that brings history to a shocking standstill, contracting it like Proust's bit of cake to a timeless point that is both pristine and wrinkled with age, is a formal prolepsis of the Messianic era that is yet only a shadow of its content. It is the Messiah himself who will create the relation between history and his own age; and to that extent 'nothing historical can relate itself on its own account to anything Messianic'.[65] Benjamin's utopia, as we have seen, is thus quite unteleological: infinitely remote from all epochs, an end rather than a goal, it moves in diametrical opposition to the profane desire for happiness. The two drives are mutually imbricated only as antitheses: by a curious negative logic, the profane, merely by being such, increases the force of the Messianic drive that runs counter to it. The 'immediate Messianic intensity of the heart' passes not through happiness but through suffering and misfortune. If happiness echoes the Messianic rhythm, it would seem to do so only in its eternal transience; it is its very fragility— its form rather than its content—that evokes by negation that total passing away which the Messiah will inaugurate.

The relative emptiness of Benjamin's utopia protects him from historicism to the precise extent that it threatens to dissolve any positive dialectic between present and future. The Judaic prohibition on investigating the future strips it of its idealist allure and turns us instead towards revolutionary remembrance; Benjamin knew that the ruling class hires soothsayers to assure itself that even the future is manipulable. The

65 'Theologico-Political Fragment', OWS, p. 155. As Rolf Tiedemann remarks, 'history exists in unsublatable (*unaufhebbarer*) tension with the Messianic kingdom' (*Studien zur Philosophie Walter Benjamins*, Frankfurt am Main 1965, p. 118).

truly arduous tasks are those of predicting the present—of reading its unique 'astrological' configuration before it has slipped away—and of prognosticating the past, deciphering its images with vigilance before they sink back into the *mémoire involontaire*. Social-democratic eschatology betrays the working class to a future that will never be realized because it exists to repress the past, robbing the class of its hatred by substituting dreams of liberated grandchildren for memories of enslaved ancestors. But to break with the treacherous utopianism whereby the future cancels out the past into a perpetual present will demand, as Benjamin remarks, a high price; and this is obvious from his own work. Nervous of the allure of positive utopia, historical happiness endlessly defers itself, a perpetually subjunctive presence that does no more than stand guard at the empty gateway through which the Messiah might at any moment enter. 'The kind of happiness that could arouse envy in us', Benjamin writes, 'exists only in the air we have breathed, among people we could have talked to, women who could have given themselves to us. In other words, our image of happiness is indissolubly bound up with the image of redemption'.[66] But the image of redemption must be oddly blank, as it must give name and meaning to the negativity of historical suffering without brutally cancelling the latter with a positivity of its own. The image of redemption for Christian mythology is not the risen Lord but the empty tomb, configurating history around that absence of the resurrected Messiah that scoops out for each epoch the space of its own self-transcendence. This 'undecidable' symbol prevents the Christian from worshipping the sufferings of Christ, so freezing history to a mere image of loss, just as much as it frustrates any impulse to plug that loss with a positive presence. An absent, indecipherable future hollows the present so that it may be filled with the salvific blood of the past. In a spiral of grim negations, a present already rendered non-identical with itself by the enigma of the missing Messiah must consciously enact that non-identity in self-slaughter, violating the myth of its own repleteness so that it may be fertilized by the self-sacrifices of a revolutionary past. 'This present may be meagre, granted. But no matter what it is like, one must firmly take it by the horns to be able to consult the past. It is the bull whose blood must fill the pit if the shades of the departed are to appear at its edge'.[67] But then

66 I, p. 256.
67 *Schriften*, vol. 2, p. 314.

for Benjamin every present is in a sense meagre, a dismally strait gate through which one must make the tiger's leap into the past to claw down a frail image before it flickers away. If this moment has the aura of utopia about it, it is perhaps more in the apocalyptic flash of its form than in the nature of its contents.

Benjamin's negative theology, like much of the negativity of Western Marxism, has its historical roots in an absence rather more determinate than that of the Messiah: the absence of the revolutionary party. For it is a traditional function of such a party that it should be the guardian of the dead, the living memory of the class in whose van it struggles. Such a memory cannot be adequately characterized in terms of either of the two psychical systems that Benjamin inherits from Freudianism: 'remembrance' (*Gedächtnis* or *mémoire involontaire*) and 'memory' (*Erinnerung* or *mémoire volontaire*). For the party knows no strict opposition between that perpetually combative 'presence of mind' bred in the shocks of class struggle, and those image-tracers stored in its 'unconscious'. Such images do not merely 'swim up at moments of danger'; they are woven as *Erfahrung* into the texture of *Erlebnis*, constantly nurtured and evoked to nourish the present. 'Memory' is thus less the chancy encounters of an isolated Marxist historian than an organized system, complete with its own texts and commemorative practices, a question of 'routine' as well as of the illuminating flash. If Benjamin could find such permanent commemoration (*Eingedenken*) in the protocols of Judaism or the nostalgias of a Proust, he could not do so in the historicist parties of the left; and the melancholic precariousness with which memory is shrouded in his thought is in part a consequence of this fact.

Bakhtin's utopia, by contrast, could not be more bulging with positive life. Indeed carnival is so vivaciously celebrated that the necessary political criticism is almost too obvious to make. Carnival, after all, is a *licensed* affair in every sense, a permissible rupture of hegemony, a contained popular blow-off as disturbing and relatively ineffectual as a revolutionary work of art. As Shakespeare's Olivia remarks, there is no slander in an allowed fool. The question to be addressed to carnival is that which Benjamin poses to the surrealists, in whose 'magical' uses of language, cityscapes of secret correspondences, enthusiasm for technology and devotion to the unconscious he found a powerful echo of his own concerns. Can their intoxicating liberation be politically directed? 'Are they successful in welding this experience of freedom to the other revolutionary experience that we have to acknowledge because it has been ours, the constructive, dictatorial side of revolution? In short, have they bound revolt to revolution?'[68] Carnival laughter is incorporative as well as liberating, the lifting of inhibitions politically enervating as well as disruptive. Indeed from one viewpoint carnival may figure as a prime example of that mutual complicity of law and liberation, power and desire, that has become a dominant theme of contemporary post-Marxist pessimism. Bakhtin's carnival, however, is so clearly a licensed enclave that the point almost makes itself; and its utopian aspects are thus largely subordinated to its satirical functions. Though it is in one sense a thoroughly 'corporatist' culture, and thus in some danger of being undialectically translated into an image of the future, in another sense it exists only through its subversive engagements with historical hegemony, wholly constituted by its contradictory relations to ruling-class culture. This makes it difficult to disengage as a self-contained image, in contrast, say, to the anarchic circus image of *Hard Times*, which blithely ignores its enclosing hegemony. It is, in effect, a kind of fiction: a temporary retextualizing of the social formation that exposes its 'fictive' foundations. To this extent, carnival promises to evade the double-bind that all utopianism sets for the unwary: the fact that its affirmative images of transcendence rest upon a potentially crippling sublimation of the drives necessary to achieve it in practice.

All social existence contains the simple ironic structure that we are both individuals and interrelated, and socialist collectivism tries to turn this potentially tragic tension to comic ends. It tries to realize the comic side of the truth that in social dialogue what I say to you somehow always already includes what you say to me, which in turn includes what I have said and may say to you. Bakhtin himself built no less than a whole theory of language around this irony;[69] and in carnival it becomes a 'dialogic' decentring of the discrete subject that explodes the authoritarian solemnities of monologue. The discourse of carnival knows no neutral terms: caught up in ambivalent evaluations of praise and abuse, marked by shifting dualities of tone, it is always speech received back from the other to whom it was addressed in the first place. Discourse is thus released from univocal constraints into the comedy of change and collectivity, the

68 'Surrealism', OWS, p. 236.
69 See V.N. Vološinov, *Marxism and the Philosophy of Language*, New York and London 1973.

subject caught up in a pleasurable play of shifting solidarity with others. Such play has a somatic root: carnival involves above all a pluralizing and cathecting of the body, dismantling its unity into freshly mobile parts and ceaselessly transgressing its limits. In a collectivizing movement, the individuated body is thrown wide open to its social surroundings, so that its orifices become spaces of erotic interchange with an 'outside' that is somehow always an 'inside' too. A vulgar, shameless materialism of the body—belly, buttocks, anus, genitals—rides rampant over ruling-class civilities; and the return of discourse to this sensuous root is nowhere more evident than in laughter itself, an enunciation that springs straight from the body's libidinal depths.

It is clear how Bakhtin recapitulates *avant la lettre* many of the leading motifs of contemporary deconstruction, and does so, scandalously, in a firmly social context. It suffices to say that we have yet to catch up properly with him, and if we continue to detach his 'deconstructionism' from his historical interests then doubtless we never will. There is a pressing need for what we might call a 'political somatics', a study of the political-libidinal production of the historical body that attends not only, in negative fashion, to its past and present imprintings, but which may learn from such sources as Bakhtin something of its revolutionary potential. It is also surely clear how Bakhtin's political somatics show up what is submerged in the work of a Benjamin. For the body is certainly present in Benjamin's work, but mainly in a negative mode. His recurrent comparison of intellectual labour to the labour of the prostitute signals, to adopt a phrase of Adorno's from a different context, the 'torn halves of an integral freedom, to which however they do not add up'.[70] This is one reason why Benjamin's decentred revolutionary subject, the *Unmensch* of the future, is notably 'emptier' than Bakhtin's. Benjamin's *Unmensch* is a purged space, a deconstructed function of historical forces. Bakhtin's carnivalesque subject, by contrast, is at once 'emptied' and 'full', reconstructed by the very transgressive surge that deconstructs it. The catharsis of laughter is, inseparably, the birth of a new form of discourse.

As far as the baroque drama is concerned, the only good body is a dead one. 'In the *Trauerspiel*', Benjamin writes, 'the corpse becomes quite simply the pre-eminent emblematic property'.[71] Like Christian myth-

70 Cit. *Aesthetics and Politics*, p. 109.
71 O, p. 218.

ology, the *Trauerspiel* revolves on a mangled body, its parts dismembered by a violence in whose sadistic shrieking the cry for a lost organicism can still be dimly heard. The baroque flays and butchers the living flesh in order to inscribe some allegorical meaning there; since the living body presents itself as an inexpressible symbolic unity, it is only in its brutal undoing, its diffusion into so many torn, reified fragments, that some provisional meaning may be ripped from its organic closure. The body thus achieves its full revelation only as a corpse; it is by death alone that the *Trauerspiel* characters can enter into the realms of allegory, shedding their flesh so that the drama may scavenge for significance among its pieces. In a curious prefigurement of Freudian theory, it is only by dividing the body, grasping it as the decentred site of contradictions between this or that cathected organ, that some potentially redemptive meaning may be released from its delusive *Gestalt*. Psychoanalysis, like *Trauerspiel* and carnival, is born at the juncture between signifier and the somatic, and all three modes explore their strange inversions: organ as signifier, signifier as sensuous practice, desire as the hollowing of the body by language itself. In the *Trauerspiel*, as in *Beyond the Pleasure Principle*, that hollowing is carried to the point of death itself: if for Freud all desire speaks of the utterly unrepresentable silence of death, so for Benjamin the *Trauerspiel* body may speak only when it has been quelled to a corpse. And indeed what is that corpse, that heap of cryptic fragments, that ambiguous image whose meaning is always elsewhere, if not the very text of the *Trauerspiel* itself, in which meaning and the material letter, voice and writing, presence and absence are at once mutually involved and about to come apart at the seams?

But this for Benjamin is the postlapsarian body, rent between meaning and matter. Before the fall, language sank its roots into sensuous practice, as a medium expressively mimetic of being itself. Adamic discourse is the word that discloses the God-given language of Nature, binding the subject into a communion with the concrete that turns on the immediacy of the creative name.[72] In this blissful state of grace, the semiotic element of discourse is merely the bearer of 'language as script'—of that 'archive of non-sensuous similarities' that is writing itself, that great web of magical correspondences secretly woven through the linear dispersals of post-

72 See 'On Language as Such and on the Language of Men', OWS, 107–123; 'On the Mimetic Faculty', OWS, pp. 160–63; and 'Probleme der Sprachsoziologie', GS, 3, pp. 452–80. See also Benjamin's letter to Martin Buber (B, 1, letter 45).

lapsarian history. Only a 'sacred' reading can shatter the profanity of such dispersals, finding in the written word's own non-sensuous correspondence to its referent a figure of those covert pacts between events that flash up before a subject at a point of historical crisis. It is in this sense that history is for Benjamin script, demanding the 'sacred' reading of historical materialism rather than the profanities of historicism. Script and Saussure are enemies: against the 'bourgeois' notion of the arbitrary, instrumental sign, which consummates that unhinging of speech from material practice under which the *Trauerspiel* labours, Benjamin will oppose the *Jetztzeit* of sign and referent that was there in the beginning and will be reborn in the Messianic age. His hope is that the word will dance once more, as it does in those angels whose bodies are one burning flame of praise before God, as it did in the 'expressive' beginnings of discourse, and as it can still be seen to do in, say, the gestural language of Naples: 'the language of gesture goes further here than anywhere in Italy. The conversation is impenetrable to anyone from outside. Ears, nose, eyes, breast and shoulders are signalling stations activated by the fingers. These configurations return in their fastidiously specialized eroticism'.[73]

From Naples to Bakhtinian carnival is not, it would seem, a great distance. What more resolutely seeks to overthrow Saussure and return discourse to its social basis than Bakhtin's philosophy of language? Yet surely Benjamin's hopelessly idealist theories of the word, solemnly sustained to the very end of his life, are not to be compared to Bakhtin's materialism? The matter is not, in fact, quite that simple. Benjamin's linguistics, in all their mystical primitivism and naive sensualism, are doubtless idealist; but the Judaic belief in the expressive unity of word and body, given a dialectical twist, can just as easily reappear as the ground for a materialist re-location of discourse within the social practices from which, as Benjamin shrewdly sees, modern semiotic ideologies have strategically isolated it. Indeed it may well be that Benjamin's first turn towards Marxism was made precisely on these grounds. Holidaying in Capri in 1924, at work on the final stages of *Origin*, his attention was drawn by Ernst Bloch to Lukács's recently published *History and Class Consciousness*. Struck at once by an apparent convergence between Lukács's ways of relating theory and practice and his own epistemological reflections, Benjamin wrote to Scholem that, 'starting out from political

73 'Naples', OWS, p. 176.

considerations, Lukács arrives . . . at certain theses on the theory of knowledge which are very close to me or which corroborate my own . . .'[74] Lukács's formulations, he comments, possess a 'hard philosophical core' that exposes every other approach as mere 'demagogic and bourgeois phraseology'; 'the political practice of communism', during his stay on Capri, has revealed itself to him in a new light. There were rather more pleasurable reasons for this illumination than ploughing his way through Lukács: on Capri Benjamin had also met Asja Lacis, the Lettish Bolshevik and theatre director whom he described as one of the most remarkable women he had ever encountered, and who was to become his lover. But it is perhaps significant that what impelled Benjamin first towards Marxism was the doctrine of the unity of theory and practice—more particularly, Lukács's anti-reflectionist view of consciousness as a transformative material force within historical development. It is not altogether surprising that the author of an essay such as 'On Language as Such and on the Language of Men', with its intensely Judaic conception of the word as creative act, should have felt such an intellectual confluence.[75] As far as idealism goes, then, Benjamin's case is as complex as that of another Jewish philosopher, Ludwig Wittgenstein, who similarly returns language to social practice at the same time as too complacently endorsing existing practices. Nor can Bakhtin be merely appropriated as a materialist. It would now appear that behind his work lies a Judeo–Christian mysticism in some ways akin to Benjamin's—that *Marxism and the Philosophy of Language* contains as its secret code a theological devotion to the incarnational unity of word and being similar to that which marks

---

74 B, 1, p. 355.

75 Gershom Scholem, in his *Walter Benjamin—die Geschichte einer Freudschaft* (pp. 259–60), fails to grasp this point, seeing a straight contradiction between Benjamin's 'magical' theories of language and his later materialism. It was, he claims, a contradiction that Benjamin himself freely conceded. Scholem notes how Benjamin was speaking in the 1930s, quite unmetaphorically, of the word of God as the ground of all theory of language, and can see no relation between this and a materialist theory. It is, admittedly, a highly curious coupling; but at the very least, 'onomatopoeic' and materialist notions of language join hands in common opposition to what Benjamin sees to be the idealism of Saussure. Habermas, moreover, believes that linguistic research has validated Benjamin's theory that the earliest roots of language were 'expressive' (Habermas, p. 204). Susan Buck-Morss notes Benjamin's own comment that he could see a problematic relationship between his philosophy of language and dialectical materialism, and rightly remarks that 'this was not despite affinities between the *Trauerspiel* method and the Kabbala, but because of them' (Buck-Morss, p. 22).

Benjamin's own mediations.[76] What seems clear at any rate is that the insertion of the signifying body into the absent space between 'base' and 'superstructure' is the occasion for a reconsideration of both terms—that within this classical schema the body, like the family, is an ambivalent, 'undecidable' category.

The most stirring image of the body in Benjamin is not, typically, a positive one. What we have in the figure of the *flâneur* is, Bakhtin aside, perhaps the most subtle instance of the ideological inscription of the body to be found in Marxist writing. The *flâneur's* every dallying step speaks ideological volumes; in the very poise of his head and rhythm of his gait Benjamin reads the imprint of the class struggle itself. Peerlessly self-composed, resisting the dismembered crowd, the *flâneur* moves majestically against that historical grain that would decompose his body into an alien meaning, reduce his numinous presence to an allegory of loss. Even so, though images of the erotic, 'insurrected' body are for the most part absent, Benjamin is not entirely without his more celebratory moments. A laboratory for the body's reconstruction could be found in Brechtian theatre, with its politics of *Gestus*; and surrealism made its contribution too. For the 'revolutionary' images that surrealism seeks include for Benjamin new metaphors of the body, transformed as it is by the technologies of industrial capitalism. 'The collective is a body, too. And the *physis* that is being organized for it in technology can, through all its political and factual reality, only be produced in that image sphere to which profane illumination initiates us. Only when in technology body and image so interpenetrate that all revolutionary tension becomes bodily collective innervation, and all bodily innervations of the collective become revolutionary discharge, has reality transcended itself to the extent demanded by the *Communist Manifesto*.'[77] The carnival imagery through which for Bakhtin the libido of collective *physis* is organized promises for Benjamin to materialize itself in the historical forces of production. For the body is at once numbered among those material forces, and is inscribed by images produced at the level of the superstructure. By exploiting technology to generate fresh images, experimental art can thus also intervene indirectly at the level of the base, rewriting the body to align it with the new tasks presented by that transformed infrastructure.

76 See Michael Holquist's forthcoming biography of Bakhtin. A minor curio of this Marxist-theological tradition is my own *The Body as Language*, London 1970.
77 'Surrealism', OWS, p. 239.

Metaphysical materialism of the Bukharinite sort, Benjamin remarks, leaves a 'residue'; and this residue is nothing less than the material body itself, which as libidinal image and material force wreaks havoc with any Marxism for which matter is not in the first place sensuous practice. For metaphysical materialism, images are the offprints of matter; for Benjamin and Bakhtin, images are material, and matter—the body above all—imagistically constructed. Like Bakhtin, Benjamin wants to subvert the psychological subject by opening a sphere of imagery 'in which political materialism and physical nature share the inner man, the psyche, the individual, or whatever else we wish to throw at them, with dialectical justice, so that no limb remains unrent'.[78] Yet by the time of his essay on surrealism such rending is the unleashing of a new collective libido, not that contemplative allegorizing of torn limbs which was the *Trauerspiel*. And it is perhaps not surprising, with the Freudian trope of tension and discharge in mind, that Benjamin should preface this whole passage from the surrealism essay by remarking, enigmatically, that with the artist who engages in such revolutionary reconstruction of the image sphere, 'the jokes he tells are the better for it'.[79]

There is, in fact, a curious encounter between Benjamin and the theme of carnival. In 1924, at work on the final stages of the *Origin*, he corresponded about the nature of tragedy with his friend Christian Rang, scholar and ex-civil servant. Rang drew Benjamin's attention to an article of his own on carnival, in which he argues a relation between that form and tragedy as equal ruptures of astrological determinism. Carnival is a breaking of fixed astrological order, 'such that ecstasy can spring forth from anguish; the free word can do without the law; the new god (Dionysus) can diminish the ancient ones'. It represents the 'triumph of the extraordinary over the ordinary, such that the drunk, ecstatic word can

78 OWS, p. 239.
79 OWS, p. 238. Benjamin had written of the necessity of humour as early as 1916. 'The critique of spiritual realities,' he writes in a letter, 'consists in distinguishing the authentic from the inauthentic. But this isn't something that language can achieve other than by the detour of a deep disguise: humour. Only by becoming humour can language become critique. The magic of true critique appears precisely when all counterfeit comes into contact with the light and melts away. What remains is the authentic: it is ashes. We laugh at it. Whoever emits light in great profusion ends up by initiating these divine enterprises of unmasking that we call criticism. It is precisely these great critics who have had such an astonishing vision of the authentic: Carvantes. A great writer who has seen the authentic so accurately that he could almost renounce all criticism: Sterne' (B, 1, p. 132).

break the circular, regular development of the *agon*, that a humanity imprisoned by forms . . . can rudely unfetter itself, that the persuasive force of living discourse inaugurates a right more lofty than the process whereby tribes war against one another with arms or absolute formulae. Divine decree is shattered by the logos and ends up in liberty'.[80] Whether Benjamin actually read Rang's essay is unclear, and Rang himself was to die a few months after writing this letter, cutting short any possibility of future collaboration. But it is striking how what for Rang has the name of carnival will become for the later Benjamin *Jetztzeit*—that moment of revolutionary redemption in which *jouissance* is snatched from suffering and the determinisms of both astrology and historicism violently fractured by the riotous rhetoric of liberation. It may well be that, by a devious route, Bakhtinian carnival and Benjaminesque apocalypse share a common root.

There is a story, perhaps apocryphal, of a worker in a canning factory whose job it was to pull a lever every few seconds. After some time it was discovered that for several years the lever had not been connected to anything. On being informed of this, the worker suffered a severe breakdown. One of the most disturbing aspects of this ghastly tale is that it is mildly funny. Freud would have had no difficulty in demonstrating why: we smile because of a yield of pleasure gained from a contrast between our own economizing on psychical expenditure and the worker's excessive investment of it.[81] In the hands of a Brecht, such a narrative would not, presumably, be tragically presented. One may speculate that Brecht would rather have cornered the psychical energy we save in such a situation and turned it to other uses—transformed it partly into pity and indignation, at least in his later work, but also displaced the object of our amusement to the farcical absurdity of capitalist production, its risible inefficiency and consequent ripeness for overthrow. This is to say that Brechtian theatre strives to combine elements of the modes known to Freud as 'comedy' and 'humour'. Comedy distantiates an action, thwarts any intense psychical expenditure and thus permits us a pleasurable economy released in laughter; it is incompatible with any strong affect. Humour, by contrast, is a substitutive device: it is 'a means of obtaining pleasure in spite of the distressing affects that interfere with it; it acts as a substitute for the generation of these affects, it puts itself in their place'.[82] The crudest

80 B. 1, p. 338.
81 *The Standard Edition*, vol. 13, p. 190f.
82 Ibid., p. 228.

example of this is so-called *Galgenhumor* or gallows humour: the firing-squad victim who refuses a last cigarette because he is trying to give them up.

Comic distantiation in Brecht is mainly a matter of the estrangement effect, which inhibits 'Aristotelian' empathy and thus leaves the audience's psychical energy unbound for potential liberation in laughter. But if Brecht is not mainly a question of laughter, this is partly because the available energy is displaced in another direction—not exactly into humour, but into thought. For Brecht, the two are in any case intimately linked, for as Benjamin comments, 'there is no better starting point for thought than laughter; speaking more precisely, spasms of the diaphragm generally offer better chances for thought than spasms of the soul. Epic theatre is lavish only in the occasions it offers for laughter'.[83] Comic estrangement allows the audience to 'think above the action', which clearly entails psychical expenditure; but since thinking itself is pleasurable, this does not wholly dissipate the comic effect. Moreover, thought is freer than pity or fear: it is a matter of thinking around, across and above the dramatic action, of a certain relaxed, digressive speculation that blends the vigilant expertise of the football fan with his or her casual at-homeness. Thought is not paralytically focused on the play's navel—for where in Brecht is that?—but permitted a certain phantasmal play, allowed to construct its own possible worlds athwart the text it encounters. The dialectical form of the drama enables such constructions, effecting at the same time a binding and release of psychical energy: the 'montage' principle encourages us to concentrate and relax, not only in sequence but in a complex rhythm whereby we also relax during the stage action and concentrate during the breaks. The Brechtian spectator, whose analytic responses must co-exist with 'sensuousness and humour',[84] for whom the historical sense must develop into 'a real sensual delight',[85] combines the psychic investments of 'presence of mind' with the psychic release of a certain productive indifference, so that the social division of labour and leisure is temporally transcended. As with Benjamin's theory of film, the viewing subject must not be allowed to escape into a fantasy unchallenged by the text: 'the spectator's process of association in view of these images is indeed

83 'The Author as Producer', UB, p. 101.
84 *Brecht on Theatre*, p. 204.
85 Ibid., p. 276.

interrupted by their constant, sudden change'.[86] The text, *pace* some
post-structuralism, exerts its own determinations, as *this* space of
possibilities rather than that;[87] but at the same time the notion of the
spectator as one 'who follows the action with every fibre of his being at rapt
attention', the structuralist delusion of the viewer as determined function
of the text, is overthrown for the image of a constructing audience 'that is
relaxed and follows the action without strain'.[88]

There is a further application of the Freudian model of comedy to
Brechtian theatre. Writing of a case of *Galgenhumor* in which a condemned
criminal dispels our pity by turning his situation to witty advantage, Freud
remarks that 'We are, as it were, infected by the rogue's indifference—
though we notice that it has cost him a great expenditure of psychical
work'.[89] The aim of much conventional comedy is likewise to achieve such
indifference while concealing from us its labour-costs. The comic drama
that erases its own process of production hopes to intensify its effects by
saving us the psychical expenditure that an exposure of those mechanisms
would involve. We smile delightedly at the effortless ease with which the
action is carried through. Brechtian theatre, however, has it both ways: its
self-deconstructions force us to think, while simultaneously achieving a
different kind of comic liberation. For the comic effect that Freud
describes as a perceived disproportion between another's excessive
expenditure and our own economy is with Brecht a question of structural
asymmetry within the performance itself, between its achieved positions
and the visible labour which went into their production. This, indeed, is the
very inner structure of the estrangement effect, which at once represents
and dislocates, offers a position and suggests its self-critique. There is a

---

86 'The Work of Art in the Age of Mechanical Reproduction', I, p. 240.

87 A point touched upon by Norman N. Holland, in his *The Dynamics of Literary Response*,
New York 1968. Brecht, for Holland, is an 'absurdist' in his quest for 'affectlessness', but fails
in this quest because 'he gives us belief in an ideology as a way of handling the unconscious
conflicts his plays arouse' (p. 178). Holland unites Freudian joke theory with elements of
literary formalism, for which 'content' is merely the motivation of form. He does indeed
allow that conscious meaning is more than 'a sop thrown to the superego' (p. 184), but it is
significant that in the case of Brecht (as against, say, Ionesco), 'meaning' has mysteriously
become 'ideology', with the clear negative implication of a 'defence' against fantasy. The
effect of this is, of course, the familiar ideological devaluation of ideology to superficially
formulable ideas. Holland does not consider the possibility that the 'unconscious' of literary
texts may be as much a strategic response to their ideological positions as *vice versa*.

88 'What Is Epic Theatre?', I, p. 149.

89 *The Standard Edition*, vol. 13, p. 230.

source of comedy in this very duplicity—in the irony by which the 'finished', economic *énoncé* is played off against the always unfinished, uneconomic business of *énonciation*. If Freud is to be believed, part of our enjoyment of Brechtian as of any other drama is the pleasure of watching others work while we do not; Brecht's insistence on a relaxedly appraising, preferably smoking audience would seem to underline this imbalance. But this is in itself a fairly trivial matter: it is the way Brecht carries such ironic discrepancy into the very form of the drama that is most original. The comedy of Brecht is something like a conscious version of the unwitting funniness of a poet's first drafts, where we can see in the desperate deletions and banal emendations how close the final polished product came to utter disaster.

If we were to submit to some structuralist *combinatoire* the great debates of the 1930s between Lukács, Bloch, Brecht, Adorno and Benjamin, it would surely become apparent that there was a missing term. What we have, if I may use the reductive terminology suitable to such schemas, is: an idealist realist (Lukács); two idealist modernists (Bloch, Adorno); a materialist modernist (Brecht); and a modernist who blends elements of both idealism and materialism (Benjamin). The unoccupied location, then, is a 'materialist realist': there is no such twentieth-century Marxist aesthetician of the stature of these others. And that this is so might suggest who, in the end, has had the upper hand. But another term stands out in this combination, to perceive which requires no structuralist sophistication. Of Bloch, Lukács, Brecht, Benjamin and Adorno, only Brecht is comic. I do not mean simply that he is humorous, although that is important enough: I mean also that Brecht stands ideologically apart from that 'Western Marxist' melancholy which in its various ways broods over the other four, and infiltrates the very sinew of their prose styles. It is not surprising that Brecht is at once unmelancholic and cultivates the alienation effect; for few things are funnier than auto-referentiality. It lays bare the inherent comedy of all discourse, which pivots on the 'virtual' presence of objects it necessarily absents. Brecht once commented that Hegel was comic because his shiftings from level to level had the effect of wit; and though we might consider such a reading of Hegel as heroic as Harriet Martineau's ability to weep tears of joy over Comte, it reveals the tenacity with which he grasped the very character of comedy.

There has been, so far as I know, no Marxist theory of comedy to date;

tragedy has been a considerably more successful contender for the attention of materialist criticism. And there are good enough reasons why Marxism has suspected the comic: for what after all could more securely rivet us in our ideological places, having provisionally jolted us out of them? But if traditional comedy shakes us out of those places only to allow us wryly to rejoin them, Brecht's theatre is comic in a more radical sense. Its comedy lies in its insight that any place is reversible, any signified may become a signifier, any discourse may be without warning rapped over the knuckles by some meta-discourse which may then suffer such rapping in its turn. To adopt one of Brecht's own phrases: if one wanted an aesthetic (of the comic), one could find it here. And all this is somewhat removed from, even if it relates to, that delight in auto-referentiality which, as in the later Barthes, turns on what is still the essentially privatized, de-politicized notion of *jouissance*. The comic, for Brecht, comes down to the double-take; it is thus in the first place a formal matter, not a question of 'content'. But in that question of comic form everything is at stake: it is here that we find the profoundest nexus between Brecht's alienation effect and his politics. Brecht's major achievement here is surely to teach us the deep comedy of meta-language, which in distantiating its object displays just where it is itself most vulnerable, revealing the vacuum into which another putative discourse could always rush to take it over.

'The theatre of the scientific age', Brecht writes, 'is in a position to make dialectics into a source of enjoyment. The unexpectedness of logically progressive or zigzag development, the instability of every circumstance, the joke of contradiction and so forth: all these are ways of enjoying the liveliness of men, things and processes, and they heighten both our capacity for life and our pleasure in it'.[90] What for Walter Benjamin is potentially tragic—the unexpected rebuff, the fragility of existence, the agony of conflict—is for Brecht the very stuff of comedy. Yet that is too sharp and simple an opposition. If there is hope for Benjamin, it lies as for Brecht in history's unruly refusal to conform to its historicist models; for both men, history can be patient of a comic emplotment once *Ananke* or tragic necessity has been unmasked for the ruling-class lie it so often is. Particular mutations may be tragic or comic, but mutability itself, at least for Brecht, is somehow comic in principle: witness his anecdote of Herr Keuner, who on being told by a long-absent friend that he hadn't changed

90 *Brecht on Theatre*, p. 277.

a bit, turned pale.[91] Contradictions are a joke not because they are not often intolerable but because without the dialectic which is, so to speak, the ironic wit of history, there could be no significant life at all. History, as it were, is comic in form; as with the Freudian theory of the joke, it is that form which strives to make palatable, because changeable, any particular tragedy of content, and whose pleasurable savouring releases the transformative forces of the historical 'unconscious'. Hitler as housepainter yesterday and Chancellor today is thus a sign of the comic, because that resistible rise foreshadows the unstable process whereby he may be dead in a bunker tomorrow. For Marxism, history moves under the very sign of irony: there is something darkly comic about the fact that the bourgeoisie are their own grave-diggers, just as there is an incongruous humour about the fact that the wretched of the earth should come to power. The only reason for being a Marxist is to get to the point where you can stop being one. It is in that glib, feeble piece of wit that much of the Marxist project is surely summarized. Marxism has the humour of dialectics because it reckons itself into the historical equations it writes; like the great heritage of Irish wit from Swift and Sterne to Joyce, Beckett and Flann O'Brien, it has the comedy of all 'texts' that write about themselves in the act of writing history.

Yet it is not of course true that all tragic contents are changeable, just as carnival is wrong to believe that anything can be converted into humour. There is nothing comic about gang rape, or Auschwitz. There are always blasphemies, words that must on no account be uttered because they defile the tongue. Those who believe that the sacred and profane belong to a benighted past need only to consider whether they would be prepared to pronounce certain words about Auschwitz even as a joke. The mode in which sacred and profane *can* co-exist is the mode of satire: Swift's *Modest Proposal* utters the unspeakable in the context of therapeutic ridicule. But tragic situations are often unchangeable in at least one important respect—unchangeable for those who are their victims. Contemporary history, for Benjamin, is the 'after-life' of a continuous tragedy, in which, as with the after-life of the artefact, we have a revolutionary chance to redeem the past by imbuing it through political action with retroactive meaning and value. But though this is a crucial *caveat* for those who would dogmatically absolutize tragedy, make the existence of Auschwitz rather than its destruction the definitive word, or arrogantly claim that the 'modern world' is too shabbily unaristocratic to be tragic at all, it remains true that such redemptions can only ever be partial. And there are also always individual tragedies, tragedies that persist like a forgotten bruise in the flesh of history, which no transcendence short of a Messiah could retroactively transform.

There is, in other words, always something that escapes comic emplotment; there is always a pure residue of difference that is non-dialectizable. But if this is true of tragedy, it is also paradoxically true of comedy itself. In his book *Revolution and Repetition*, Jeffrey Mehlman sees the elegant dialectical schemas of Marx's *The Eighteenth Brumaire of Louis Bonaparte* as fissured by an uncouth, irreducible cackle of farce: the farce of Bonaparte himself, the non-representative joker in the dialectical pack, riding to power on the shields of a drunken soldiery. The ruin of the Marxist notion of the state as class-representative, Bonaparte prises a crack in that conceptual architecture through which floods a heterogeneous swarm of lumpenproletarians, a flood that threatens to swamp Marx's own orderly text under the semiotic excess it lends to his language. 'The upshot', Mehlman comments, '[is] a Marx more profoundly anarchical than Anarchism ever dreamed'.[92] It is not in fact clear how far Mehlman's own text escapes into a realm of pure difference from those ruling ideologies that have an interest in abolishing dialectics and rewriting Marxism as textual productivity. For Bonapartism is not of course anarchism, and, *pace* Mehlman, there is nothing 'uncanny' about it. The state for Marxism is not the direct representation of a class interest (which Bonaparte can then be thought to rupture), but, as Nicos Poulantzas argued, 'the strategic site of organization of the dominant class in its relationship to the dominated classes'.[93] It is a contradictory condensation of class forces—the space of a continual struggle, which nonetheless 'represents and organizes the long-term political interests of a *power bloc*'.[94] The contradictory nature of Bonapartism, which works by 'materially encouraging yet politically repressing the bourgeoisie, depending the while for political support on a peasantry whose interests are at loggerheads with [the] material encouragement of the bourgeoisie',[95] is

92 Berkeley 1977, p. 41.
93 *State, Power, Socialism*, p. 148.
94 Ibid., p. 127.
95 John Maguire, *Marx's Theory of Politics*, Cambridge 1978, p. 112.

simply a stark example of the state's normally contradictory character, one that Marx's study of English history was itself enough to establish. The fond hope that the belly-laughter of Bonapartism brings the Marxist theory of the state toppling into the gutter is not, regretfully, well-founded.

What 'escapes' in *The Eighteenth Brumaire* is not an irreducible anarchist excess within the present, but the poetry of the future: 'the social revolution of the nineteenth century cannot draw its poetry from the past, but only from the future. It cannot begin with itself before it has stripped off all superstition in regard to the past. Earlier revolutions required recollections of past world history in order to drug themselves concerning their own content. In order to arrive at its own content, the revolution of the nineteenth century must let the dead bury their dead. There the phrase went beyond the content; here the content goes beyond the phrase.'[96] From the viewpoint of a Walter Benjamin, Marx's apparent dismissal of the past may sound unduly brisk. But he is speaking of course of past *bourgeois* revolutions, whereas Benjamin has in mind the past struggles of the exploited; and in any case the passage must be taken with what Marx has written just before: 'but unheroic as bourgeois society is, it nevertheless took heroism, sacrifice, terror, civil war and battles of peoples to bring it into being. And in the classically austere traditions of the Roman republic its gladiators found the ideals and the art forms, the self-deceptions that they needed in order to conceal from themselves the bourgeois limitations of the content of their struggles and to keep their enthusiasm on the high plane of the great historical tragedy. Similarly, at another stage of development, a century earlier, Cromwell and the English people had borrowed speech, passions and illusions from the Old Testament for their bourgeois revolution. When the real aim had been achieved, when the bourgeois transformation of English society had been accomplished, Locke supplanted Habakkuk.

'Thus the awakening of the dead in these revolutions served the purpose of glorifying the new struggles, not of parodying the old; of magnifying the given task in imagination, not of fleeing from its solution in reality; of finding once more the spirit of revolution, not of making its ghost walk about again.'[97] Marx's text is symptomatically incoherent. Bourgeois

96 Marx and Engels, *Selected Works*, London 1968, p. 99.
97 Ibid., p. 98.

society may be 'unheroic', but bourgeois revolution is not; its exponents are indeed 'gladiators', though their ideals are self-deceptive; their enthusiasm, nevertheless, does genuinely belong to the high plane of historical tragedy. The English revolution is a matter of both passions and illusions; disinterring the dead is no hollow parody but a real source of revolutionary spirit; but the *Brumaire* opens by telling us that such historical rehearsals are mere 'caricature' and 'farce', and goes on to castigate their purpose as purely opiate.

It could be claimed that Marx's text is not incoherent but dialectical— that he is contrasting the heroism of the earlier bourgeois revolutions with the sordid farce of Louis Bonaparte, opposing form to content, and grasping both positive and negative moments of such dramatic re-enactments. This is true, but insufficient. For *The Eighteenth Brumaire* does after all open with a *general* pronouncement about such political recurrences—historical tragedy always repeats itself as farce—which it then instantly specifies in terms of the contemporary French events: 'Caussidière for Danton, Louis Blanc for Robespierre, the *Montagne* of 1848 to 1851 for the *Montagne* of 1793 to 1795, the Nephew for the Uncle'. So this is an instance of a general truth—or is it? If Caussidière, Blanc and the Nephew are farce, what about Danton, Robespierre and the Uncle, who are also repetitions? Is there no *Nachträglichkeit* at work? The first paragraph of the text would seem to rescue these latter figures from farce while implicitly including them in the universal truth of it, opposing them to that of which they are part, idealizing them to an origin while treating them as an after-life.

There follows another famous general pronouncement: 'men make their own history, but they do not make it just as they please; they do not make it under circumstances chosen by themselves, but under circumstances directly encountered, given and transmitted from the past'. If this is a materialist truth, then all generations would seem to be implicated in it, and their compulsion to repeat determined by the nature of history itself. As such it is a 'neutral' fact; but suddenly in the next sentence it is not: 'the tradition of all the dead generations weighs like a nightmare on the brain of the living'. The doctrine of material determination by the past with which Marxism counters idealism is, politically speaking, a source of potential tragedy: history would seem to condemn men and women to parodic repetition, so that 'just when they seem engaged in revolutionizing themselves and things, in creating something that has never yet existed, precisely in such periods of revolutionary crisis they anxiously conjure up the spirits of the past to their service and borrow from them names, battle cries and costumes in order to present the new scene of world history in this time-honoured disguise and this borrowed language'.[98] They *seem* engaged in revolutionizing themselves, though this is in fact a ritual repetition of the old; yet even so these are 'periods of revolutionary crisis'. Are they, then, 'genuinely' revolutionary or only apparently so? How can their *apparent* 'creating [of] something that has never existed' be reconciled with the fact that this is indeed a 'new scene of world history'? Is it really new or not? The subsequent imagery of borrowing and disguise offers to resolve this dilemma: the 'contents' are new but the 'forms' are not. Luther 'donned the mask' of the apostle Paul, and the French revolution of 1789 to 1814 'draped' itself alternately in the trappings of the Roman republic and the Roman empire. Here the past is seen as mere external lendings; but just as it becomes so the metaphor shifts. 'In like manner a beginner who has learnt a new language always translates it back into his mother tongue, but he has assimilated the spirit of the new language and can freely express himself in it only when he finds his way in it without recalling the old and forgets his native tongue in the use of the new'. What Marx means by the new language, presumably, is the novel revolutionary reality, which by a kind of epistemological break must seek new forms of expression. But in another sense the *old* imagery of the past has now become the *new* foreign language, so that the trope really says the reverse of what the text will say later about the need to bury the dead. There the old language of the past must be repudiated for the 'poetry of the future'; here the new language, which is metaphorical of the past's trappings, must be lived into until the mother tongue is forgotten. The metaphor unwittingly valorizes a rhetoric of the past which the text also wants to spurn. The 'natural'—the 'mother tongue'—is now discarded for the 'artificial'—the new language—which will become 'naturalized' in its turn; the language of the future is suddenly identical with the discourse of the past, in a turn which the text clearly does not 'mean' to make. This move is enabled by the transition from an imagery of masking, draping and disguise to one of language: for the relations between a cloak and the body it conceals are obviously not applicable to the relations between one language and another. The semiotic problematic has shifted: Marx implies an equivalence between cloak/body and mother tongue/foreign tongue which cannot be sustained. In the 'mythical' connotative system of the bourgeois revolutions, the signifier 'Roman cloak' has as its signified 'Roman heroism', while the whole sign acts as the signifier of 'bourgeois heroism'; in the meta-linguistic situation Marx goes on to describe, the reverse happens and the mother tongue becomes the signified of the new language.[99] But in the second case, the distance between old and new sign-systems is rapidly diminished as the speaker grows into the new language; the new absorbs the old and thereby becomes autonomous. If this image is then transplanted to the relations between the political present and the rhetoric of the past, it has a 'contaminating' effect: it suggests that the past's insignia are not quite so extrinsic to the present as the dualist metaphors of disguise and draping would insinuate. There, too, the discourse of the new might absorb the spirit of the old to the point where no simple binary model of opposition or correspondence would be adequate.

From 1848 to 1851, the ghosts of the old French revolution walk abroad once more. Bonaparte 'hides his commonplace repulsive features under the iron death mask of Napoleon'. But is this merely the symbolic resummoning of the dead or a literal regression, a matter of text or history? 'An entire people, which had imagined that by means of a revolution it had imparted to itself an accelerated power of motion, suddenly finds itself set back into a defunct epoch . . .'[100] So it was the revolution that was imaginary and the regression that was real; but the next image contradicts this in turn, comparing the French situation to that of the mad Englishman in Bedlam who believes that he is living in the time of the Pharaohs. History *has* regressed, even if it is madness to believe so. Having been told that Louis Bonaparte merely assumes the disguise of his uncle, we now learn that the sign is in fact at one with the referent: '[the French] have not only a caricature of the old Napoleon, they have the old Napoleon himself, caricatured as he must appear in the middle of the nineteenth century'.[101] Bonaparte is not just a parody of Napoleon; he is Napoleon parodying himself. He is the real thing dressed up as false, not just the false

99 See Roland Barthes, *Elements of Semiology*, London 1967, p. 34; and *Mythologies*, St Alban's 1973, p. 114f.
100 *Selected Works*, p. 98.
101 Ibid., p. 99.

thing tricked out as real. What is in question now is not a regressive caricature but a caricaturing regression. Once more, the representational model of a form external to its content, a sign detachable from its referent, threatens to fail at the very point where the farcical incongruity of the two is being enforced. This semiotic disturbance is caught up in the contradictory articulation of society and state: 'instead of *society* having conquered a new content for itself, it seems that the *state* only returned to its oldest form, to the shamelessly simple domination of the sabre and the cowl'. It is a 'revolution' of the signifier only, which regresses while society stands still. If previously a turbulent content concealed itself in static forms, it is now the signified that congeals into inertia, passing its energies to a signifier that 'seems'—or does it 'really'?—to move rapidly backwards.

This curious disruption of the sign seems endemic to bourgeois revolution. 'Bourgeois revolutions, like those of the eighteenth century, storm swiftly from success to success; their dramatic effects outdo each other; men and things seem set in sparkling brilliants; ecstasy is the everyday spirit; but they are short-lived; soon they have attained their zenith, and a long crapulent depression lays hold of society before it learns soberly to assimilate the results of its storm-and-stress period'.[102] So it is not just that bourgeois revolution swathes itself in theatrical costume: it *is* theatrical in essence, a matter of panache and breathless rhetoric, a baroque frenzy whose poetic effusions are in inverse proportion to its meagre substance. It is not just that it manipulates past fictions: it *is* a kind of fiction, an ill-made drama that expends itself in Act Three and totters exhausted to its tawdry conclusion. If bourgeois revolutions trick themselves out in flashy tropes it is because there is a kind of fictiveness in their very structure, a hidden flaw that disarticulates form and content. It is not that bourgeois nature seeks an artificial supplement from the past; on the contrary, that historical supplement reveals what was artificial about it in the first place, filling and yet not filling a lack that was already there.

The crux of this ambiguity can be found in the famous enigma that Marx proposes in the text's final pages: when is a class not a class? The small-holding French peasantry are a class in so far as they share the same economic conditions of existence; but 'in so far as there is merely a local interconnection among these small-holding peasants, and the identity of their interests begets no community, no national bond and no political organisation among them, they do not form a class'. Unable to install themselves within the state apparatuses, the small-holding peasantry need political representation; and that representative is Louis Bonaparte. By virtue of Bonaparte the peasantry becomes a class proper, discovers a signifier that redefines its status. Marx's political insight, in other words, is the ruin, not of representation, but of a naive semiotic conception of it. It is not that political signifiers have become free-standing, as the formalism of a Mehlman (or his post-Marxist English equivalents) would suggest; such a claim merely falls prey to the ideology of Bonapartism itself. Bonaparte is indeed a signifier of class interests, but a complex, contradictory one that politically *constitutes* the very interests it signifies. Such complex articulation can be grasped neither by a purely empiricist model of the sign, in which the signified grabs for a signifying form extrinsic to it, nor by the kind of formalism that slides signified under signifier, where the resultant friction wears the former to nothing.

The ambiguities of Bonaparte, then, have a relation to Marx's ambiguous handling of historical repetition. Confronted in the contemporary figure of Bonaparte with a sordid case of *farcical* repetition, Marx's view of the positive features of such recurrences *in general* is continually refracted through this negative optic, to the point where his text symptomatically hesitates. The borderline between sheer historical plagiarism and what Harold Bloom has called 'creative misprision' is constantly blurred. This, as I have tried to show, takes the form of a semiotic puzzle: on the one hand, prosaic contents seem cynically to hijack poetic forms; on the other hand, as the signifier transmits its energy to the signified, those forms cannot after all be quite as external to their contents as they seemed to be. Bourgeois revolution are fictions that rewrite fictions; and it is difficult for us not to feel, coming after Brecht, that there is also something 'textual' in the model of socialist revolution that Marx counterposes to them: 'on the other hand, proletarian revolutions, like those of the nineteenth century, criticize themselves constantly, interrupt themselves continually in their own course, come back to the apparently accomplished in order to begin it afresh, deride with unmerciful thoroughness the inadequacies, weaknesses and paltrinesses of their first attempts, seem to throw down their adversary only in order that he may draw new strength from the earth and rise again, more gigantic, before them, recoil ever and anon from the indefinite prodigiousness of their own aims, until a situation has been created which makes all turning back impossible, and the conditions themselves cry out: *Hic Rhodus, hic salta!*'[103] Critical self-reflexiveness, self-interruption, ceaseless provisionality, oblique and zigzag progression: Marx's description of the form of proletarian revolution could equally well be an account of the form of epic theatre. It is the '*Hic Rhodus, hic salta!*' that the liberal enthusiasts of that medium are less likely to stomach.

Bonaparte is certainly a joke; but he is funnier than Mehlman thinks. For the joke his buffoonery incarnates is not the collapse of class representation in a snort of libertarian laughter, but what Brecht calls the 'joke of contradiction'. By allowing him into power, 'the bourgeoisie confesses that its own interests dictate that it should be delivered from the danger of its *own rule*; that, in order to restore tranquillity in the country, its bourgeois parliament must, first of all, be given its quietus; that in order to preserve its *social* power intact, its political power must be broken; that the individual bourgeois can continue to exploit the other classes and to enjoy undisturbed property, family, religion and order only on condition that their class be condemned along with the other classes to like political nullity; that in order to save its purse, it must forfeit the crown, and the sword that is to safeguard it must at the same time be hung over its own head as a sword of Damocles.'[104] It would be odd to find a liberal critic enjoying *this* joke with quite Marx's relish; for in the long term the joke is certainly on him. The 'joke of contradiction' that is Louis Bonaparte is history's humour at the expense of a crippled bourgeoisie, compelled to surrender its political power in order to protect its material existence. And if it happened once, it can happen again—next time, perhaps, to add spice to the comedy, with an insurgent proletariat still on the scene. The 'forepleasure' afforded by such witty conundrums can release the deeper forces that effect their practical resolutions; and it is in such forces that Marx finds prefigured what he calls the 'poetry of the future'. If there is always that which escapes, always that difference irreducible to dialectics, it is not only the irredeemably tragic or the insolently anarchistic but the very content of the comic society of the future, the very end-product of dialectics itself. The truly comic dislocation of signifier and signified is not the regressive farce of Bonapartism but its obverse: that ceaseless self-

103 Ibid., p. 100.
104 Ibid., p. 132.

surpassing or productive 'content', unconfinable within any past or present 'phrase', which is for Marx the realm of freedom and abundance.[105]

The riot of carnival, the impudence of inversion, the cackling of iconoclasm: these for historical materialism are moments within, not alternatives to, that deeper comedy which is the joke of contradiction and its pleasurable release. No finer example of this could be found than in the complex structure of Brecht's *The Caucasian Chalk Circle*, which frames the Bakhtinian buffoonery of an Azdak within the potential tragedy of class society, and then frames all that in turn within the comedy of a 'socialist' society. But it is not of course a question of Chinese boxes: the different actions are deftly articulated. Azdakian anarchy is in part the desperate funniness of *Galgenhumor*, the irrepressible roguishness of the victim whom the ruling class has deprived of everything but his wit. For revolutionaries, who live continually in the shadow of the gallows, this negative comedy is not to be underestimated. Joking with the rope around your neck is a feeble way of transcending your oppressors, but it is a sort of transcendence all the same, which someone else may always find a use for. Walter Benjamin's own death, according to Gershom Scholem, proved useful in this way: disturbed by his suicide, the border authorities allowed his fellow fugitives through. But since Azdak's humour is resourceful rather than defeatist, it offers more than a narrow margin of freedom within a realm of *Ananke*. His rough justice and devious opportunism may be in one sense mere functions or inverted mirror-images of class society, but the play also relates them structurally to the greater comedy of social contradictions and their successful resolution. Living provisionally yet self-protectively, having a quick eye to the main chance, bowing humbly to the mighty only the more effectively to butt them in the stomach,

105 Perhaps I may quote some earlier remarks of my own on this subject, to clarify the point: '. . . for *The Eighteenth Brumaire*, it is not simply a matter of discovering the expressive or representational forms 'adequate to' the content of the socialist revolution. It is a question of rethinking that opposition—of grasping form no longer as the symbolic mould into which content is poured but as the 'form of the content': which is to say, grasping it as the structure of a ceaseless self-production, and so not as 'structure' but as 'structuration'. It is this process of continual self-excess—of 'the content go[ing] beyond the phrase'—which is for Marx the poetry of the future and the sign of communism, as it is for us the secret of a materialist analysis of the literary text' (*Criticism and Ideology*, p. 184). In other words, what is implied by Marx's 'poetry of the future' is not simply an image of utopia but a wholly new political semiotics.

entangling the enemy in his own rhetoric: all these may be qualities of the clown, but they are qualities of the revolutionary too, and Brechtian drama continually invites us to ponder their identity and difference. If bourgeois revolution for Marx conceals its unheroic proportions beneath an epic splendour, sheathes its drooping dagger in a virile scabbard, socialist revolution is another genre altogether—an epic without heroes, a poetry of the *Unmensch*, of the 'unmanned' who lay no claim to heroic 'manhood' but grasp their condition as the overturning of all manhood and all heroism. Socialist revolution presents a scenario of traditionally tragic depth and import, only to cast it with the low, cunning, unheroic characters of traditional comedy.

In *Beyond Good and Evil*, Nietzsche opposes the 'stupidity of moral indignation' to what he calls a 'philosophical sense of humour'.[106] 'Cynicism', he remarks, 'is the only form in which common souls come close to honesty; and the higher man must prick up his ears at every cynicism, whether coarse or refined, and congratulate himself whenever a buffoon without shame or a scientific satyr speaks out in his presence'.[107] Whenever anyone speaks 'badly but not ill' of a human being as a belly with two needs and a head with one, crudely deflating metaphysical solemnities, then 'the lover of knowledge should listen carefully and with diligence'.[108] The *buffo* and satyr, Nietzsche laments, are strangers to the ponderous German spirit, lacking as it does the 'boisterous *allegrissimo* of a Machiavelli, the liberating scorn of a wind that makes everything healthy by making everything *run*!'[109] If Bakhtin is the *buffo*, Marx is the scientific satyr, and the brio of *The Eighteenth Brumaire* his crowning comic achievement. Walter Benjamin found support for his anti-historicism in the work, alluding to it in his *Theses*: 'History is the object of a construction whose site is formed not by homogeneous, empty time, but rather by time filled by the presence of the now. Thus, to Robespierre ancient Rome was a past charged with the time of the now which he blasted out of the continuum of history'.[110] But Benjamin did not learn greatly from Marx's philosophical humour, despite his citing of that virtue; and it is in this sense that Marx, in his brusque 'let the dead bury their dead', and Bakhtin,

106 Harmondsworth 1979, p. 38.
107 Ibid., p. 40.
108 Ibid., p. 40.
109 Ibid., p. 42.
110 I, p. 263 (translation amended).

in his carnivalesque celebrations, remind us of a dimension of historical materialism which Western Marxism has damagingly lost.[111] Benjamin, like Gramsci, admired the slogan 'Pessimism of the intellect, optimism of the will', and in what Brecht called the 'new ice age' of fascism one can see its point. But Marxism holds out other strategic slogans too. Having taken the point of the first, it might then be possible to say, without voluntarist or Kautskyist triumphalism: 'Given the strength of the masses, how can we be defeated?'

111 One of the severest critics of Benjamin's suspicion of 'progress' is Jürgen Habermas, who comments that 'before Benjamin's Manichean gaze, which is able to discern progress only in the solar prominences of happiness, history extends like the revolving of a dead star upon which every now and then lightning flashes down' (Habermas, p. 218). Whatever the limitations of Habermas's general critique of Benjamin's work, his commentary here draws attention to the possibilities of a real, if partial, progress which Benjamin's apocalyticism would seem to devalue.

6

In the year of Benjamin's death, another exiled Jewish revolutionary intellectual met his fate at the hands of political reaction. Victims respectively of fascism and Stalinism, and conjoint sign of their lethal complicity, Walter Benjamin and Leon Trotsky reveal a set of parallelisms that remain to be seriously studied. We know that Benjamin read Trotsky with acclaim: he thought highly of *Where Is Britain Going?*,[112] and 'breathlessly' devoured *My Life* and *History of the Russian Revolution*, declaring of these latter works that he had assimilated nothing with such intensity for years.[113] The two men's political views were in many respects identical. Both opposed the ultra-leftist insanity of the Third Period, urging the imminent threat of fascism in the teeth of the Comintern's murderous complacency; both equally rejected the alternative illusions of social democracy, as is apparent in Benjamin's mordant comments on the capitulation to fascism of the German SPD.[114] The Popular Front conception of anti-fascist struggle against which Trotsky never ceased to polemicize is well enough characterized in Benjamin's scorn for left illusions of 'progress' and alliances with traditional culture.[115] The conception of history as a triumphal progression of cultural treasures, one odious to Benjamin, is a typical feature of Popular Front ideology. Writing of the French Popular Front in 1937, he speaks of a 'fetish of the left majority' that fails to find itself embarrassed by a politics that, if practised by the right, would provoke riots.[116] His 'Conversations

112 B, 1, p. 409.
113 B, 2, p. 553.
114 I, p. 260.
115 See I, p. 258.
116 B, 2, p. 732.

with Brecht' record Brecht's own close interest in Trotsky's writings, his sceptical response to the dogma of 'socialism in one country' and the degeneration of the Soviet workers' state.[117] In the realm of cultural revolution, Trotsky and Benjamin are equally concordant, though the latter is to the left of the former. Both reject *Proletkult*,[118] seeking to salvage aspects of traditional culture while remaining critically open to the *avant-garde*; both welcome the findings of Freud and make active alliance with the surrealists; both combine the erudition and sensibility of 'traditional' intellectuals with an insistence on the 'organic' tasks of socialist culture, whether these be literacy campaigns or the essential proletarianization of the artist.

There is a sense in which it would be demeaning to the memory of Leon Trotsky to pursue this parallel much further. For Trotsky was one of the two greatest Marxist revolutionaries of the twentieth century, incomparably more significant for the course and destiny of socialism than a mystical, politically quiescent, temperamentally sluggish art-reviewer in the Weimar republic. Whatever the genius and poignancy of Walter Benjamin, a full comparison of him to the architect of the Red Army and the Fourth International has the ring of a category mistake about it. For the two men were formed in distinct periods of modern Marxism: the one in the heroic phrase of political struggle culminating in the October revolution; the other in the bleaker epoch of 'Western Marxism', where those political struggles had received their political quietus at the joint hands of Stalinism, social democracy and the bourgeoisie.

117 UB, pp. 117–18.
118 See Benjamin's comments in 'Surrealism', OWS, p. 236. In his recently published *Moscow Diary*, he describes the pessimism of his friend Bernhard Reich over the 'reactionary turn' of the Soviet party in cultural matters. Reich, he reports, fears that the left movements, used at the time of war communism, will now (in late 1926) be totally dropped. The proletarian writers, against Trotsky's wishes, have recently become state-recognized; and the case of Llelewitsch, whose work on methods of Marxist literary criticism has met with disfavour from the authorities, signifies a move against the Left Front in Art (*Moskauer Tagebuch*, Frankfurt-am-Main 1980, pp. 19–20). Charles Rosen (cf. n. 32 above) shrewdly points out that Benjamin's famous essay 'The Author as Producer', first delivered as a lecture to a Communist front organization in Paris, 1934, could hardly have been entirely congenial to its audience in its resolute elevation of a cultural strategy associated with the Left Front in Art over 'tendency' literature. It should be pointed out, on the other hand, that Benjamin appears to have continued to support the Soviet state, and to cherish illusions as to its political character, at least up to his sharply disillusioned response to the Nazi–Soviet pact of 1939.

There is, however, a contrast possible between Benjamin and Trotsky which is more to the former's credit. Trotsky, whatever his keen interests in artistic modernism, was like Marx, Engels, Lenin and Lukács fundamentally an heir of the Enlightenment. Classical Marxism largely shares that Enlightenment rationality—that web of historical assumptions as to what is to count as truth, reason, meaning, value and identity, which now runs so deep as to be entirely ineradicable from our slightest gestures. That such a problematic should simply be 'eradicated' in any case is highly suspect; and that it was—and is—historically necessary for Marxism to fight mainly on its terrain is surely clear. Most of the alternatives so far proposed have been, to say the least, primitivist and unpalatable. Yet one may surely also question the grave constraints of this problematic, in so far as we can identify them, without indulging in intellectual suicide. Benjamin and his friend Adorno are 'modernist Marxists', poised on some ultimate threshold of meaning where it might just be possible to think Marxism through again in terms often bizarrely remote from mainstream Enlightenment assumptions.[119] The results, as we might expect, are partial and varied; but they outline a daunting, exhilarating project whose shape we are perhaps only dimly beginning to discern. It is a project that might prove fully feasible only on the other side of revolutionary change. If much current theoretical modernism has ended up by abandoning all hopes of such change, it may be less that it is incompatible with Marxism than that the material conditions for such an interchange do not as yet properly exist. It may be that it will only be in the realm of freedom that Reason will have full leisure to transform itself, in terms that will no doubt bear at least some reference to the 'alien' rationalities of other world civilizations.

I have argued that much of 'Marxist aesthetics' is nowhere more symptomatic of Western Marxism than in its curious cross-breedings of materialism and idealism, and that no figure within that aesthetic lineage could in turn be more exemplary of this liaison than Benjamin himself. Benjamin's idealism assumes multiple forms, but one in particular demands some brief discussion here. A tendency towards technologism— the assigning of historical determinacy to technical forces abstracted from

119 For Benjamin's own critique of Enlightenment—and especially Kantian—thought on the grounds of the 'pre-rational' thought-forms it suppresses, see his 'Über das Programm der kommenden Philosophie', GS, 2/1, pp. 157–71.

their social contexts—has often been noticed in his work; but it has perhaps not been sufficiently stressed that this is one term of an antithetical couple, of which the other is 'culturalism'. Benjamin, in short, tends at once to objectivize the economic base and subjectivize the superstructure, swinging with a minimum of mediation between 'material forces' and 'experience'. Technical forces are sometimes idealized, just as the materiality of the superstructure sometimes threatens to dissolve into the 'immediacy' of 'experience' itself, whether as *Erlebnis* or *Erfahrung*. The relation between base and superstructure becomes essentially one of 'expression'—of a 'correspondence' or sensuous mimesis, as in Benjamin's theories of language. This doctrine, ironically, is often a feature of the very historicism which he fought so relentlessly: if he rejected historicism's diachronic axis—its determinist teleologies—he came close at times to reproducing its synchronic vision of history as a homogeneity of 'levels'. Base and superstructure unite in the encompassing reality of history, of which modes of production are one side, 'experience' another. Indeed Benjamin takes an historicist view of his own Marxism, which is, he remarks, 'nothing, absolutely nothing but the expression of certain experiences in my thought and life'.[120] Theory is nothing but the self-consciousness of 'experience' or practice.

To leave the matter here would be to do Benjamin a serious injustice. For if he sometimes sees 'experience' as a kind of direct impress or distillation of physical or technological forces, it remains true that he conjures out of such reflexiveness a subtlety of perception marvellously in excess of the model's own crudity. Moreover, his insistence on the personally experiential nature of his own communist commitment is deliberately aimed against that 'sterility of a "credo"' that is Stalinism. To be 'true' to Marxism in such conditions meant being to some degree 'necessarily, symptomatically, productively false'. Nor is it entirely true that Benjamin's work lacks a mediation between technology and experience: what else is the concept of class struggle? Yet even this mediation is often an attenuated one. The *Theses* are a superb revolutionary document; but they consistently evoke class struggle in terms of consciousness, image, memory and experience, and are almost wholly silent on the question of its *political* forms. Between 'base' and 'experience', the political instance is mutely elided; Habermas is not far

120 B, 2, p. 604.

from the mark when he comments that 'Benjamin conceived the philosophy of history also as a theory of experience'.[121] The surrealists, Benjamin writes, perceived an ecstatic or anarchic component in every revolutionary act; but, he quickly adds, 'to place the accent exclusively on it would be to subordinate the methodical and disciplinary preparation for revolution entirely to a praxis oscillating between fitness exercises and celebration in advance'.[122] Precisely such a subordination scars Benjamin's own work, all the way from the spasmodic Sorelian violence espoused in his early ultra-leftist apocalypticism to the revolutionary Messianism and political poetry of the *Theses* themselves.

This, of course, is more than a theoretical lapse. It has its roots in the very political character of Benjamin's epoch. Stranded between social democracy and Stalinism, his political options were narrow indeed. There was little left to him but 'experience', and even that was sickeningly fragile. Benjamin's anti-historicism, then, is in collusion with his idealism: the *Jetztzeit* ceases to figure simply as a symbolic element within historical materialism and comes to stand in for the rigours of revolutionary practice. Between the coming of the masses and the coming of the Messiah, no third term is able to crystallize. The revolutionary prophet substitutes himself for the revolutionary party, able to fulfil its mnemonic but not its theoretical and organizational tasks, rich in wisdom partly because poor in practice. If Trotsky has the Transitional Programme, Benjamin is left with the 'time of the now'. No revolutionary movement can afford to ignore signs of steady progress, rhythms of gradual development, or (in a non-metaphysical sense of the term) questions of teleology; Benjamin's 'homogeneous time', thought from the standpoint of Bolshevism, looks somewhat less repellent. If not even the dead are safe from fascism, not even the Messiah is safe from socialism. The Messiah is the last instance that never comes, but even if he were to come it would not be an event within historical materialism.

William Blake, writing before the emergence of historical materialism, cast his critique of industrial capitalism in theological terms. For all its consequent limits, no materialist artefact has ever exceeded its power. Benjamin, as we have seen, can likewise progress by his idealist side: like his great mentor in Marxism, Georg Lukács, he summons the ambivalent resources of idealism to do battle with a considerably more pernicious

121 Habermas, p. 207.
122 'Surrealism', OWS, p. 236.

positivism. The measure of this achievement may be taken by a simple parallel. Twentieth-century Marxism contains an anti-historicist theory that speaks like Benjamin of amalgamating archaic with more contemporary forms, and which grasps historical development not as linear evolution but as a shocking constellation of disparate epochs. It was this hypothesis—the hypothesis of Trotsky's *Results and Prospects*—that adumbrated the destiny of the Russian revolution, and which, generalized as the theory of permanent revolution, remains of the utmost importance for socialist strategy today. If it had been heeded by a Marxism mesmerized by a 'stagist' theory of history, Walter Benjamin conceivably would not have died when he did. The theory of permanent revolution slices sideways into historical homogeneity, finding within the era of bourgeois-democratic struggle the 'weak Messianic impulse' that turns it heliotropically towards the sun of socialism rising in the future. What remains an image in Benjamin becomes a political strategy with Trotsky: the proletariat, assuming leadership of the bourgeois-democratic revolution in hegemonic alliance with other subordinated classes and groups, releases the dynamic that will carry the revolution beyond itself into workers' power. The epochal strata laid neatly end to end in an official Marxist imagination are seized and stacked rudely one upon the other, transfiguring the geology of revolution by a violent upheaval. Assumed hierarchies are impudently subverted: the weakest link in the imperialist chain, viewed from the standpoint of revolutionary irony, now becomes the strongest, the heterogeneous chip of history that might unbalance the whole top-heavy capitalist structure. With its eyes turned towards the future, the revolution makes a tiger's leap into the past—the archaic feudalism of Tsarist Russia—in order to configurate it violently with the present. The result, as Benjamin notes in his essay on Moscow, is a 'complete interpenetration of technological and primitive modes of life'.[123] A ripe moment of the homogeneous time of bourgeois revolution becomes the strait gate through which the proletariat will enter, the *Jetztzeit* in which differential histories—feudalist, bourgeois-democratic, proletarian—are impelled dramatically into contradictory correspondence.

Once installed in power, the workers' state continues to rub history against the grain. The sedate narrative of homogeneous history is transformed into a tangled text: 'outbreaks of civil war and foreign wars

123 OWS, p. 190.

alternate with periods of "peaceful" reform. Revolution in economy, technique, science, the family, morals and everyday life develop in complex reciprocal action and do not allow society to achieve equilibrium'.[124] The practice of socialist revolution demonstrates the 'synchronic' as well as 'diachronic' displacements and condensations of history: 'in a revolutionary break in the life of society', writes Trotsky, 'there is no simultaneousness and no symmetry of process either in the ideology of society, or in its economic structure'.[125] Revolutionary time is neither self-identical nor purely diffuse; so too with revolutionary space. The socialist revolution begins on national foundations, but cannot be completed within them: in the deadliest of all constellations for the international bourgeoisie, the powers released by the national revolution begin to take effect elsewhere, warp the global space of capitalism and condense its apparently discrete national areas into the landscape of international socialist revolution. Only when the whole of this 'text' is written can its component national narratives be properly recounted; only when the national revolution is blasted out of the continuum of its own time and terrain into global terms can we be sure that it is not lost irrevocably to history. For every image of revolution that is not recognized by the international proletariat as one of its own concerns threatens to disappear irretrievably.

Seen in the light of the theory of permanent revolution, Benjamin's anti-historicism becomes more than an engaging notion. On the contrary, its reactivation in our own epoch may be quite literally the warrant of our survival. Since the American defeat in Vietnam, world imperialism has suffered a series of grievous rebuffs at the hands of revolutionary nationalism. But without the proletarian leadership which could alone guarantee the transformation of such insurrections into the foundations of socialism, these societies will continue to be trapped within the precarious deadlock of Stalinism and imperialism. In the imperialist homelands, the conditions against which Benjamin warned are once again in sway: a reformist mythology continues to grip whole sectors of the working class, in a global crisis of capitalism that places the threat of fascism once more on the agenda. In such a situation, it is more than ever necessary to blast Benjamin's work out of its historical continuum, so that it may fertilize the present.

124 Leon Trotsky, *The Permanent Revolution*, New York 1969, p. 132.
125 Idem, *Literature and Revolution*, Ann Arbor 1971, p. 159.

Homage to
Walter Benjamin

'So we went, changing countries
oftener than our shoes . . .'
Blue-lipped angel
lurching on ruined wings
down cracked arcades, blown auras
morsels of unmade texts
spilling like runes
death pills in pocket
hurtling backwards to Port Bou

—something these shocks
were allegorical of—

Flüchtling, flâneur
rattling your suitcase of quotations
at a strait gate
you would always never enter
emblem *involontaire*, nailed
to a *nunc stans*, the dialectical
Jew at a standstill, declaring
the small hoarse sound
of the Torah
          in the customs shed

A pit in the Pyrenees
you brimmed with villeins' blood
twisting your own neck
in voluntary liquidation
your flesh become
new forces of production
madeleines of remembrance
where Bolsheviks storm Belsen

Courteous myopic angel, how
you press upward in me
to light these humble bits
of you I cook the books with.
Stand now: be spilled, unmade.

Index

Printed in the United States
By Bookmasters